Developing Design Tools and Standards for Blast-Resistant Windows

Parekh

Copyright © 2024 by Parekh

TABLE OF CONTENT

Part I

Introduction & State of the Art

CHAPTER 1. INTRODUCTION

1.1 General

The Canadian Safety and Security Program (CSSP) provided research funds to the University of Ottawa to develop blast-resistant window retention anchors to improve Canada's preparedness and prevention capabilities against blast threats. The project, entitled "Development of Blast Resistant Window Anchor Systems," included research and development on window retention anchors to develop new design tools and a national CSA (Canadian Standards Association) Standard on the topic. One of the important objectives of the project was to generate research data on the performance of blast-resistant window anchors. The research consisted of experimental and analytical components, forming the driving force behind the research for the current doctoral investigation.

1.2 Background

The windows and doors are part of the building facade that are defined as non-structural elements and are usually fabricated and mounted on the building without a structural design. During recent blast incidences around the world, it was continuously observed that most injuries and casualties are caused by flying debris and fragmentation of building components, including broken glass shards. Several types of glass assemblies are used to form building windows, such as single or multi-light punched windows, insulated glass units (IGU), monolithic or laminated glass units, and curtain walls. Punched windows are widely used in old and new residential, commercial, and public buildings. Curtain walls are commonly used in new and modern office, commercial, and public buildings.

Punched windows usually consist of a frame that can be flexible (aluminum or wood) or rigid (steel), glass panes (made of annealed, heated strengthened or fully tempered glass) in the form of monolithic glass panes, insulated multi-pane glass units and laminated blast-resistant glass panes. The glass panes are the first components of the window system to receive the applied blast pressure and transmit it to the protective film, which in turn transfers the load to the frame and the anchors. The glass panes are fabricated in different configurations such as monolithic glass units, insulated glass units (IGU) or laminated glass. Laminated glass pane can be part of a multi-pane IGU.

The laminated glass is strengthened by an intermediate elastic layer, usually in the form of PVB that is installed in between two glass layers to keep glass shards intact upon breakage. Another method of keeping broken glass shards together and thereby preventing them from entering in the building is the installation of protective films on the inner pane of glass. This is a surface mounted protective layer that can be applied on monolithic glass units, IGUs, or laminated glass panes. The protective film is glazed to the window frames using various glazing techniques. The most common glazing types are wet-glazing using structural silicon, or mechanical glazing using metal elements supported against the glass panes along the frame, secured on the frame elements.

Most of the previous research has focused on appropriate methods of keeping the fragmentation within the protective glass pane and preventing the glass shards from entering the building. Limited attention was paid to the anchorage of windows on substrates, that usually appear in the form of wall panels. Glazed window panes transmit the applied pressure to the frame, which may not have sufficient anchorage. If the glazed window sustains the applied blast pressure, the failure may occur in the frame connection region, leading to the detachment of the entire window unit, which may fly in to the building, causing serious injuries and fatalities of the occupants. Designing the anchorage of window is an important subject that has not been comprehensively investigated (Saatcioglu et al. 2016).

1.3   Problem Definition

The behaviour of blast-resistant window retention anchors has not been well-established due to lack of research and the limitations in the current body of knowledge. While there has been some research on window glazing and overall performance of blast-resistant window systems, the performance of window anchorage has not been well researched. It is unclear how the retention anchor forces can be obtained for design purposes. Furthermore, it is unclear how the resistance of the window systems is influenced by the anchor capacity and anchor patterns (number and size and spacing of anchors). Challenges created by anchorage on different types of substrates with significantly different mechanical properties (reinforced concrete, steel, block masonry, stone masonry) increases the complexity of the problem. Additional complexities are introduced by nonlinear response of the window systems with different characteristics for glazing, glass panes, window frames and the substrate. Post-breakage performance of glazed windows with the resulting membrane action compounds the problem, creating additional challenges in determining the anchor design forces. Current procedures employed in the construction industry provide empirical procedures for anchor strength to develop full glazing capacity, without specific methodologies for quantifying design forces under combined flexure, shear and axial tension associated with pre-break and post-break behaviour of windows, including the membrane response. Lack of sufficient knowledge on window anchor behaviour is compensated in these empirical design procedures by excessively conservative approaches, while sometimes resulting in unsafe practices. It is clear that significant gaps exist in the current body of knowledge on blast resistant window anchor performance. Both experimental and analytical research is needed to establish the performance characteristics of blast-resistant window retention anchors.

1.4 Objective and Scope

The primary objective of the current research project is to develop analysis and design information for blast-resistant window retention anchors in different substrates. The objective includes generation of much needed test data on performance of blast-resistant windows and their anchorages, as well as analysis techniques suitable for the assessment and design of blast resistant windows and window retention anchors.

The above objectives are achieved by following the steps given below, which form the scope of the investigation.

- Literature review to establish the state of the art on blast-resistant window retention anchors.

- Construction, instrumentation, and tests of 23 full-size windows under simulated blast loads using the University of Ottawa Shock Tube. Two tests are conducted on each window under two levels of blast pressure-impulse combinations, resulting in a total of 46 blast tests. The tests provide data on the effects of window substrates that consist of steel, reinforced concrete, concrete block masonry and stone masonry; window size and aspect ratio; glazing techniques; protective film thicknesses; and retention anchor characteristics (number, pattern, and anchorage length).

- Evaluation of test data and the assessment of overall window glazing system performance, as well as the specific behaviour of window retention anchors, while also investigating the effects of test parameters.

- Selection of the general-purpose computational fluid dynamics (CFD) and finite element (FE) software LS-DYAN for numerical analysis of windows with emphasis on window anchor behaviour.

- Construction of analytical models for windows using the available modelling techniques in LS-DYNA and the validation of the analytical models against test data generated during the experimental phase of investigation.

- Analytical parametric investigation using LS_DYNA to assess the significance of design parameters consisting of window size and aspect ratio, window frame rigidity, substrate type, anchor fixity, number and distribution of anchors, blast threat level.

- Development of a non-linear SDOF analysis approach for blast-resistant window systems and the construction of window resistance functions to compute anchor design forces.

- Validation of the SDOF analysis against experimental data and the available window design software WINGARD and BRADS.

- Presentation of results and design recommendations.

1.5 Research Methodology

The research program comprises of three main phases; experimental research using shock tube as blast simulator, numerical parametric investigation based on three-dimensional FEM analysis, and development of non-linear dynamic analysis procedure for window systems based on a SDOF simplification. The research work begins with the experimental phase that includes the construction of four types of substrates (reinforced concrete, steel, concrete block, and stone masonry), preparation, instrumentation and glazing of 23 windows using either wet-glazing or mechanical glazing. A total of 46 tests are conducted under two different threat scenarios. The test windows consist of three different sizes and aspect ratios. The evaluation of test data is performed using the recorded pressures, strain gauges and the high-speed camera images.

The numerical investigation involves FEM modelling and analysis of selected test windows. The FEM models are first validated against test data. The models are then used to conduct an analytical parametric investigation. The parameters in this phase include; substrate type, window frame rigidity, anchor fixity level in the substrate, window aspect ratio and size, anchor spacing, and blast pressure-impulse combination. The results demonstrate the significance of design parameters on window response, while also defining anchor force distribution along the window frame.

The third phase of research includes the development of a simplified SDOF method of analysis for window systems, incorporating the effects of anchor flexibility and substrate rigidity on the non-linear response of the window and its anchorage. The analysis approach includes the construction of window resistance functions in pre-break and post-break phases of response, where the latter stage of response is dominated by the membrane action of protective film. The analysis results provide anchor design forces for use in design.

The above three phases generate much needed research data for the assessment and design of blast resistant windows and their anchorages.

1.6　Organization of book

The book consists of six chapters as presented below:

- Chapter 1 presents research needs, background information, research objectives and scope, as well as a summary of research methodology followed in the three main phases of research.

- Chapter 2 provides the review of available research on blast-resistant windows, including both experimental and analytical research. It also provides an overview of available guidelines and standards on the topic.

- The next three chapters (Chapters 3 to 5) are presented in journal article format.

    o Chapter 3 (Article 1) **"Experimental Investigation of Blast-Resistant Window Anchors."** This chapter provides an overview of the experimental research, with further details included in Appendices A and B of the book.

    o Chapter 4 (Article 2) **"Numerical Investigation of Blast-Resistant Window Anchors."** This chapter provides an overview of the numerical investigation using LS-DYNA software and the FEM modeling implemented, with further details included in Appendix C of the book.

    o Chapter 5 (Article 3) **"SDOF Analysis for Anchorage Design of Blast-Resistant Windows."** This chapter provides an analysis procedure for non-linear SDOF analysis using step-by-step linear acceleration method and the construction of window resistance functions for use in window retention anchors. The procedure incorporates pre-break flexural analysis and post-break membrane analysis, providing corresponding anchor forces for use in design.

- Chapter 6 provides conclusions and a summary of findings of the research project.

CHAPTER 2. STATE OF THE ART

2.1   General

Blast resistant window systems is a topic of research that may be traced back to the last quarter of the 20th Century. Significant research has been conducted on different aspects of window systems subjected to blast loads with an emphasis on window glazing. Research on window retention anchors remains to be scarce in the literature. Previous research on behaviour of anchors in different materials is limited to static loads for static load applications. This has resulted in limited understanding of window anchor behaviour under blast loads.

Previous studies in the general area of blast-resistant windows provide some understanding of the behaviour and design of window anchors. In addition, the limited number of books that have become available in recent years on blast-resistant buildings also provide limited information on glazing design and performance of windows (Mays et al. 2003; Bangash et al. 2006; Krauthammer 2008; Dussenberry 2010; Uddin 2010). This chapter provides an overview of the mechanism of blast resistance in window systems, review of previous literature on blast resistant windows, and a summary of design standards and guidelines on the topic.

2.2   Mechanism of Blast Resistance in Windows Systems

Blast-resistant windows consist of glass pane(s), protective film or interlayer, window frame and window retention anchors. The protective film is anchored to the window frame (sometimes through window stoppers) using wet or mechanical glazing. Wet glazing is done using structural silicon; and mechanical glazing is done using metal pieces that secure the film to the frame along the glass perimeter by means of bolts or screws. Upon the application of blast loads, the pressure is collected by the window pane, which initially provides elastic resistance until breakage. Breakage of glass results in a sudden drop in load resistance as the pressure is transferred from glass to the protective film or the interlayer, which develops membrane resistance. During the post-break phase of response, the broken glass fragments remain in contact with the film or the interlayer. The blast pressure is transferred from the window pane to the frame, which is anchored to the substrate by means of window retention anchors. During dynamic response to blast loads, the window, anchors, and the substrate may develop inelastic deformations as the load is transmitted from the window pane(s) to the substrate (Zhang et al. 2015).

2.2.1 Window Frames

Window frame is a critical element that may require special design to resist blast pressures transferred from glass pane(s) (Weissman 1978). Among different types of window frames, wood and aluminum frames are widely used in practice due to their availability and low cost. Flexible aluminum frame elements with hollow profiles or wood frames develop significant out-of-plane bending, resulting in unequal distribution of anchor forces with higher forces near the middle of the window and lower anchor forces near the corners. Steel frames, often required for blast-resistant windows, are rigid frames. They deform less, generating close to uniform distribution of anchor forces (Zhang. X 2016).

2.2.2 Glass

Glass is frequently used as window panes because of its transparency, allowing light to pass through without much scattering. The glass used in modern building construction is labelled as "float glass," named after the manufacturing process used, which involves floating molten glass on a bed of metal so that a glass with uniform thickness and flat surface is manufactured. Regular glass is referred to as "annealed" glass, which has limited bending capacity and exhibits brittle failure when the capacity is reached. When higher strength is needed, glass is tempered or toughened through thermal or chemical treatments. Tempered glass can have four times higher strength than annealed glass, and hence it is often used as safety glass. Tempering process induces compression in the outer surface and tension in the interior face. This results in a safe manner of breaking making the glass crumble into smaller granular pieces instead of splintering into sharp shards. When the glass breaks under high blast pressures, it generates high-velocity flying and falling shards, posing threat to building occupants and people nearby. Thus, when an explosion occurs in populated areas, most casualties are caused by the glass fragments. The selection of glass panes is the first step to design blast-resistance windows. Several types of glass panes are available in the market as discussed by (Weissman 1978; Smith 2010). The common types of glass panes used for windows include monolithic, laminated and insulating multiple panes. Glass-clad polycarbonate is also used for blast resistance. Types of blast resistant windows are illustrated in Figure 2.1. More information on glass types and manufacturing processes can be found elsewhere (Weissman 1978; Smith 2010).

Monolithic glass

Monolithic glass is used for windows in the form of a single glass pane, having a thickness ranging between 1/8 in (3 mm) to ¾ in (19 mm). When annealed glass is used as a monolithic glass pane without a protective film, it generates high-velocity jagged glass shards upon breakage. Such shards place inhabitants to very high risk for serious injuries and death. Therefore, it is not recommended to be used as a safety glass unless glazed when the blast threat is present.

Laminated glass

Laminated glass is a composite of two or more glass panes made of either annealed, strengthened, or fully tempered glass in combination with one or more interlayers of elastomeric PVB material. The use of this type of glass provides significant ductility beyond breakage. The glass fragments are controlled by the PVB interlayer, which reduces or eliminates flying glass shards. Typical blast-resistant windows for new construction consist of laminated glass.

Insulating glass

Insulating glass units (IGU) are comprised of two or more glass panes with air-gap(s) in between, providing improved energy performance. The glass panes are produced with a variety of thickness, separated from each other by a sealed spacer bar, forming a single unit. The window panes could be a combination of insulating and laminated glass panes; however, it is critically important to place the laminated glass pane as the interior pane to protect the inhabitants.

Glass-clad polycarbonate

Polycarbonate is an alternative material to glass. It can be as clear as glass but has the added advantages of being light and very strong. It can be up to 200 times stronger than glass and will not shatter at failure. Hence it can be used as a security window. It can also be used as a lamination for glass panes. Two or more plies of glass with polycarbonate interlayer provides a blast-resistant window pane. The polycarbonate layer is glued to the glass panes with epoxy, which enhances the tearing strength of the interlayer.

2.2.3 Protective Film

Protective window film is a thin laminate installed on the interior surface of a window. It helps glass maintain its integrity after breakage. Therefore, it is especially suitable for blast-resistant windows. The security film is generally made from Polyethylene Teraphthalate (PET), which is a thermoplastic polymer from the polyester family. These films are completely clear and can be scratch resistant for improved performance when applied on glass. Multiple layers of film can be applied for increased resistance. They are used in homes, commercial buildings, and vehicles to protect people against injuries caused by broken glass shards. The application of protective film on an existing window pane is a cost-effective retrofit technique compared to the replacement of windows with laminated and stronger glass panes.

2.2.4 Window Glazing Assemblies

Window glazing plays a key role in unifying window components and anchoring them to the supporting frame to resist the applied blast pressures. The security film on a window pane needs to be anchored to the window frame through a proper glazing technique to maintain the integrity of the window pane with the window frame. The effectiveness of glazing is control by the frame bite. Longer bites provide stronger glazing. It is recommended to design a glazing system that can flex with the applied force. The glazing procedures used for blast-resistant window panes can be categorized into types:

Mechanical glazing:

Generally, the mechanical glazing is applied around the edges of the glass pane using metal frames or connectors sealed with gaskets to absorb applied pressure. When protective films are placed with mechanical anchoring connections, the film is extended around the metal connector, anchored to the frame. The film ends are trimmed or overlapped around the metal connections. The mechanical connectors are usually anchored to the window frames with special anchors available in different shapes and colors.

Wet glazing:

Wet-glazing is performed by using structural silicon around the window pane along the frame, ensuring the integrity of the film ends with the frame. The structural silicon is required to have a minimum thickness of ½ in (13 mm) to sustain blast pressures. In contract to mechanical glazing, wet-glazing offers a cost-effective method of glazing if the blast pressures are relatively low (in the current investigation wet glazing performed well under 4 psi (28 kPa) but not under 10 psi (69 kPa).

2.2.5   Retention Anchors

Retention anchors are provided to attach the window through its frame to the substrate. Specifications and dimensions of retention anchors are not available in the literature. Other than limited empirical guidelines. Detailed investigation of retention anchor behaviour, analysis and design forms the scope of current research, with is discussion in detail in the following chapters.

2.3   Literature Review of Blast-Resistant Window Systems

The following sections provide a review of available literature on different aspects of blast-resistant window behaviour, including those that specifically address window retention anchors, however limited it may be.

2.3.1 Window Retention Anchors

2.3.1.1 Ward and Jordan (2006):

(Ward et al. 2006) studied window retention anchor behaviour under blast loads. The authors found that there were three factors affecting the window frame anchors to hold in substrates including, i) friction, ii) bearing, and iii) bond or adhesion. To generate proper friction between the anchor and the surrounding substrate, it is recommended to use an anchor that applies an expansion force to the substrate. The anchor base resistance is created by bolt heads, nuts, washers, or bolt plates that are secured in the opposite direction of the substrate. The authors proposed the use of epoxy to provide adhesive bond while producing a form of undercut to enhance the friction with a keying action. Figure 2.2 illustrates a typical installation for window anchors on a masonry wall with drilled holes indicated for blast-proof window installation.

The blast load transmission within the window, the frame, anchors, and the substrate to the ground is discussed and present in the flowchart of Figure 2.3. The authors focused on optimized system design that is cost effective and protective against blast shock waves. Relatively, if one of the system components is under or over design in accordance with the neighboring element, an adverse failure can occur.

It was found that the glass and the interior PVB layer for the laminated glass helped in dissipating the blast energy before the blast load is transferred to the window frame. This indeed, reduced the force on retention anchors compared with applied static loads. However, as the window size increased, the anchor forces became significantly higher. The analytical investigation illustrated results of windows analyzed with different numbers and patterns of retention anchors. The window shown in Figure 2.4, with 28 anchors at 200 mm on centers was modeled under 87 kPa reflected pressure and 537 kPa-ms of impulse, which corresponds to 100 kg of TNT at 21 m. Figure 2.5 illustrates shear forces recorded along the window sides. When the number of anchors was reduced, a minor change was noticed on anchor shear forces, which indicated that windows with fewer anchors could be used in practice.

The paper referred to the analytical research conducted by (Ward et al. 2006) and concluded that windows in practice are engineered and placed with a large number of anchors with small spacing that could cause damage to the substrate. Using this number of anchors is also time consuming, whereas the attention should be paid to the quality of window installation without weakening the substrate.

2.3.1.2   A. Braimah, E. Contestabile, and R. Guilbeault (2009):

The authors first introduced the importance of adhesive steel anchors because their failure could lead to complete failure of window systems, resulting in injuries and casualties. The forces transmitted from the window frame to the substrate depend on the efficiency of the anchors. The modes of failure for steel anchors are also discussed in the same study indicating five main modes of failure, including concrete cone failure, bond failure, combined concrete cone and bond failure, concrete substrate splitting, and steel anchor fracture (Braimah et.al 2009). The researchers also provided a brief literature review of existing analytical models for finding ultimate loads on adhesive anchors in concrete.

An experimental investigation was conducted to evaluate the dynamic performance of adhesive steel anchors placed in concrete and stone masonry. Tests were conducted under impulsive loads using a drop test frame on adhesive steel anchors having 6.4 mm and 9.5 mm diameters, and 908 mm and 458 mm embedment lengths. The anchors penetrated with two different angles of inclination (45° and 90°). Figure 2.6 shows the specimens tested.

The results indicate that the dynamic increase factor (DIF) decreases with increasing embedment length. DIF for anchors in concrete was established to be 1.2 and 3.2 for 90^0 (normal to concrete surface) and 45^0 inclinations, respectively. In contrast, the DIF for anchors in limestone was 1.2 and 2.5 for normal and inclined anchors. The anchors in concrete consistently failed due to the steel rupturing whereas those embedded in limestone showed mixed failure modes; sometimes resulting in the rupturing of steel and other times inducing masonry failure.

2.3.1.3   Braimah, Guilbeault and Contestabile (2014):

(Braimah et al. 2009) extended their previous research on adhesive steel anchors in concrete and stone masonry, reported in the preceding sub-section, to adhesive steel anchors in clay brick and concrete masonry. Figure 2.7 illustrates the test samples. The researchers conducted an experimental investigation with the objective of assessing dynamic response of adhesive anchors embedded in concrete block and clay brick masonry while also comparing the results with static tests. The comparison was intended to determine dynamic increase factors. Tests were carried out using a drop test frame on standard concrete blocks of (190 mm X 190 mm) and clay bricks with dimensions of (W57 X L190 X H90 mm). The steel anchors penetrated in 90^0 and 45^0 inclination angles with variable embedment lengths. The results indicated that the clay brick substrate showed very brittle manner, which resulted in a dynamic increase factors of around 1.0, while DIF was above 1.0 in concrete masonry substrate under high rates of loading, such as those typically seen in blast and impact scenarios.

2.3.2   Glass and Glazing

2.3.2.1   Smith (2003):

The paper summarized different research projects conducted on mitigation of blast hazards. Part of the study involved presentation of typical glass available in industry while indicating advantages of each type and glazing used for each. Accordingly, the following glass types are available for manufacturing windows:

- Plain float annealed glass is the most common glass type with an ultimate design strength of 4,000 psi. (28 MPa)

- Heat strengthened glass with partial temperature treatment to increase the ultimate design strength to 7,600 psi (52 MPa)

- Fully thermally tempered glass to increase the ultimate design strength up to 16,000 psi (110 MPa).

The paper reported that the blast resistance of glass increases with the use of security film. It was also reported that the security film is typically manufactured in four different thickness including 4, 6, 7, or 11 mils. Films could be installed using four different methods that are depicted in Figure 2.8:

Day-Lite or Day Light: The film is only applied to the interior pane, extending up to the frame without extending into the window bite. This type of film has the least cost of application.

Edge-to-Edge: The film has extensions that go into the window frame. The film application requires glass removal. It generates membrane action when a deep rebate is provided.

Wet Glazed: The film is attached to the frame using structural silicone. The resulting film-frame anchorage may create membrane action.

Mechanically Attached: The film is anchored to the window frame by means of bolts, washers and nuts having mechanical splices. This anchorage provides membrane action.

2.3.3   Experimental Investigations

2.3.3.1   Meyers, Baldwin and Mlakar (1994):

The authors provided an overview of 63 tests on full-scale windows, while also summarizing 19 software codes developed over the preceding 10 years to study the blast-resistant design of windows and window frames. The experimental results were compared with design outcomes. The design process used was that outlined in the US Department of Defense (DDESB 2004), the US Army TM5-1300 (TN5-1300 1990), the US Navy NAVFAC P-397 (NAVFAC 1990), the US Air Force AFR 88-22 (NAVFAC 1990), the Naval Physical Security Equipment Manual (NFESC 2000) and the Corps of Engineers Security Engineering Manual Handbook (US Army Corps of Engineers 1957). The authors concluded that the design results based on single degree of freedom method underestimated the windows strength. It was recommended to design window frames to develop higher strength than the glazing. Figure 2.9 illustrates the generic details for window glazing and frame details.

2.3.3.2   Weissman, Dobbs, Stea and Price (1978):

The authors summarized several static and dynamic loading tests conducted on windows with two sizes of (0.72 m x 1.10 m) and (0.84 m x 1.22 m). The windows that were tested under static loads had 6.35 mm thickness for regular and tempered glasses. The glasses were mounted on either wooden or regular and retrofitted aluminum frames. The dynamic tests included two different glass thicknesses of 6.35 mm and 9.52 mm for the tempered and regular glasses attached to wooden and regular aluminum frames as well as 6.35 mm thick tempered glasses mounted on retrofitted aluminum frames.

Generally, the test results exhibited an ultimate blast strength of 30.3 kPa incident overpressure for 6.35-mm thick tempered glass lites installed on strong frames having a glass area of 1.86 m². When tempered glass was secured on aluminum window frames, the aluminum frame failed, exhibiting (8.27 kPa of ultimate strength) for regular frames. The retrofitted frame showed 17.9 kPa of maximum capacity. These conclusions indicated that window frame is the critical element that should be designed to develop the full capacity of glass. It was found that the regular glass is limited to maximum overpressures of about 3.4 kPa. The fragmentations resulted from regular glass tests were more hazardous compared with those observed from tempered glass. The 9.52 mm thick tempered glass showed no failure when subjected to repeated overpressures up to 30.3 kPa at 40 msec except for one glass failed at 10.8 kPa reflected pressure at 20 msec.

2.3.3.3 Hao and Zhang (2015):

The publication provides overview on previous experimental window studies as well as their laboratory tests conducted on monolithic and laminated window glasses. The behaviours of monolithic and laminated glass windows under blast loading and windborne debris impact were evaluated by experimental and site tests. The authors highlighted the accuracies of analysis and design approaches used for window glass subjected to blast and impact loads and compared with the test data. Analytical investigation was also conducted to simulate the dynamic behavior of glass and interlayer material using FEM. The authors discussed the effectiveness of the interlayer anchorage and the sliding of window boundary in the frame for blast risk mitigation.

2.3.3.4 Anderson and Dover (2003):

The publication provides a brief discussion on a study conducted by the US Air Force Research Laboratories (AFRL) for the development and evaluation of "membrane windows" that were expected to resist higher blast pressures, compared with typical blast-resistant windows for remaining sealed during chemical or biological attacks. The protection of the new windows developed was due to several reasons, including: i) polymer membranes, ii) a damping chamber, and iii) special anchors. The windows provided significant capacity that was needed for large store fronts with perfect transparency unless subjected to blast waves. The test windows were fabricated using interior and exterior glass panels with a film laminate attached to each panel. The blast pressure flexed the exterior panel that compressed the air in between the two panels in the damping chamber as illustrated in Figure 2.10. The damping chamber dissipated part of the applied pressure, and the rest was transferred to the interior panel with reduced magnitude, which indeed, helped the interior glass survive the pressure. The window system was tested under high blast pressures up to 100 psi, and the concept was validated. Several tests were also conducted on sealed blast resistant window systems that could survive high blast pressures and resist secondary blasts and chemical-biological threats that may take place after the initial attack.

2.3.3.5 EQE International, GDA, DRES and CERL:

A comprehensive experimental program was carried out with contributions from EQE International, Grendon Design Agency (GDA), Defense Research Establishment Suffield (DRES) and the Canadian Explosives Research Laboratory (CERL) to evaluate the behaviour of protective film configuration based on GSA and ISC previsions.

A total of 70 live explosive window tests were conducted at DRES Fuel-Air Site at Medicine Hat, Alberta. The windows consisted of 48 in x 66 in (1220 mm X 1676 mm) commercial frames and had ¼ in (6.3 mm) annealed glass. The glasses were protected by safety films with a thickness of 4, 7, 8, 10 and 15 mils. Three types of glazing were used: mechanical, wet glazing, or daylight application (shorter than the glass dimensions, using 7 mil films). Anchorage bars were used on 1, 2, or 4 sides, and different types of catch bars were installed. The windows were tested under nine blast loads consisting of 5 at GSA Category C loads that recommended 425 lbs (193 kg) NM charge at 180 feet (55 m), 1 at GSA Category D loads with 2500 lbs (1134 kg) NM charge at 200 feet (61 kg), 2 satchel charge shots of 3 kg C-4 at 5.5 m and 1 experimental shot. The use of daylight technique exhibited GSA Level 3B rating (low to medium protection) when the application was with or without catch bars. Generally, the catch bars decreased the fragment levels from high to medium. The anchorage of 4 sides provided the most effective protection and resulted in low amount of fragment, while 1-side and 2-side anchorage showed high and medium level of fragments, respectively. The application of wet glazing along the edges resulted in GSA Level 3 rating having medium fragments level. The results demonstrated that as the film thickness was increase from 4 to 7, 8, and 10 mils, the number of fragments decreased. Figure 2.11 shows the behaviour of test windows.

2.3.3.6 Panzerfilm Tests by Trundle of Grendon Design Agency (2002):

The experiments included three windows prepared with different glazing characteristics and tested under live explosives. The windows were rectangular with 1590 mm height and 1190 mm width of frame and glass dimensions of 1480 mm by 1080 mm. Tests were conducted by applying a reflected pressure and an impulse of 56 kPa and 410 kPa-ms, which was equal to 100 kg TNT at 32 metres.

The three windows were fabricated differently where the window (L1) consisted of a 10 mm heat-soaked toughened safety glass that was glazed using Panzerfilm Crystal 200 (FT800) film. The film was anchored on four Pilkington Planar mountings with Pentagon Filmtek Bolted Glass Anchor and washer system. The window was secured to the cubical by means of 4 M10 mild steel bolts. When the test was performed, the glass with film supporting system completely detached from the cubical and fell on the ground 1.5 m away from the cubical. The middle window (C2) consisted of double glass made of toughened glass with a 16 mm air gap in between. The window was also glazed with Panzerfilm Crtystal 200 (FT800) as (L1). Gullwing Profile L was attached to four sides and supported by UPVC frame with Dow 895 silicon sealant. Later, the Gullwing Profile was supported on the glass using FrameGard security grade adhesive tape. The Gullwing Profiles were placed on the steel frame of the cubical along the four vertical corners using angled mounting brackets as depicted in Figure 2.12(a). The brackets had dimensions of 50 mm x 50 mm x 6 mm and was made from mild steel secured with M 10 mounting bolts. When the window was subjected to the blast pressure, the outer pane shattered and landed outside the cubical. External glazing beads ejected out, and fell out of the cubical, but the inner pane kept intact by the glazing, matching the GSA 3a level of hazards. The combination of Gullwing Profiles and glazing technique showed satisfactory performance and kept the window in place. Figure 2.12(b) illustrates the distortion of about 3 mm for the angle brackets. It also shows that the unanchored side of Gullwing Profiles failed and moved by about 20 mm. The window (R3) was fabricated as the window (L1) except that there was no safety film. The glass used was heat-soaked toughened safety glass with 10 mm thickness, placed on 4 No

Pilkington Planer glass mountings. Also, 4 bolts of M 10 mild steel bolts were used to secure the window. When the window was tested, the glass broke completely, and the toughened glass fell inside the test cubicle, as illustrated in Figure 2.13.

2.4 Standards and Best Practice Guidelines

2.4.1 Testing Standards

2.4.1.1 ASTM F 1642-96 Standard:

The ASTM F 1642-96 standard was developed in 1966 for glazing and glazing system tests under Air-Blast loading. The air-blast was created by either a live explosive testing arena or a shock tube. The blast-resistant window was evaluated based on performance of the window during the test. If the glazing broke and allowed the pressure to propagate inside the building, or the fragments passed through the aluminum foil located at 305 mm away from the window, the glazing was considered to have failed.

2.4.1.2 GSA Standard (1996, 2003):

The US General Services Administration (GSA) developed standards for testing Glazing and Glazing systems subjected to Air-blast loading in 1996 based on the ASTM 1642-96. The standards were modified in 2003 and the loading function on the glazing system was changed to Dynamic Overpressure Loadings. The title of the standards was also changed to "GSA Standard Test Method for Glazing and Window Systems Subject to Dynamic Overpressure Loadings" (GSA 2003).

The new GSA standard evaluates the performance of windows using a specific rating based on the fragments and debris location after the test relative to the pre-test position of the window. The air-blast loading is created either from an open arena or a blast simulator (shock tube). The standards developed a method to capture the post-test fragments using a witness panel located 3 m (10 ft) away from the window, as shown in Figure 2.14. The rating of the window hazards is presented in Table 2.1. GSA indicated that the blast loading, including the pressure and impulse used in the test, should match the specification of the building occupancy. Thus, the design security criteria of GSA as well as the ISC Security Design Criteria for New Federal Buildings and Major Renovation Projects (2001) are used by the GSA test standards. Table 2.2 provides the recommended pressure by GSA and the corresponding building classification used for US Government Buildings.

2.4.1.3   ISO 16933 and ISO 16934:

In 2006, the International Organization for Standardization (ISO) developed two bomb blast standards for blast testing (ISO 16933 and ISO 16934). ISO 16933 specifies the pressure and impulse values for arena blasts resulting from vehicle bombs and hand carried satchel bombs, as presented in Tables 2.3 and 2.4. The shock tube blast pressure and impulse were tabulated in ISO 16934 and shown in Table 2.5.

2.4.1.4   ASTM F 1642-12 Standard:

The ASTM Standard F1642 was modified in 2012 to implement a test procedure similar to that developed by (GSA 2003), presented earlier. Figure 2.15 indicates the hazard levels recorded after a blast test as per ASTM F 1642-12. The method focuses on the position of the post-test window fragments and debris compared with its pre-test location.

2.4.2   Design Standards

2.4.2.1   The Interagency Security Committee (ISC):

The Oklahoma City bombing in 1995 created a major concern for the US government to develop a new test method and design specifications that led to the formation of the Interagency Security Committee (ISC). The GSA Security Criteria in 1997 was the reference of the ISC Security Design Criteria that was outlined in 2001. The new design criteria of ISC was accepted by 26 US federal agencies. They categorized the US government building into five types as outlined in Table 2.2.

2.4.2.2   ASTM F2248 and ASTM E1300:

The ASTM F2248-12 was developed to establish design loads acting on laminated glass windows. The standard was named "Standard Practice for Specifying an Equivalent 3-Second Duration Design Loading for Blast Resistant Glazing Fabricated with Laminated Glass" (ASTM F2248-12). The standard was limited to laminated glass, and filmed glass used for retrofitting windows was not included. The standard was intended for blast resistant glazing that consisted of laminated glass, such as single pane laminated glass or insulating glass having laminated glass for the inner pane. Figure 2.16 shows the chart used to obtain design loads based on different charge weight and standoff distance combinations developed by ASTM F2248-12.

ASTM E1300 was developed to obtain resistance of windows to ensure the capacity exceeds the 3-second duration equivalent design load specified in ASTM F2248. The standard assumes that the glazed window is anchored to the frame with structural silicone or glazing tape. The width of the structural silicone bead is recommended be either equal to 10 mm or the glass thickness, and it should not exceed twice the glass thickness. However, the structural silicone bead thickness is recommended not to be less than 5 mm. UFC 4-010-01 limits the deflection of the glazed window to L/160, where L is the span length in the direction in which the deflection is computed based on the equivalent static load acting on the window tributary area. For the intermediate mullions, the deflection is checked based on the longest supported length with simple support condition. The ASTM F2248 standard is used to design window frames. The Standard limits framing member deflection not to exceed L/60 under twice the glazing capacity for inward deflection obtained from ASTM E1300. It is consistent with that used for (UFC 4-010-01 2013). The anchorage between the window frame and glazing should be of mechanical type. The window system design concept is based on the concept of balanced design, ensuring glazing failure to occur prior to the failure of the window frame and its anchorage to the substrate. The window anchors are design depending on uniform load applied on the window with a magnitude satisfying the following conditions:

- If the blast pressure obtained from ASTM F2248-12 is greater than 1.5 of the glazing capacity as computed from ASTM E1300, the applied design uniform pressure on the window shall be twice the load resistance of glazing.

- If the blast pressure obtained from ASTM F2248-12 is less than 1.5 of the glazing capacity as computed from ASTM E1300, the applied design uniform pressure on the window shall be equal to the load resistance of glazing.

2.4.2.3   The ISC Security Design Criteria (2001):

The ISC (Interagency Security Committee) "(Security Design Criteria 2001) for new federal office buildings and major modernization projects in the US" conducted a comprehensive study with a multidisciplinary project teams to investigate security measures for buildings and their locations, among which blast-resistant windows were part of the study. Based on their level of protection, windows were categorized into windows with limited protection and protected windows. The first category was windows with limited protection that should not be designed for blast loads. Nevertheless, the glazing materials are required to be designed and used to mitigate blast hazard. Protected window systems have several types of glass, including filmed annealed glass on the interior pane anchored to the frame using wet glazing, or other heat-treated glass types with lamination. Furthermore, the monolithic annealed or heat-treated glass and wire fabric glass are considered as hazardous systems. The film thickness used for annealed glass applications should not be less that 4 mils. The window frame should be designed to have a higher capacity than the glazing, the window retention anchors to be stronger that the window frame, and the substrate is required to be stronger than the retention anchors. According to the security design criterion, the thermally tempered glass exhibit 4 times the annealed glass strength while the heat strengthened glass develop 2 times the annealed glass strength. The optimized design based on the (ISC Design Criteria 2001) for the walls, window retention anchors, and window frames should allow the glazing materials to develop its capacity. It is recommended to use dynamic structural analysis software and experimental data to ensure that the glazing could sustain the applied pressure or the post event damage of the window to be within the condition outlined in Table 2.1 for the (GSA 2003) standard. The design criteria also indicate that window frames with sufficient bite depth show better performance as observed by experimental data. The structural silicon application requirements include the use frame bite of ½-inch (12 mm). The design criteria do not limit the window opening size, but it is recommended not to exceed 40 % of the wall (substrate) area. The recommendation advises the implementation of the optimum window frame design that allows for developing maximum resistance of the selected glazing up to 750 breaks per 1000 without failure. The retention anchor should stay functional during a car bomb attack without failure.

2.4.2.4 British MCTPSM - Manual for Counter Terrorist Protective Security Measures (2003):

The design guidelines included in the British MCTPSM Manual provides a simplified design procedure for glazing protection in supplement Four, Annex C and D. The procedure includes two design stages. In the first stage the threat and the standoff (S.O) distance based on the explosive device size and standoff distance that causes 4 mm annealed glass failure is establish, as specified in Table 2.6. This condition defines the S.O for the reference window. In the second stage, comparative performance of the window is determined relative to the reference window and was obtained depending on the reference standoff distance, which is S.O for 4 mm annealed glass. This explained as follows:

Comparative Performance = (S.O for 4 mm annealed)/(S.O measured)

The appropriate glazing type for the window is based on the above relationship and presented in Table 2.7. The annealed glass with 4 mm thickness is the reference window in the Table with Comparative Performance of 1.0 unit. As the Comparative Performance ration increases, the quality of the protection improves. An example is provided in the British Manual (MCTPSM 2003) for glazing of a window subjected to 1000 kg of home-made explosive (HME) car bomb parked in front of a building with a standoff distance of 36 m. It is found from Table 2.6 that the reference S.O for 4 mm annealed glass for 1000 HME is 120 m. The comparative performance becomes 120/36=3.3.

Based on Table 2.7, the glazing type is either 11.5 mm laminated or 6.0 mm annealed + 7.5 mm laminated glass.

Window frames can be designed based on the (MCTPSM Supplement Four 2003), where the equivalent ultimate static frame loads (w) with different glass thicknesses, window pane sizes, and minimum glazing rebates are listed as presented in Table 2.8. The average frame edge reaction is obtained as follows:

$$F = (W \times A) / P \qquad\qquad 2.1$$

where F is the average frame edge reaction along the length, A is the surface area of the entire window, including the frame face, in m^2, and P is the perimeter of the window in m.

According to the MCTPSM Supplement Four, the frame and the supporting members are designed to account for two types of actions taking place at the same time; first a line load equal to 1.0F kN/m applied on the frame perpendicular to the window generating shear forces; and second a line load equal to 0.5F kN/m working in the plane of the window generating axial tension.

Table 2.8 gives examples for frame strength based on tests conducted using blast pressures of 100 kPa to 200 kPa and impulse of 500 kPa. If steel frames are used, they should be designed depending on their ultimate yield strength while aluminum frames could use 0.2% proof stress for design. Also, the frame design should be able to survive 75% of the loads in rebound under negative pressure. The design for shear connectors and fixing loads for nominal blast resistance of laminated glass are also provided in the MCTPSM Supplement Four. An example for the recommended design loads is depicted in Table 2.9. A laminated glass with 1.52 mm PVB thick interlayer with 35 mm bite depth is used for the specified load in Table 2.9. Steel bolts, screws or anchors can be used to resist forces at ultimate or yield with magnitudes 7kN, 14 kN, and 21 kN for 6 mm, 8 mm and 10 mm diameter bolts, respectively.

2.4.2.5 Royal Institute for British Architects (RIBA) Guidance on Designing for Counterterrorism (2011):

In 2011, the Royal Institute for British Architects (RIBA) provided design guidelines for counterterrorism and hazards related to terrorist attacks, also including planning guidelines. The guidelines recommend the use of appropriate materials for glazed facades for safety. It provides limited specifications window glazing design.

2.4.2.6 NaCTSO Recommendations of UK:

National Counter Terrorism Security Office (NaCTSO) in the UK published a total of 26 articles as Counter Terrorism Protective Security Advice series for communities, businesses and different places of gatherings and their infrastructure between 2006 and 2015. The focus of the recommendations was on soft security measures and hazards related issues. The published recommendations included limited information on the design of security window systems.

2.4.2.7 Physical Security Management Guidelines – Security Zones and Risk Mitigation Control Measures, Australian Government, (2013):

The Australian guidelines issued in 2013 recommended alarm systems in various security forms, soft measures for access control, and various counter terrorist measures. The recommendations called for appropriate building hardening elements and blast resistant measures without specific details.

2.4.2.8   Canadian Standards Association (CSA) S850-12 (2012):

The Canadian Standards Association (CSA) issued a new standard in 2012 for designing new buildings and evaluating existing buildings under blast loads. The intent was to mitigate blast risk, minimizing property damage and casualties of building occupants. The performance criteria, analysis methods, and design for building materials and elements are included in the standard. A section is also devoted to window design. The standard requires window glazing assessment and design using either standard tests or analysis by a third party. The test results are expected to conform to the performance requirements of either one of ASTM F1642, GSA-TS01 or ISO 16933. If testing is not available, dynamic analysis of the glazed window is required. Several types of glazing systems and catchment systems, including glass with safety film, thermally tempered glass, laminated glass, or polycarbonates and catchment systems are recommended to be used to reduce glass fragmentations. The window frame, mullions, and sashes should be designed using dynamic analysis or tested experimentally to check their capacities. They should be made from aluminum, steel, or other appropriate materials. The window system should be designed such that the frame is stronger than the glazing, anchors are stronger than the window frame, and the substrate is 1.5 stronger than the window frame.

2.4.2.9   PWGSC Design Guidelines (2005):

The PWGSC (Public works and Government Services Canada) design guidelines were developed by CERL (Canadian Explosives Research Laboratory) for appropriate method of installation of protective film for blast risk mitigation. The Guidelines specifies the safety film in different thicknesses, ranging from 4 mils to 7 mills, with possible installation in plies having a total thickness of 7 mils to 21 mils. The characteristics of the film material and the adhesive used are presented in detail with proper methods of installation depending on the expected level of protection. The guide highlights tests used for film material assessment and protective film performance based on the US General Services Administration (GSA 2003) methodology and other testing standards. The guild also provides types of glazing that are typically used to anchor the protective film to the window frames, including wet-glazing and mechanical anchoring techniques.

2.4.2.10 AAMA 510-06 (2006):

The American Architectural Manufacturers Association (AAMA 2006) issued AAMA 510-06 Voluntary Guide Specification for Blast Hazard Mitigation for Fenestration Systems. The document presents available test procedures and window design previsions while emphasizing the components of window protection systems. The specification gives design recommendations and guidelines for best practices, as well as project-specific and product-specific certifications for practitioners. The specifications are required to conform with the ASTM F1642, AAMA 510 and UFC 4-010 requirements.

2.4.2.11 AAMA (2008):

Design procedures used for blast resistant window system are provided in (AAMA 2008) with appropriate references made to existing design standards. The blast mitigation approaches of window systems are classified into four criteria including: limitation of flying shards, glass retention, frame support, and wall integrity. According to (AAMA 2008), window anchors should be evaluated for each product and the surrounding substrate. The glazing that satisfies their design criteria can be divide into four categories: laminated glass, window film, polycarbonate, and insulating glass unit. The document also illustrates laminated glass for possible use with different interlayer and laminate configurations, as shown in Figure 2.17. It also refers to (UFC 4-010-01 2013) specifications for minimum glass and lamination thicknesses. It is indicated that ¼" (6.3 mm) is the minimum recommended glass thickness with 0.75 mm interlayer for lamination. Window films are recommended for existing windows. Several challenges are mentioned for use of laminations in glass, such as the UV effects and possible discoloration (yellowing) and poor connections to the frame. The minimum bite is specified as 3/8" (9.5 mm) if structural glazing is used, and 1" (25 mm) bite otherwise based on the (UFC 4-010-01 2007) recommendations.

The use of polycarbonates poses challenges when it is applied for larger lites due to their relatively high flexibility, which would need large window bites. It is indicated that insulated glass shows the best protection from shards, but it may not be a cost-effective solution. Therefore, the use of one-sided lamination has lower cost, and the other lite can be annealed, heat strengthened or fully tempered glass.

2.4.2.12 CERL (2015):

The Canadian Explosives Research Laboratory (CERL) provided a guide to using protective film for security upgrade of glass windows for the Department of Foreign Affairs and Trade and Development (DFATD) in 2015. The design guide aims to meet either the GSA Performance Condition 3a, as illustrated in Figure 2.14 at a Protection Level C, or Low Hazard rating under (ISO 16933 2007). The performance criteria mentioned above can be achieved using a protective film on the inner pane of double pane insulated glass or on single glass window. Then, it is required to anchor the film to the window frame, and the window frame should be secured to the substrate. The film thickness should not be less than 0.18 (7 mil) for four-sided anchoring based on the DFATD requirements. The authors also mentioned that the frame retention anchors to the substrate should have sufficient strength to develop the maximum capacity of the film, which in turn needs to have a minimum tensile strength of 193 MPa. If laminated glass is used, it should be of 6.8 mm thickness with a heavy window frame having 30 mm bite. The typical film to frame anchoring technique is illustrated in Figure 2.18.

The document indicated the acceptable design for window frame anchorage to substrate where the maximum anchor spacing of 300 mm is allowed for Level I protection depicted in Figure 2.19. The tighter anchor spacing depends on the surrounding substrate and frame construction details. The conditions of the substrate construction on site might affect the design of anchors, and the substrate must be strong to avoid disintegration prior to the window failure. DFATD also provides an example for window designs in Table 2.10 where number of anchors, anchor diameter and anchor embedment lengths are specified for a standard GSA size window with 1200 mm by 1700 mm window dimensions. These results are only applicable for anchors that are critical in shear. The anchoring details for different wall media are shown in Figure 2.19.

2.4.2.13 Graham Architectural Products Specifications (2012a, 2012b):

The (Graham Architectural Products Specifications 2012a; 2012b) highlights manufacturing and design specification for blast mitigation of operable aluminum windows and their components (2012a) and fixed windows (2012b). The specifications follow existing requirements published in various documents such as the US Government UFC and GSA, American Architectural Manufacturing Association (AAMA), American Society of Testing Materials (ASTM), American National Standards Institute, and Glass Association of North America standards) for different hardware components. Based on the above requirements, the maximum deflection is limited to L/160, where L is the frame length in the direction of deflection calculations. The frame anchors are designed to survive 2 times the 3-second duration design loads specified in (ASTMF2248 2012).

2.4.2.14 Standards Design Group (2007):

A study was conducted by (Standards Design Group, Inc. 2007) using computer software "Blast Resistant Glazing Design 2007," (BRGD 2003) on a rectangular laminated glass and insulating glass construction manufactured with a single laminated glass pane to survive blast loads. The publications authored by (Scott et al. 2001), ASTM F2248-03 and ASTM E 1300-02/03 were the references for the blast software. The hazard levels are defined based on GSA Level C and Level D or can be defined as threats level associated with a certain charge weight and standoff distance. The threat levels are converted in the software to a 3-second duration equivalent design loads.

The output from the software includes recommendations for the appropriate dimensions of sealant bead to anchor glazing to the window frame, as well as applied forces on the connections used to anchor the window frame to the substrate. In the software, a user can enter several parameters including the hazard level, rectangular dimensions of the window and the type of glass. It is assumed in the software that the glazing should be continuously supported along four sides of the window frame. The glazed window is fabricated with a laminated glass that consists of annealed or heat strengthened glass panes having a PVB interlayer. Also, insulating glass type can be used having a monolithic glass pane for the outer side of the building and a laminated glass pane in the interior side or laminated glass, mounted on both sides.

2.5 List of Blast Resistant Glazing Standards and Specifications

Industry Standards:

AAMA 510-06: "American Architectural Manufacturers Association (AAMA) Voluntary Guide Specifications for Blast Hazard Mitigation for Fenestration Windows".

US Government Standards

US General Services Administration (GSA): "Standard Test Method for Glazing and Window Systems Subject to Dynamic Overpressure Loadings".

ISC Security Design Criteria for New Federal Buildings and Major Renovation Projects, "the Interagency Security Committee, 2001".

DoD United Facilities Criteria (UFC)

UFC 4-010-01: "Minimum Antiterrorism Standards for Buildings".

UFC 4-010-02: "Minimum Antiterrorism Standards for Buildings (RESTRICTED)".

UK Government Standards and Manuals

"MCTPSM - Manual for Counter Terrorist Protective Security Measures, Supplement Four, Annex C and D (2003)".

"Security Facilities Executive Special Services Group – Explosion Protection, Glazing Hazed Guide (1997), Cabinet Office, London, England".

ASTM Standards

ASTM E1300: "Standard Practice for Determining Load Resistance of Glass in Buildings".

ASTM F1642: "Standard Test Method for Glazing and Glazing Systems Subject to Airblast Loadings".

ASTM F2248: "Standard Practice for Specifying an Equivalent 3-Second Duration Design Loading for Blast Resistant Glazing Fabricated with Laminated Glass".

International Organization for Standardization

ISO 16933: "(2007) Glass in building - Explosion-resistant security glazing - Test and classification for arena air-blast loading".

ISO 16934: "(2007) Glass in building - Explosion-resistant security glazing - Test and classification by shock-tube loading".

2.6   Summary of Previous Research

A review of existing literature and design recommendations/guidelines/standards was conducted to identify research gaps and research needs. The following provides an overall summary of the available literature.

- There is lack of sufficient experimental and analytical research to devise a design standard and make design recommendations for blast-resistant window retention anchors; hence, the rational for the development of CSA Standard S852, which is partly based on the current research project reported in this PhD book.

- Several standards were developed for testing glazed window systems such as the GSA Standard (GSA 2003) and (ASTM F1642 1966) that use a similar window test procedure having the same performance criteria and equivalent hazard levels. However, these standards are limited to test protocols, and do not provide information for design.

- The majority of previous research has been on glazed window performance, glazing design, and to some extent on window frame design and overall window system performance. There is very little research conducted on blast-resistant window retention anchor design.

- The lack of availability of research on retention anchors has promoted empirical design with larger number of anchors, closely spaced along the perimeter of the window opening, which may be detrimental to substrate performance near the vicinity of windows.

- Window blast risk can be mitigated with the use of laminated blast-resistant windows and/or use of protective films on existing windows.

- The DoD Unified Facilities Criteria (UFC 4-010) gives detailed design information, based on the (ASTM F2248 2012) design loads for window systems.

- The window resistance can be computed using ASTM E1300, and the design loads acting on window frames and frame anchors can be obtained from (ASTM F2248 2012).

- The international guidelines including UFC 4-010, AAMA 510-06 (American Architectural Manufacturers Association Voluntary Guide) and DFATD Design Guide provide limited design information for window retention anchors.

- A simplified design method is proposed by Manual for Counter Terrorist Protective Security Measures (MCTPSM) of the UK for window retention anchor design based on equivalent static loads.

- A conservative retention anchor design can be obtained using an equivalent static loads procedure that may cooperate the performance of window frame.

The review of previous studies indicated the need for design specifications and guidelines of window retention anchors under blast loads to securely mount window frames to the surrounding substrates.

Table 2.1 GSA Ratings of window hazard (GSA 2003)

Performance condition	Protection level	Hazard level	Description of Window Glazing Response
1	Safe	None	Glazing does not break. No visible damage to glazing or frame.
2	Very High	None	Glazing cracks but is retained by the frame. Dusting or very small fragments near sill or on floor acceptable.
3a	High	Very low	Glazing cracks. Fragments enter space and land on floor no further than 3.3 ft. from the window.
3b	High	low	Glazing cracks. Fragments enter space and land on floor no further than 10 ft. from the window.
4	Medium	Medium	Glazing cracks. Fragments enter space and land on floor and impact a vertical witness panel at a distance of no more than 10 ft. from the window at a height no greater than 2 ft. above the floor.
5	Low	High	Glazing cracks and window system fails catastrophically. Fragments enter space impacting a vertical witness panel at a distance of no more than 10 ft. from the window at a height greater than 2 ft. above the floor.

Table 2.2 GSA Protection levels (ISC 2001)

Building Description				Maximum Over-pressure	Maximum impulse
Type	Occupants	Square Feet	Tenants		
A	<10	<25k	Recruiting Office	0	0
B	<150	<80k	Social Sec. Admin.	0	0
C	<450	<150k	Law Enforcement	4 psi	30 psi-msec
D	>450	>150k	Courts, Justice	10 psi	90 psi-msec
E	>450	>150k	Pentagon, CIA	Classified	Classified

Table 2.3 Vehicle bombs (ISO 16933)

Mean peak air blast pressure kPa	Mean positive phase impulse kPa-ms
30	180
50	250
80	380
140	600
250	850
450	1200
800	1600

Table 2.4 Hand carried satchel bombs(ISO 16933)

Mean peak air blast pressure kPa	Mean positive phase impulse kPa-ms
70	150
110	200
250	300
800	500
700	700
1600	1000
2800	1500

Table 2.5 Shock tube pressure and impulse combinations for glazed window tests (ISO 16934)

Minimum values	
Peak pressure P_c kPa	Impulse I_c kPa-ms
30	170
50	370
70	550
100	900
150	1500
200	2200

Table 2.6 Stand-off distances to produce internal flying glass (British MCTPSM 2003)

Device	Stand-off for 4 mm annealed glass in meters
Small package	10
Small briefcase	14
Large briefcase	20
Suitcase	26
Car	60
Small van	120
Large van	140
Small lorry	160
Large lorry	200

Table 2.7 Recommended glazing types in the British approach (British MCTPSM 2003)

GLAZING TYPE	COMPARATIVE PERFORMANCE
ANNEALED GLASS (A)	
4mm	1.0
4mm + ASF[1]	1.7
4mm + ASF + BBNC[2]	2.0
TOUGHENED GLASS (T)	
6mm	2.0
6mm + ASF	2.5
8mm	2.5
8mm + ASF	2.9
10mm	2.9
10mm + ASF	3.3
LAMINATED GLASS (L)[3]	
6.8mm	2.5
7.5mm	2.9
11.5mm	3.3
DOUBLE GLAZED UNITS[3]	
6mm T + 6mm T	2.5
6mm A + 7.5mm L	3.3
6mm T + 7.5mm L	4.0

[1] ASF – Anti Shatter Film, 100 microns thick.

[2] BBNC – Bomb Blast Net Curtains.

[3] For laminated glass to be effective it must be securely fixed into its frames Preferably with structural silicon and the frames must have 25mm minimum deep glazing rebates. However in special frames with deeper (3.5mm) rebates the % improvement will increase. The frames in turn must be securely sixed to the surrounding structure.

Table 2.8 Strength of frames, mullions and transoms required for nominal blast resistance using laminated glass (British MCTPSM 2003)

LAMINATED GLASS THICKNESS mm	APPROX GLASS PANE SIZE m^2	EQUIVALENT ULTIMATE STATIC FRAME LOAD W kN/m^2	MINIMUM GLAZING REBATE mm (35mm preferred)
6.8	0.6	8.0	25
(0.8 mm pvb)	1.8	4.0	25
	3.0	4.0	30
7.5	0.6	12.0	25
(1.5 mm pvb)	1.8	7.0	30
	3.0	6.0	30
11.5	0.6	18.0	25
(1.5 mm pvb)	1.8	11.0	30
	3.0	9.0	30

Note: PVB is polyvinyl butyral interlayer in laminated glass.

Table 2.9 Recommended shear fixing loads (British MCTPSM 2003)

Nominal shear fixing loads for windows with sealant laminated glass having 1.52 mm thick pvb, set in 35 mm deep rebates					
Window size m^2	Approx. Aspect ratio	Design Load kN/m^2	Total Load kN	Assumed Perimeter m	Line Load kN/m
0.7	1.25	150	105	3.5	30
2.0	1.25	60	120	6.0	20
4.0	1.0	30	120	8.0	15

Table 2.10 Acceptable wall anchorage solutions for a 1200 mm by 1700 mm standard GSA window on solid substrate, when anchors are loaded in shear (CERL 2015)

Wall	Number of Anchors (Spacing)		Total Number of Anchors	Anchor Diameter (mm)	Anchor Embedment (cm)
	Top/Bottom	Sides			
Steel Frame	4 + 4 (30 cm)	6 + 6 (30 cm)	20	10	3.0
Rubble Infill	4 + 4 (30 cm)	6 + 6 (30 cm)	20	16	20
RC	4 + 4 (30 cm)	6 + 6 (30 cm)	20	10	15
CMU	4 + 4 (30 cm)	6 + 6 (30 cm)	20	16	20

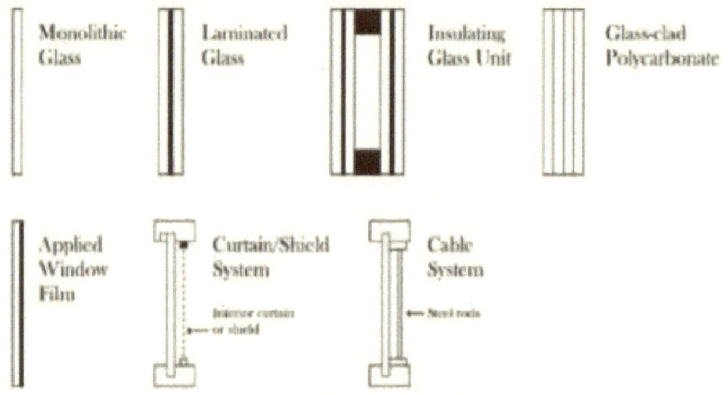

Figure 2.1: Types of blast resistant windows (Smith et al. 2010)

Figure 2.2: Typical installation for window anchor on masonry wall

(Ward and Jordan 2006)

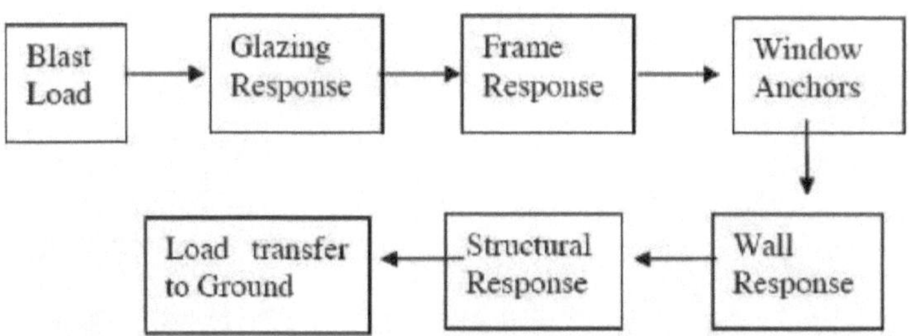

Figure 2.3: Mechanism of blast resistance in window systems (Ward et al. 2006)

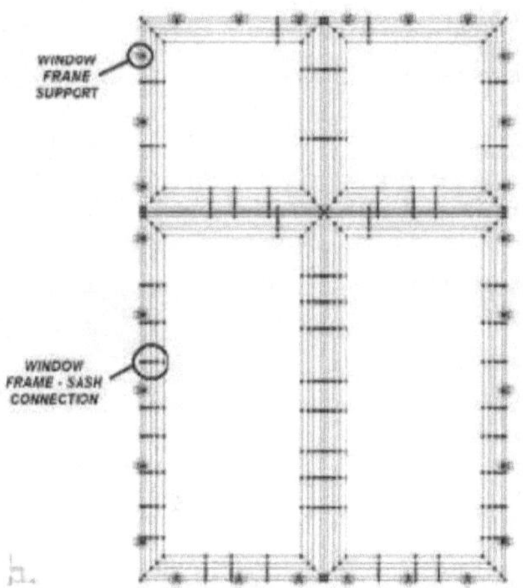

Figure 2.4: Building frame used for blast analysis (Ward et al. 2006)

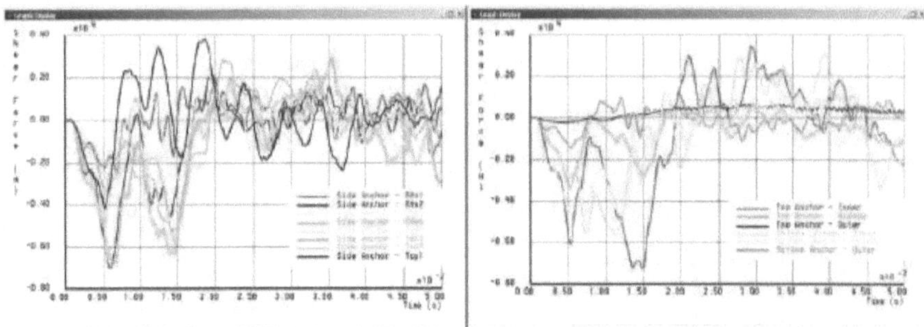

Figure 2.5: Analysis results showing force distribution along anchors (Ward et al. 2006)

a) Concrete samples

b) Limestone masonry samples

Figure 2.6: Typical specimens in concrete and lime stone substrates (Braimah et al. 2009)

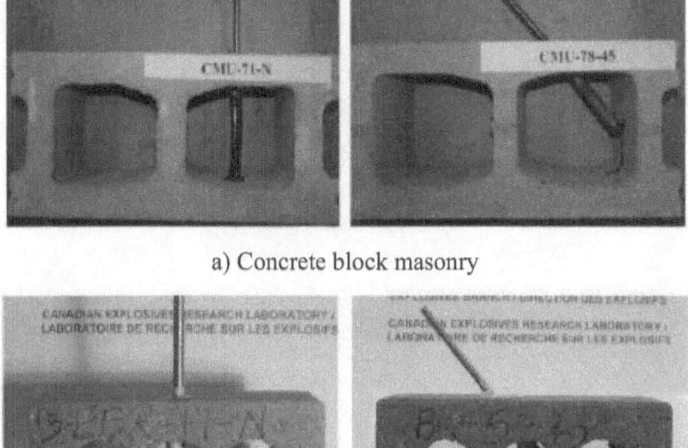

a) Concrete block masonry

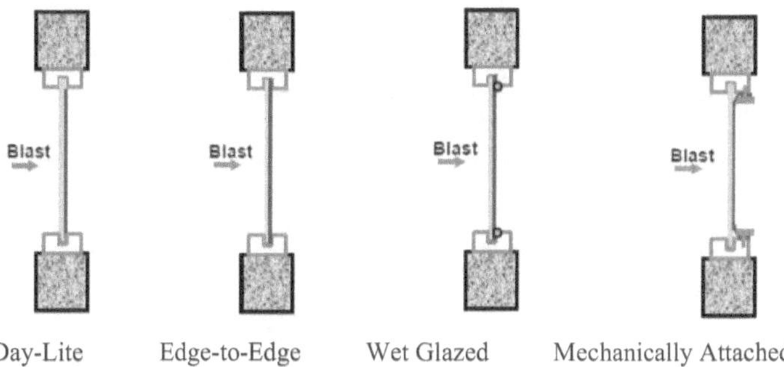

b) Clay brick masonry

Figure 2.7: Typical test specimens embedded in masonry (Braimah et al. 2014)

Blast   Blast   Blast   Blast

Day-Lite   Edge-to-Edge   Wet Glazed   Mechanically Attached

Figure 2.8: Different applications of protective film (Smith 2003)

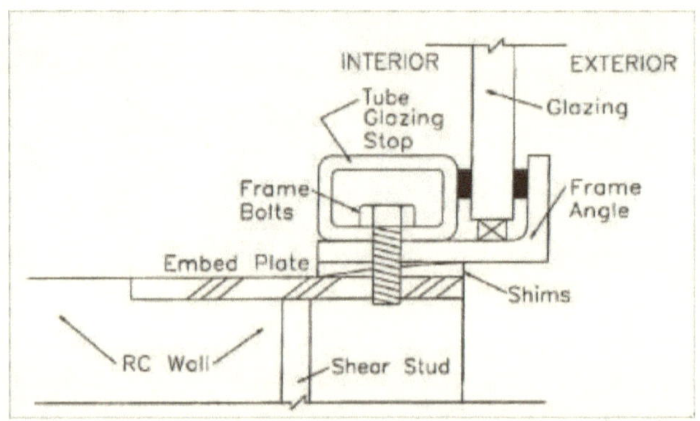

Figure 2.9: Generic window glazing and frame details (Meyers et al. 1994)

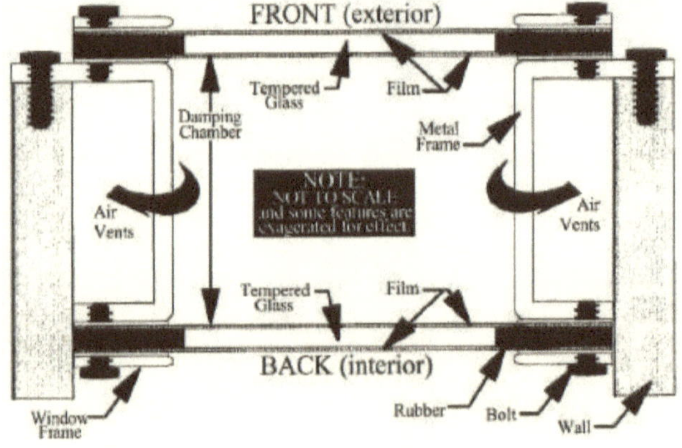

Figure 2.10: Sealed blast-resistant window (Anderson et al. 2003)

7 mill daylight film - 4psi; 30 psi-ms

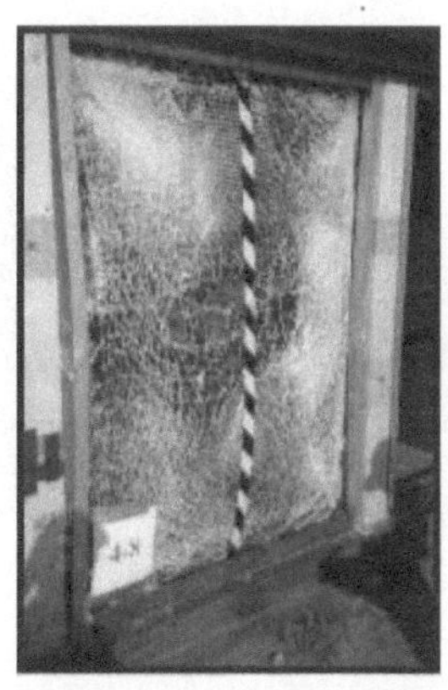

10 mill anchored film - 4 psi; 30 psi-ms

15 mil anchored film - 9 psi; 90 psi-ms

7 mil anchored film - 35 psi; 35 psi-ms
(close-in)

Figure 2.11: Window performance of daylight application and anchored films on four sides
(Anderson et al. 2003)

a) Gullwing profile attached to steel test cubical by means of angle brackets

b) Rupturing of the bottom Gullwing profile

Figure 2.12: Window C2 with Panzerfilm glazing and silicone anchored Gullwing profiles (Panzerfilm Tests 2002)

Figure 2.13: Windows L1; C2; and R3 (left, centre and right, respectively) after live testing (Panzerfilm Tests 2002)

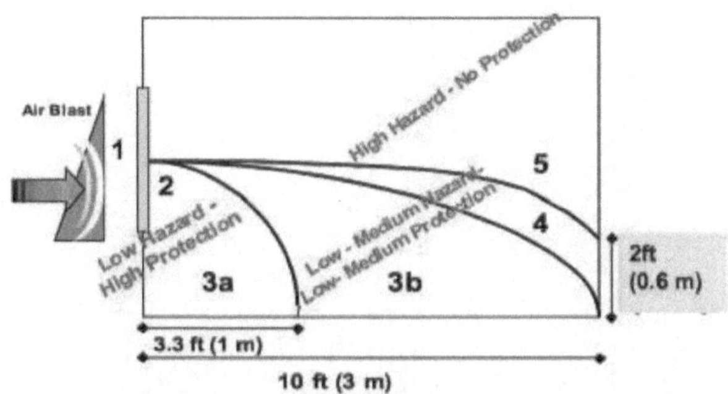

Figure 2.14: GSA post-test performance for window system (GSA 2003)

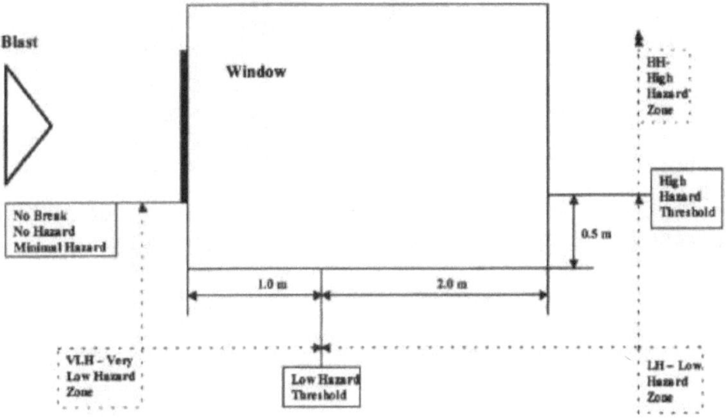

Figure 2.15: ASCE F1642-12 Window test set-up and hazard levels (ASTM F 1642-12)

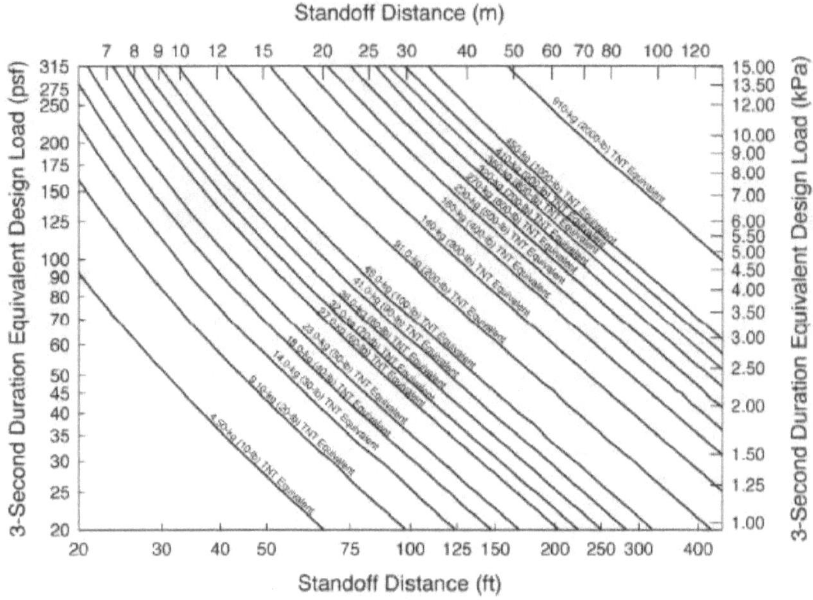

Figure 2.16: Three-second equivalent design load (ASTM F2248-12)

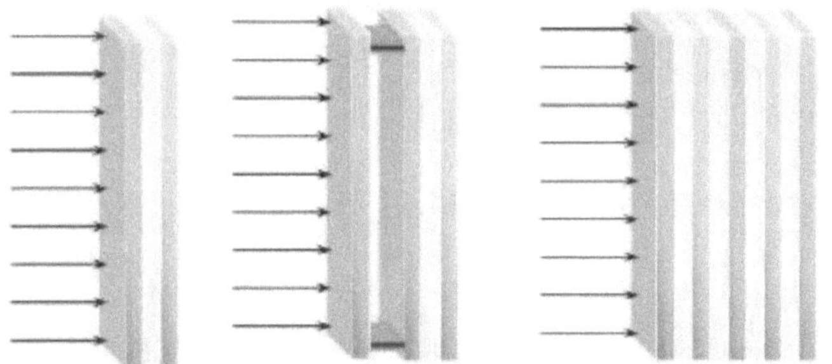

a) Single Light   b) Laminated Insulated   c) Multiply Laminated

Figure 2.17: Laminated glass (AAMA 2008)

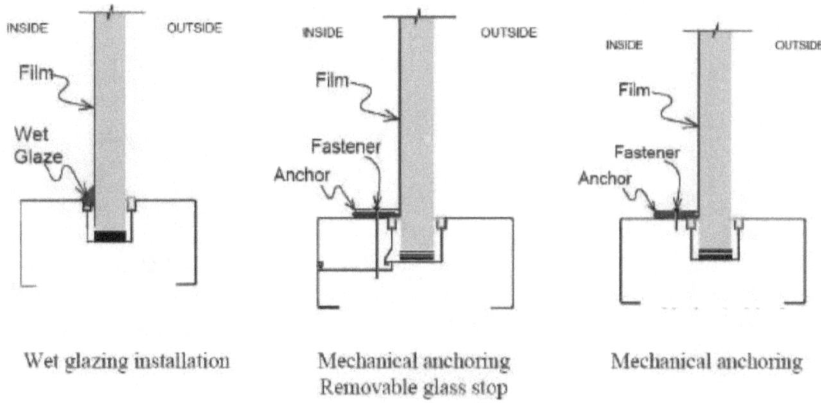

Wet glazing installation   Mechanical anchoring   Mechanical anchoring
                                Removable glass stop

Figure 2.18: Typical film-to-frame anchoring techniques (CERL 2015)

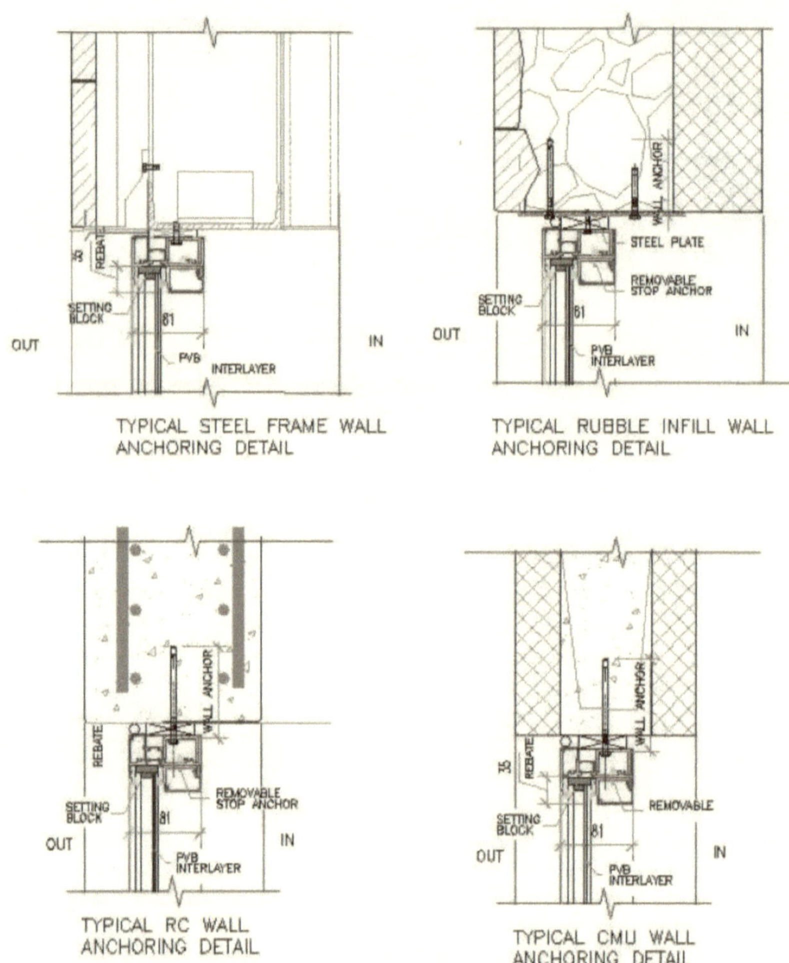

Figure 2.19: Anchoring details in different substrates (CERL 2015)

Part II

Experimental Research

CHAPTER 3. EXPERIMENTAL INVESTIGATION

OF BLAST-RESISTANT WINDOW ANCHORS

3.1 Introduction

Critical infrastructure subjected to blast loads may suffer varying degrees of damage to their structural and/or non-structural components. Windows are one of the most vulnerable elements of a building infrastructure, posing serious threats to building occupants. High intensity blast overpressures generated by external sources of explosives cause significant damage to windows, potentially producing lethal glass shards or other window fragments flying into the occupied areas of buildings at supersonic velocities. Therefore, design of blast-resistant windows is paramount for blast risk mitigation of buildings. Significant research and development has been conducted on window protection systems, including use of protective films, laminated glass, types of glazing (wet or mechanical glazing systems), as well as blast-resistant window frames and substrates (Mays et al. 2003; Bangash et al. 2006; Krauthammer 2008; Dussenberry 2010; Uddin 2010; Hao et al. 2015; Weissman et al. 1978). However, research on window retention anchors is scarce in the literature. The previous literature summarized by (Saatcioglu et al. 2015) indicate lack of sufficient experimental and analytical data for designing window retention anchors under blast loads. Ward et al. 2006) indicated that the windows used in practice are engineered and placed with a large number of anchors, with mostly very small spacing that could cause damage to the substrate without quantifying the magnitude and distribution of retention anchors. The researchers reported on the results of analyses of windows with different number and patterns of window retention anchors. The results showed significant variation of shear forces among the anchors. They concluded that the total number of anchors commonly used in practice could be reduced. Other researcher projects, including those conducted by (Smith et al. 2010) and (Smith 2003) studied the failure mechanism of retention anchors on different substrates and the effect of dynamic increase factor (DIF) on anchors without providing specific recommendations on anchor types, distribution patterns, or the anchorage techniques. A state of the art on blast-resistant design of windows and window frames is presented by (Meyers et al. 1994) with verifications of design results against available tests. The researchers listed a total of 19 computer codes, developed for blast-resistant design of windows between 1984 and 1994. In addition, the results of 63 successful full-scale window blast tests were reported. It was indicated that a design procedure based on single-degree-of-freedom analysis provide sufficiently conservative values. The Canadian Explosives Research Laboratory (CERL) developed a guide for the Department of Foreign Affairs, Trade and Development (DFATD) in Canada using protective film for security upgrade of glass windows (CERL 2015). The DFATD design guide also provides design information for anchoring window frames to substrates, recommending an acceptable window frame anchoring scheme with 300 mm anchor spacing for a specific level of protection. It is indicated that tighter spacing of anchors may be required depending on wall and frame construction details.

Several standards were developed for testing glazed window systems, such as the (GSA 2003) and (ASTM F1642 2012) standards, providing a testing protocol and performance criteria for experimental approval of windows in blast-resistant construction. The DoD Unified Facilities Criteria (UFC3-340 2008) gives detailed design information on blast-resistant design of infrastructure, but they limit their window anchor design provisions to those recommended by (ASTM F2248 2012).

A comprehensive research program was conducted at the Blast Research Laboratory of the University of Ottawa with the objectives of generating design data and a design procedure for blast-resistant window retention anchors. The research program consisted of experimental and numerical components. The current paper reports on the experimental phase of research. A companion paper reports on the numerical investigation (Alameer et al. 2020). It is worth noting that the focus of the current investigation is on the behavior and design of window retention anchors, in terms of the magnitude and distribution of force and deformation components as effected by design variables used as test parameters. Substrate failure in the anchorage zone, in the form of substrate cone failure, loss of friction/adhesion or the failure of unreinforced concrete, masonry and stone are not included in the current investigation, though observed failure modes are presented. Design of anchorage regions of substrates and their design requirements are covered in various standards (ACI 318-19 2019), and their behavior was widely researched in the past (Colak 2001; Ammann et al. 1991; Cannon et al. 1981; Collins et al. 1989; Cook et al. 1993; Cook et al. 2001; Eligehausen et al. 1988; Elingehausen 2001; Sankiw et al. 1991; Klinger et al. 1982; Lin et al. 1996; McVay et al. 1993; Peier 1983; Rodriguez et al. 2001). An extensive review of literature was reported by (Chen 2004) on performance and design of adhesive anchors.

3.2 Experimental Research

The University of Ottawa Blast Research Laboratory was used for experimental research. The laboratory is equipped with a pneumatically driven shock tube as a blast simulator with a maximum reflected pressure capacity of 100 kPa and an ability to simulate blast shock wave durations ranging between 5 ms to 50 ms. Figure 3.1 illustrates the shock tube used for testing the full-size punched windows that formed the experimental component of current research. Further details of the shock tube can be found elsewhere (Lloyd et al. 2010).

3.2.1 Test Windows

A total of 23 full-size windows were prepared for testing. The windows were anchored to reinforced concrete, structural steel, concrete block, or stone walls as four types of substrates. Figure

3.2 depicts the geometric characteristics of the window systems tested. Three different window height-to-length aspects ratios (ℓ_y/ℓ_x) were considered, though the majority of the tests were conducted on square and rectangular windows with aspect ratios of 1.0 and 3.0, respectively. The windows were manufactured by a local company as double pane insulated glass units (IGU) having anneal glass with a 12 mm air gap between the panes. The window frame consisted of aluminum sections and U-shaped aluminum clip-on window stops with an aluminum wall thickness of 1.5 mm. Tables 3.1 (a) and (b) provide a list of all the windows tested and their properties. The window properties were selected based on several parameters known to impact the behavior of window anchors. The parameters considered included the glazing type (wet glazing versus mechanical glazing), protective film thickness, window aspect ratio, the number and arrangement of anchors, blast pressure-impulse combination, and substrate type.

The windows were glazed and assembled prior to being mounted on the substrates. The inner pane (the protected side, facing outside the shock tube during testing) was glazed with protective films. After the installation of the films, the windows were either wet-glazed using structural silicone, or mechanically glazed using aluminum window stops secured to the window frames by bolts. Wet glazing was applied on edge-to-edge films by means of structural silicone with a minimum bead thickness of 13 mm along the perimeter of the glass. For wet glazed windows, the original clip-on window stops were used after being strengthened by inserting solid aluminum bars and bolting on the window frame. The majority of the windows tested were mechanically anchored using 25 mm square hallow aluminum sections having a wall thickness of 5 mm, replacing the original U-shaped clip-on stops. The mechanical anchoring was done using 6.3 mm (1/4 in) diameter 38 mm (1.5 in) long bolts to secure the films to the frame. These bolts were equally spaced at 100 mm between the window retention anchors. Figure 3.3 shows the details of the glazing process employed.

The glazed windows were secured to window substrates using steel bolts as window retention anchors. The anchor consisted of 9.5 mm (3/8 in) diameter high-strength (Grade 8) bolts, having either 76 mm (3 in) or 127 mm (5 in) lengths, secured in steel, reinforced concrete, concrete block, or stone substrate. For steel substrates, nuts were used to tighten the bolts at substrate ends. For concrete, concrete block, or stone substrates, drop-in-anchors shown in Figure 3.4 were used. Tables 3.1 (a) and (b) show the anchor spacing and embedment length for each window.

Two of each of reinforced concrete, concrete block masonry and stone masonry walls were designed and built as window substrates for the two window sizes with aspect ratios of 1.0 and 3.0. Three structural steel walls were prepared to accommodate all the three window sizes. All the walls had a 2.0 m square geometry. They were bolted on the shock tube test area along their top and bottom edges prior to testing to behave in the one-way mode, representing a portion of a continuous wall between two structural slabs. All the walls were designed to sustain substantially higher pressures than the 69 kPa maximum pressure applied during the test program. The reinforced concrete walls with a 150 mm thickness remained essentially elastic during the tests but developed some hairline cracks when subjected to the higher of the two blast loads considered. Steel substrates were built using a combination of 150 mm hallow square sections (HSS), 75 mm HSS and steel plates. They had the highest strength and rigidity among all the substrates considered and remained elastic. The concrete block walls were built as unreinforced masonry infill walls. They were built using standard size 200 mm x 200 mm x 400 mm (8 in x 8 in x 16 in) concrete blocks. The walls were strengthened around the window openings by providing 2- 10M bars vertically in the closest block cells on both sides of the window and by filling these cells with concrete, essentially creating two reinforced concrete columns, one on either side of the opening. Similarly, lintel blocks were used above and below the window opening with 2-10M bars in each lintel and filled with concrete. They provided sufficient resistance during the tests, developing cracks in some mortar joints. Some of the blocks were observed to show slight dislocations near the top and bottom support regions after repeated use, without any effect on window performance. The stone masonry walls were constructed using a combination of three different sandstone sizes. They were built as sneaked masonry walls with keyed stones to have a 200 mm thickness. The window openings either had square or rectangular shapes to accommodate 1220 mm x 1220 mm (48 in x 48 in) square or 560 mm x 1676 mm (22 in x 66 in) rectangular windows. They performed well under blast pressures, showing some mortar joint cracking. However, when a square window with a larger tributary area was exposed to 69 kPa pressure, failure of the anchorage region was experienced. This was expected because of the unreinforced nature of the window openings.

3.2.2 Preparation and Instrumentation

The preparation of window assemblies for testing involved securing the glazed windows to the substrates using the retention anchors at pre-drilled holes along the perimeter of window openings. The test assemblies were instrumented to measure anchor forces during response to blast loads. A number of options were considered to overcome the challenges associated with measuring forces in the anchors. The first 8 windows tested were instrumented with strain gauges placed on tension sides of frame elements. They were positioned either at anchor locations (support locations) or between the anchors (maximum deformation locations). The former gave tensile strains under negative bending and the latter gave tensile strains under positive bending. Because the flexural strains can be linked to moments, and moments on frame elements can be linked to the shear forces associated with anchors, the strain gauge readings would indirectly provide estimates of anchor shear forces. Four linear variable differential transducers (LVDT) were also used to monitor anchor deflections in the direction of blast pressure, and the deflection of the frame at nearby locations. The data on anchor deflections provided additional information to compute shear forces by modelling the anchors with appropriate end conditions as cantilever elements. Figure 3.5(a) illustrates the locations of strain gauges and the displacement transducers. Figure 3.5(b) shows typical instrumentation used in a rectangular window. Although this set of instrumentation led to indirect computation of anchor shear forces, axial tension generated by the membrane action in the post-break range could not be recorded. Therefore, an improved instrumentation technique was developed and used for the subsequent 15 windows tested. Representative anchors were instrumented with strain gauges. Holes were drilled into the anchor bolts longitudinally so that the lead-wires could be threaded through the holes for protection against damage during installation. This is illustrated in Figure 3.5(c).The strain measurements recorded on opposite sides of an anchor at maximum stress locations led to the computation of applied bending moment and axial tensile force, which could be resolved into all the force components acting on the anchor. LVDTs were also placed at the tip of the instrumented anchors, as well as on substrate locations near the anchors to assess anchor displacements relative to the substrates. The second set of instrumentation proved to be successful as subsequently illustrated.

3.2.3 Blast Loads and Test Procedure

The tests were conducted under the General Services Administration (GSA) recommended test procedure (GSA 2003). A witness panel was used to assess window performance in terms of GSA-specified performance criteria. The GSA specifies building occupancy classification for US

Government Buildings. It recommends pressure-impulse combinations expected to be resisted by each type of building. The two pressure-impulse combinations specified in the GSA specification are 28 kPa (4 psi) – 207 kPa-ms (30 psi-ms) and 69 kPa (10 psi) – 621 kPa-ms (90 psi-ms). Each window system was subjected to these two levels of reflected pressure-impulse combinations as the first and the second shots. Figure 3.6 shows representative pressure-time relationships used.

3.2.4   Test Observations and Failure Modes

The window assemblies tested in the experimental program have six components that can be critical under blast loads; i) glass, ii) protective film, iii) glazing type (wet or mechanical) iv) window frame, v) window retention anchors, and vi) substrate. The current design standards require anchors to be stronger than the rest of the glazed window components, with a safety margin of 1.5 (ASCE/SEI 59-11 2011; CSA S850-12 2012; CSA S852-18 2018) to prevent global failure of the window system as a whole. The substrate is also expected to be stronger than the window system. The test program was designed to investigate the effects of test parameters on anchor performance, including the modes of failure.

The unprotected glass pane, facing the exterior of the building (exposed to blast pressures), was damaged and failed in the majority of the windows tests. Figure 3.7 illustrates typical failure of an exterior glass facing the inside of the shock tube after a test. The unprotected glass in few rectangular windows survived the 28 kPa pressure. This was attributed to the relatively small, exposed area of the rectangular windows, coupled with protective reactive pressure that was generated by the air gap between the two glass panes, which was especially effective under certain combination of design parameters. The use of security film on protected glass panes prevented the failure of glass in the post-break phase of loading in all cases, provided that the window glazing was done properly, i.e., sufficient film thickness with proper anchorage to window frame was ensured. Minimum film thicknesses of 12-mil in rectangular windows with exposed surface area of 0.9 m^2, performing in one-way mode, and 23-mil in square windows with exposed surface area of 1.5 m^2, performing in two-way mode, were sufficient when they were mechanically glazed. Figure 3.8 shows a typical film rupturing that occurred in a square window.

The windows were glazed by securing protective films to window frames either using structural silicone (wet glazing) or through bolted mechanical anchors (square aluminum HSS sections). Both types of glazing were successful in maintaining the integrity of the window system under 28 kPa (4psi) blast pressure, irrespective of window dimensions. However, the wet glazing could not survive the pressure at 69 kPa (10 psi). In these windows, the protected glass pane flew in towards the witness panel without any sign of premature film rupturing. Examples of wet glazing failures are shown in Figure 3.9. Mechanical glazing performed extremely well until the failure of either the substrate or the retention anchors. Figure 3.10 shows an example of successful performance of a glazed window.

The aluminum window frames strengthened with enhanced window stops performed well during the tests. One of the square windows tested on a rigid steel substrate had fewer retention anchors (3 per side) at a wider anchor spacing (500 mm). This led to stress concentrations at anchor locations, as opposed to well distributed anchors in other comparable windows and resulted in the failure of the frame. This is shown in Figure 3.11. Other window frame failures were only observed in the form of secondary modes of failure, following either the failure of the substrate anchorage zone or the failure of the window anchors.

The anchorage zone of the retention anchors forms critical regions against pull-out forces or material failures, especially if these regions are unreinforced. Steel substrates offered stiff and strong anchorage zones. However, reinforced concrete, concrete masonry and stone masonry substrates had unreinforced anchorage zones near the window openings. The retention anchors consisted of 9.5 mm (3/4 in) diameter high-strength (Grade 8) bolts, having either 76 mm (3 in) or 127 mm (5 in) lengths. The initial set of anchors used had a 76 mm length with 38 mm embedment length into the substrate. They were bolted to steel substrates and performed well without any damage in the substrate. The same anchors were also used in the first 4 windows tested on reinforced concrete substrates. They performed well when the anchors were well distributed with 250 mm anchor spacing. When the anchor spacing was increased to 500 mm the increased force per anchor caused failure of the concrete anchorage zone during the second shot under higher pressure, as depicted in Figure 3.12. The anchor length in subsequent tests was increased to 127 mm with a 90 mm embedment length. The increased embedment length in drop-in anchors resulted in superior performance without any damage to concrete. Similarly, favorable behavior was observed in the anchorage region of concrete block masonry substrate, with 127 mm (5 in) anchors. It should be recalled that the concrete masonry substrate was reinforced around the window openings. This explains the absence of damage to the anchorage region. However, the stone masonry substrate suffered extensive damage to the anchorage zone, as shown in Figure 3.13 because of lack of reinforcement around the window opening.

Observations made during the tests indicated no damage in steel and reinforced concrete substrates except for limited hairline cracks detected in the reinforced concrete substrates. However, the masonry walls suffered significant softening in response due to the cracking of mortar joints. Some masonry units experienced movements within the wall without adversely affecting the integrity of the substrate. The stone masonry walls showed more softening than the concrete masonry wall. Figure 3.14 illustrates the observed damage.

Window retention anchors generally performed well except for windows with a small number of anchors, especially on steel substrates under 69 kPa pressure. One of the effects of substrates on anchor performance was the magnitude of force as affected by substrate rigidity. Steel substrate was the most rigid of all the substrates considered, followed closely by reinforced concrete. Anchors on steel substrates developed the highest forces, some failing in shear under 69 kPa pressure, while others flying as far away as the witness panel. A great majority of anchors developed permanent inelastic deformations at 69 kPa (10 psi), though many remained elastic under 28 kPa (4 psi), with some developing limited inelasticity. Many anchors pulled out and became loose after 69 kPa (10 psi), while some were lost after the test, though the windows remained attached to the substrate, indicating these pressure levels were representative of elastic and inelastic anchor capacities. Anchors on concrete substrates often developed bending under flexural stresses, indicating yield and post-yield behavior. Figure 3.15 illustrates the observed anchor deformations after the tests.

3.3   Test Data and The Effects of Test Parameters on Anchor Performance

The primary objective of the current research project was to assess anchor forces under dynamic blast loads. Anchor forces and out-of-plane displacements were measured using two different instrumentation techniques as previously discussed. The anchor forces were computed from the strain readings recorded during the post-break stage of loading as shear and axial tension force components when glazed windows developed membrane action. Of significance was the magnitude of axial tension relative to shear, as well as the effects of test variables on magnitude and distribution of anchor forces along the edges of window frames.

The anchors that were instrumented had two strain gauges, one placed on the extreme tension and the other on the extreme compression fibre at the critical section. The critical section was defined as the anchor section at the face of the substrate where they experienced the highest bending moment (as verified by observed deflected shapes of anchors after the tests). The tensile strain readings were higher than those in compression because of the accompanying axial tension associated with the membrane action. The maximum tensile strains recorded under 28 kPa reflected pressure varied between 5500 $\mu\varepsilon$ and 6500 $\mu\varepsilon$ for anchors at mid-vertical height of windows, and 3000 $\mu\varepsilon$ and 5500 $\mu\varepsilon$ for anchors at mid-length of the horizontal windows edge. Considering Grade 8 bolts which had 960 MPa yield strength and 5000 $\mu\varepsilon$ yield strain (based on 0.2% offset method) the anchors were at or slightly above the yield at this stage of loading. The computed anchor deflection at mid-height of window frame was approximately equal to 20 mm at this stage. The anchors under 69 kPa reflected pressure developed significant yielding with maximum tensile strains ranging between 7000 $\mu\varepsilon$ and 10000 $\mu\varepsilon$ on anchors of square windows, and 4000 $\mu\varepsilon$ and 7000 $\mu\varepsilon$ on anchors of rectangular windows. The recorded strain readings were resolved into two components; i) constant axial tension (T) (found by taking the difference between tensile and compressive strains), and ii) flexural component (based on linearly varying strain profile between tension fiber (ε_t) and compression fiber (ε_c), as illustrated in the stress profile depicted in Figure 3.16. The forces were computed for both levels of applied reflected pressure; 28 kPa and 69 kPa. The flexural strain profile was used to find moments generated at the critical section. The anchor shear force (V_a) was calculated using the computed moments and the applicable shear spans (length of anchors between the critical section and the point of application of force) and assuming cantilever behavior (as observed in deflected shapes of anchors after tests). Anchor deflections were computed from moment-curvature analyses and moment area theorems. The deflections computed showed good agreement with experimentally recorded values. However, there was discrepancy between the measured and computed displacements for windows on steel substrates when subjected to high pressures. This was attributed to the behavior of the anchors on steel substrates. These anchors were fully fixed prior to tests using nuts at substrate ends. They remained fully fixed during the first shot at 28 kPa. But they lost their full fixity during the second shot (became somewhat loose) and developed additional deflections at their loaded ends due to the rigid-body rotation of what was assumed to be fully fixed support in the analytical calculations. Figure 3.17 shows the variation of computed and measured deflections as a function of shear forces applied during the tests. These relationships were used to obtain shear forces in earlier tests where the anchors did not have strain gauges but had LVDTs to measure tip deflections. It is noteworthy that a bilinear relationship was used for anchors on steel substrates to allow for the softening observed during the second shots due to support rotations. The details of the data analysis are provided elsewhere (Alameer et al. 2020). Tables 3.1 (a) and (b) includes anchor shear forces and anchor deflections for mid-length anchors along vertical and horizontal window edges. Deflections, shear forces and axial tension for anchors near the window corners are presented and discussed later under the heading of "anchor force distribution" and "axial tension caused by membrane behavior."

3.3.1   The Effect of Window Aspect Ratio

The window aspect ratio (ℓ_y/ℓ_x) considered in the test program was either 1.0 (square windows) or 3.0 (rectangular windows) with one window having an aspect ratio of 1.7. Square windows exhibited two-way action, with similar anchor displacements recorded along vertical and horizontal frame elements as illustrated in Figure 3.18. The rectangular windows exhibited one-way action and developed higher anchor displacements along the longer edge as more blast loads were transferred in the short direction. This is illustrated in Figure 3.19. The anchor forces along the vertical edges divided by the applied static load on the window (the static load is the applied static blast pressure times the window surface area) of a square and a rectangular window are compared in Figure 3.20. The anchors along the vertical edge of a rectangular window developed higher percentages of total window resistance as the applied blast loads are almost entirely resisted by the anchors along the two vertical edges, as opposed to the square window, which equally shared window resistance along all four edges. The comparisons of anchor deflections and shear forces listed in Table 3.2 shows the same trend in all other window tests.

3.3.2   The Effect of Anchor Spacing

Anchor spacing, and the number of anchors used per side of a window frame was one of the primary parameters investigated. Figure 3.11 shows a square window with three retention anchors per side that resulted in the failure of anchors and the window frame. The use of well-distributed anchors, with closely spaced anchors exhibited superior performance. Figure 3.21 shows the comparison of anchor displacements recorded in two square windows on steel substrates with 3 or 4 anchors per side. Clearly, the anchor deflections increase multiple times when fewer anchors are used, as expected. A similar comparison is made in Figure 3.22, where the anchor forces are compared in two square windows with steel substrates one with 400 mm spacing of 4 anchors and the other with 500 spacing of 3 anchors per side. The former shows less force per anchor and a better distribution of forces. For the size and properties used in the experimental program, it is recommended to use a minimum anchor spacing of 400 mm along the long side.

3.3.3   The effect of Protective Film Thickness

The effect of protective film thickness on anchor deformation and force response has two effects; the effect on the strength of glazed glass and the effect on the stiffness of the windowpane. Three film thicknesses were considered; 5 mils (single ply), 14 mils (3 plies), and 23 mils (5 plies). One rectangular window was glazed with 12 mil (2 plies) thick film (Test C5 and C6). The required number of plies hence the required strength depends on the window size. Square windows had the largest surface area and needed the larger number of plies of film. Three plies (14 mil thickness) were found to be sufficient to resist 69 kPa (10 psi) pressure for the rectangular windows. However, the square windows required five plies of film (23 mil thickness). The effect of film thickness and associated change in stiffness is two-fold; first, thicker film results in a smaller central panel deflection with reduced anchor deflections and forces, second, the increase in panel stiffness results in reduced window period of vibration and higher dynamic load factor, increasing dynamic effects on anchor forces and deformations. These two factors were approximately equal for the windows tested under 28 kPa of reflected pressure, thereby cancelling their effects on window response. Figure 3.23 shows two sets of windows, one set with a window aspect ratio of 3.0 and the other 1.7, both on steel substrates, both were tested under 28 kPa reflected pressure. One window in each set had a protective film thickness of 5 mils, and the other had 14 mils. As can be seen, the anchor displacement response was not affected by the film thickness, displaying approximately the same response wave form. In contrast, Figure 3.24 shows the comparison of two windows with an aspect ratio of 1.0, both mounted on a steel substrate, but were subjected to the higher reflected pressure of 69 kPa. One window was glazed with a 14-mil film, whereas the other had a 23-mil film thickness. In this case, the higher dynamic effects associated with thicker film (hence increased panel stiffness) and associated reduction in window period outweighed the effect of reduced central panel deflection and related reduction in anchor deflection. Furthermore, in this comparison, the window with 23-mil thickness had an extra anchor per side, which would decrease force per anchor and the deflection of the anchor. In spite of the expected decrease in anchor deflection, the results indicated a marked increase in deflection, which can be attributed to the significantly high dynamic load factor, underlining the important role the film thickness plays on dynamic response of the protected glass pane in the post-break phase of response.

3.3.4   The Effect of Substrate

Four different types of substrates were investigated in the experimental program, i.e., reinforced concrete, steel, concrete block masonry, and stone masonry. While the substrate response and strength were beyond the scope of the experimental program, the effect of substrate on window anchor response was very much part of the current investigation. The substrates played important roles on two aspects of window anchor behaviour; i) strength of the anchorage region, ii) flexibility of the substrate and its effect on anchor forces. Sufficient strength of the anchorage zone near the window opening is paramount for the functioning of the window retention anchors under blast loads. The design of substrate anchorage region and the strength of anchorage in different types of substrates are widely addressed in the literature and design standards (Klingner et al. 1982; Abrishami et al. 1996; Eligehausen et al. 1988; Lotze et al. 2001; ACI 318 2019; CSA A23.3 2019). They are outside of the scope of the current investigation.

It was experimentally observed that rigid substrates resulted in lower deflection but higher relative anchor deflections. Flexible substrates developed lower relative anchor deflections and anchor forces. Among the substrates considered, the steel substrate was the most rigid, followed by reinforced concrete, block masonry and stone masonry walls. Two sets of deflections were measured in out-of-plane direction. One set was measured by LVDTs placed at mid-height window frame location on the substrate. The other set was measured by LVDTs on the tip of the anchor at the same location. The difference between the two readings provided anchor deflection relative to the substrate. Figure 3. 25 shows measured substrate deflection and the relative anchor deflection at the frame mid-height location for selected windows. It should be noted that the deflected shapes shown in the figure represents a parabolic variation between the top and bottom substrate supports with measured values indicated only the maximum deflection point. Figure 3.25 indicates that the highest anchor deflections and hence the highest anchor shear forces occurred when rigid steel substrates were used. The total anchor forces per edge listed in Table 3.3 also indicate highest anchor forces for windows on rigid steel substrates and lowest forces on flexible stone masonry substrates. Indeed, it was observed after the tests that the anchors on steel substrates either failed or deformed excessively when subjected to 69 kPa pressure, whereas those on more flexible masonry substrates suffered less deformations, sometimes remaining elastic after the tests.

3.4 Dynamic Analysis and Computation of Anchor Forces

Anchor forces can be computed through dynamic inelastic analysis of window systems. Single degree-of-freedom (SDOF) analysis may be employed for this purpose with appropriate assumptions based on the experimental observations. Dynamic response of a double pane window system with inner protected pane (either in the form of laminated glass or with the application of security film) undergo two phases of response; pre-break phase and post-break phase. Figure 3.26 illustrates a typical window resistance function (CSA 852-18 2018). The pre-break phase involves elastic response of glass until breakage. During this phase, the window responds with the stiffness of the double-pane glass having appropriate support conditions and geometry. The mass in the pre-break phase is dominated by the mass of glass in both windowpanes. Upon cracking of the glass and the failure of the unprotected outer glass pane, the resistance drops sharply, as depicted in Figure 3.26. The subsequent phase of response is provided by the inner protected window pane, which has been cracked but remained attached to the protective film (or interlayer), providing substantially reduced stiffness while developing membrane action.

The window systems tested can be modelled as a SDOF system for the purpose of computing maximum response. This requires the computation of the stiffness of the window, which is attached to the substrate through steel anchors. The aluminum window frame offers very little rotational restraint along the window edges. Hence, it may be reasonable to assume that the glass panes are simply supported along their edges without a significant restraint against rotation. The window retention anchors develop out-of-plane flexural bending as illustrated in Figure 3.15, resulting in out-of-plane displacements of the window support. Furthermore, the substrate that provides support to the anchored window system also develops out-of-plane deformations. The window system and the substrate, with their respective mass and stiffness, result in a two-degree-of-freedom (TDOF) system. However, it was experimentally observed that the peak deflection response of the substrate occurred at about the same time as that of the window system. Figure 3.27 shows response time histories of the substrate and the attached window anchor in one of the windows tested, confirming that the peak displacements occur at about the same time. The same behaviour was also observed in the numerical investigation reported elsewhere (Alameer et al. 2020). This enables the simplification of the TDOF system as an equivalent SDOF system. The resulting analytical spring-mass model is illustrated in Figure 3.28, where the effective spring stiffness consists of contributions from three springs in series.

The springs represent the stiffness of; i) window pane(s), ii) window retention anchors, and iii) substrate.

The stiffness of the window pane(s) during the pre-crack phase can be computed using the window geometry and the elastic property of glass. Figure 3.29 shows the cross-section view of a double pane glass window with insulating air gap in between (IGU). The spring stiffness of the IGU can be computed using the stiffness coefficients for panels supported along all four sides (Biggs 1964). The use of median values of stiffness coefficients for windows with different aspect ratios was suggested by (CSA Standard S852 2018) as a simplification, and can be used for window stiffness in the elastic range of window panel (pre-break phase), as shown below:

$$k_1 = 225 \, \frac{E \, I_a}{a^2} \qquad\qquad 3.1$$

(for windows with simple supports on all four sides)

where; E is the elastic modulus of window pane and can be taken as E = 69000 MPa, I_a is the moment of inertia of window section per unit width and "a" is the length of the short side of the window panel.

The moment of inertia for a unit width of a double pane IGU can be expressed as follows:

$$I_a = 2 \left\{ \frac{t_g^3}{12} + t_g \left[\frac{t_a + t_g}{2} \right]^2 \right\} \qquad\qquad 3.2$$

where; t_g is the glass pane thickness, and t_a is the in-between air-gap thickness. Attention should be given to the level of composite action that can be developed between the two panes. The recommendation of the Applied Research Associates, Inc. is to use 75% of the computed moment of inertia for double pane IGUs as partially composite sections (ARA, 2005).

During the post-break phase, the stiffness of window panes (k_1) is equal to the stiffness of the glazed inner window, which is governed by the membrane action. The computation of stiffness in the tension membrane phase is a complex problem. It is dominated by the axial rigidity of the security film or laminate ($t_f E_f$). (CSA S852 2018) provides empirical expressions for the effective stiffness in this phase of response, obtained by fitting curves to resistance functions derived by using software WINGARD (ARA 2005). Accordingly, the effective stiffness (k_{eff}) in the post-break phase of response is as follows.

$$k_{eff} = \beta t_f E_f \tag{3.3}$$

t_f: total thickness of protective film or laminate

E_f: elastic modulus of protective film or laminate

β : empirically obtained stiffness coefficient, presented below for two-way and one-way windows.

For two-way windows:

$$\beta = 3.2 \left(\frac{a}{b}\right)^2 - 5.2 \, \frac{a}{b} + 2.7 \text{ for windows with } 0.4 \leq \frac{a}{b} \leq 1.0 \tag{3.4}$$

$$\beta = 4.0 - 7.4 \, \frac{a}{b} \text{ for windows with } \frac{a}{b} \leq 0.4 \tag{3.5}$$

$\frac{a}{b}$: window aspect ratio (ratio of shorter to longer lengths of window pane).

For one-way windows:

$$\beta = 0.46 \frac{l_s}{l_o} \tag{3.6}$$

l_s: window length along the supported edge

l_o: window length along the unsupported edge

The flexural stiffness of window retention anchors as cantilever elements and substrates as one-way panels between top and bottom simple supports can be computed from the following expressions.

$$k_2 = \frac{3 \sum EI}{L_a^3}$$ 3.7

$$\delta_{wall} = \frac{5L^3 F_{wall}}{384EI}$$ 3.8 (a)

$$k_3 = \frac{5F_{window}}{3\delta_{wall}}$$ 3.8 (b)

where, flexural rigidity terms (EI) represent rigidities of the steel anchors and the substrate. L_a is the cantilever anchor length, and L_s is the length of the substrate between its supports.

The forcing function for blast loading is in the form of a rapidly increasing reflected pressure that diminishes quickly with time. It can be idealized as a triangular impulsive forcing function as shown in Figure 3.30(a). The solution of the differential equation that defines dynamic equation of motion under triangular impulsive forcing function is widely available in the literature. For the computation of maximum anchor forces, it is sufficient to compute maximum dynamic response, which can be achieved by applying the maximum dynamic increase factor $(DLF)_{max}$ to the maximum static displacement or the maximum resistance. The $(DLF)_{max}$ can be expressed as a function of the ratio of the duration of load (t_d) to the period of the SDOF system (T), as illustrated in Figure 3.30(b). This necessitates the computation of the fundamental period T using the equivalent stiffness (k_e), representing three springs in series; load-mass factor C_{LM}, which is required to model uniformly distributed mass as a lumped mass model, and the total window mass, m.

$$T = 2\pi \sqrt{\frac{C_{LM}m}{k_e}} \qquad 3.9$$

Two levels of pressure were applied to each window during the experimental program; 28 kPa (4 psi) and 69 kPa (10 psi). The first level of pressure (28 kPa) was applied to the undamaged window with elastic glass properties. This level of pressure did not induce cracking of the glass in rectangular windows on concrete and masonry substrates. Hence, these windows performed in pre-break range, developing support shear forces associated with elastic window response with very little membrane action and in-plane tension. All other windows experienced cracking of glass, responding in the post-break response of the inner protected pane. Beyond the breakage of glass, the stiffness and mass of the inner glazed window pane are used for computing $(DLF)_{max}$. The higher of the pre-break and post-break shear forces governs the anchor design. It should be noted that the pre-break shear forces are limited by the failure capacity of glass for which expressions are given in (Biggs 1964) and (CSA S852 2018). Windows subjected to 69 kPa pressure (second shot) beyond the breakage of the outer unprotected glass and cracked inner glazed pane provide resistance in membrane action.

Anchor shear forces can be calculated from the window support reactions. Window support reactions along each side of window frame can be expressed in terms of window resistance (R) and applied static force (F) for long and short sides as V_A and V_B, respectively (Morison 2007). The following expressions, adapted from (Morison 2007), were used for the two window aspect ratios considered and the two levels of reflected blast pressures applied.

For window aspect ratio of 1.0 (square windows):

For $P_r = 28$ kPa $\qquad\qquad V_A = V_B = 0.08F + 0.11R \qquad\qquad$ 3.10 (a)

For $Pr = 69$ kPa $\qquad\qquad V_A = V_B = 0.03F + 0.165R \qquad\qquad$ 3.10 (b)

For window aspect ratio of 3.0 (rectangular windows):

$$V_A = 0.08F + 0.22R \qquad\qquad \text{3.11 (a)}$$

For $Pr = 28$ kPa

$$V_B = 0.07F + 0.022R \qquad\qquad \text{3.11 (b)}$$

$$V_A = 0.07F + 0.26R \qquad\qquad \text{3.11 (c)}$$

For $P_r = 69$ kPa

$$V_B = 0.035F + 0.045R \qquad\qquad \text{3.11 (d)}$$

Where,

$$F = P_r\, A_t \qquad\qquad 3.12$$

$$R = F \times (DLF)_{max} \qquad\qquad 3.13$$

A_t = Tributary area of window subjected to blast reflected pressure P_r.

Average shear force per anchor, V_{ax} and V_{ay} along x and y directions of the window frame can be computed by dividing the window edge support reactions V_x and V_y along x and y directions by respective number of anchors, n_x and n_y in each direction.

$$V_{ax} = \frac{V_x}{n_x} \qquad\qquad \text{3.14 (a)}$$

$$V_{ay} = \frac{V_y}{n_y}$$
3.14 (b)

An important aspect of post-break inelastic response is the development of membrane action of the protective film (or the internal laminate), which induces axial tensile forces at window supports in the plane of the window. (Timoshenko 1940; Vallabhan 1983) developed expressions for membrane resistance by balancing the strain energy in the membrane with work done by uniform static pressure. These expressions were used by computer software WINGARD (ARA, 2005), and are also adopted here as given below. Accordingly, the strains (ε_x and ε_y), and membrane forces (T_x and T_y) in two orthogonal directions (x and y) are expressed as follows:

$$T_x = \frac{Et}{1-v^2}\left(\varepsilon_x + v\varepsilon_y\right)$$
3.15

$$T_y = \frac{Et}{1-v^2}\left(\varepsilon_y + v\varepsilon_x\right)$$
3.16

$$T_{ax} = T_x \ell_y / n_x$$
3.17

$$T_{ay} = T_y \ell_x / n_y$$
3.18

Where:

E = Modulus of elasticity of the protective film or laminate

ℓ_x = Window frame length in x direction

ℓ_y = Window frame length in y direction

n_x = Number of anchors along the window edge in x direction

n_y = Number of anchors along the window edge in y direction

t = Membrane thickness

T_x =Axial tension force per unit length in x direction

T_y =Axial tension force per unit length in y direction

T_{ax} =Average axial tension force per anchor in x direction

T_{ay} = Average axial tension force per anchor in the y direction

v = Poisson's ratio

The strains (ε_x and ε_y) in x and y directions can be computed from the strain energy expressions given below (ARA, 2005).

$$\varepsilon_x = \frac{d_u}{d_x} + \frac{1}{2}\left(\frac{d_w}{d_x}\right)^2 = \frac{u_0\pi}{b/2} = \frac{-(\frac{a}{2}).\pi.\left(2.C_3.(\frac{b}{2})^4.(\frac{a}{2})^2.C_2 - C_5.C_4\right)}{4.(\frac{b}{2})^6.(\frac{a}{2})^6.C_2^2 - C_5^2}.w_0^2 \qquad 3.19$$

$$\varepsilon_y = \frac{d_V}{d_y} + \frac{1}{2}\left(\frac{d_w}{d_y}\right)^2 = \frac{V_0\pi}{a/2} = \frac{-(\frac{b}{2}).\pi.\left(2.C_4.(\frac{b}{2})^2.(\frac{a}{2})^4.C_2 - C_5.C_3\right)}{4.(\frac{b}{2})^6.(\frac{a}{2})^6.C_2^2 - C_5^2}.w_0^2 \qquad 3.20$$

Where,

a = the short dimension of window

b = the long dimension of window

w_o = maximum window deflection at the center of the window

$C_1, C_2, C_3, C_4,$ and C_5 are coefficient that can be calculated using the expression given below:

$$C_1 = \left(18.\left(\tfrac{b}{2}\right)^2.\left(\tfrac{a}{2}\right)^2 + 81.\left(\tfrac{b}{2}\right)^4 + 81.\left(\tfrac{a}{2}\right)^4\right).\pi^4 \qquad\qquad 3.21(a)$$

$$C_2 = (10368 - 1152.v).\pi^2 \qquad\qquad 3.21(b)$$

$$C_3 = \left(-3072.\left(\tfrac{a}{2}\right)^3 + 768.v.\left(\tfrac{b}{2}\right).\left(\tfrac{a}{2}\right)^2 - 768.\left(\tfrac{b}{2}\right).\left(\tfrac{a}{2}\right)^2 + 1536.v.\left(\tfrac{b}{2}\right)^2.\left(\tfrac{a}{2}\right)\right).\pi^2 \qquad 3.21(c)$$

$$C_4 = \left(-3072.\left(\tfrac{b}{2}\right)^3 + 768.v.\left(\tfrac{b}{2}\right)^2.\left(\tfrac{a}{2}\right) - 768.\left(\tfrac{b}{2}\right)^2\left(\tfrac{a}{2}\right) + 1536.v.\left(\tfrac{b}{2}\right).\left(\tfrac{a}{2}\right)^2\right).\pi^2 \qquad 3.21(d)$$

$$C_5 = (16384v + 16384).\left(\left(\tfrac{b}{2}\right)^3.\left(\tfrac{a}{2}\right)^3\right) \qquad\qquad 3.21(f)$$

The maximum mid-membrane deflection of a glazed window pane, w_o is calculated by applying the (DLF)max to the static panel deflection. Anchor shear and axial tension forces in the post-break phase can be computed by following the above procedure. Analytically computed and experimentally measured anchor forces are presented and compared in Table 3.3 for selected windows with different aspect ratios and different substrates. The comparison indicates reasonably good agreement between the computed and measured forces, validating the above procedure for analytical predictions of anchor forces.

It should be noted that the anchor forces provided in Table 3.3 are the total anchor force along one side of window frame. It was experimentally observed that the distribution of anchor forces along the window frame is not uniform. This is illustrated in Figures 3.20 and 3.22. The anchors at mid-length and mid-height locations produce higher forces than those near the corners. The distribution of anchor forces depends on the rigidity of the window frame. It is conceivable that windows with rigid steel frames generate near uniform anchor forces. The effect of frame rigidity was investigated numerically through finite element analyses. Further discussion of anchor force distribution is presented in the companion paper (Alameer et al. 2020), where the results of numerical analyses are presented. The results indicate that the anchor forces, both shear and axial tension, show a parabolic or a half-sine variation along the length of flexible aluminum window frames, and closer to uniform force distribution when more rigid steel frames are used. Well distributed and closely spaced anchors exhibit more uniform variation of forces even in windows with aluminum frames.

3.5 Conclusions

The following conclusions can be drawn from the window tests and analyses reported in this paper.

- Window retention anchors develop out-of-plane shear forces and in-plane axial tension forces when subjected to blast loads. The magnitude of shear forces can be significantly different from those computed based on static analysis. The windows considered in this investigation indicated lower anchor shear forces than those computed under static pressures due to the inertia resistance provided by the window mass, implying that the use of static analysis would yield conservative anchor design forces.

- Anchor tension forces generated by the membrane action can be multiple times higher than the anchor shear forces. Membrane forces change with the level of pressure applied, as well as the thickness of the protective film. The effect of film thickness is to change the post-break stiffness and period of vibration, affecting the dynamic response of window. A minimum thickness of protective film is required to ensure the integrity of glazing without rupturing the film. This depend on the magnitude of the membrane forces that develop under a given level of blast threat. The windows considered in the experimental program required a minimum film thicknesses of 12-mil in rectangular windows with exposed surface area of 0.9 m^2, performing in one-way mode, and 23-mil in square windows with exposed surface area of 1.5 m^2, performing in two-way mode, when all the windows were mechanically glazed along all four sides.

- The rectangular windows with an aspect ratio of 3.0 resulted in one-way panel behavior, increasing anchor forces along the long sides of windows. Square windows showed similar anchor forces along all four sides.

- Anchor forces show parabolic distributions of forces along window edges with highest forces near the middle of the window frame. Well-distributed and closely spaced anchors developed a more uniform force distribution. For the windows tested, a maximum anchor spacing of 400 mm can be recommended.

- The effect of substrate type is to change the magnitude of anchor forces, depending on the substrate rigidity. The windows on rigid steel and reinforced concrete substrates developed higher anchor forces than those on more flexible concrete block and stone masonry substrates. The substrates must be reinforced around window opening to prevent the failure of the anchorage zone, especially under higher blast threat levels.

- Wet glazing of windows with structural silicone have limited capacity. For the windows tested, wet glazing performed well under 28 kPa - 207 kPa-ms threat level. However, they suffered from failure at 69 kP - 621 kPa-ms threat level. The mechanical anchorage, consisting of 25 mm square aluminum tubes of 5 mm wall thickness, secured using 38 mm long - 6.3 mm dimeter bolts at 100 mm spacing, performed well in all cases.

- The SDOF simplification for dynamic analysis of window systems with supporting segments of substrates provide good estimates of anchor force response. The glazed windows show two phases of dynamic response, pre-break elastic response and post break inelastic response. The effects of the latter phase of response can be estimated using effective elastic stiffness of glazed windowpane.

Table 3.1: Properties of windows tested

(a) Windows on reinforced concrete and steel substrates

Test No.	Aspect ratio	Film thickness (mils)	Glazing type and anchor spacing (mm)	Window retention anchor spacing (mm)	No. of retention anchors	Anchor embed. length (mm)	P_r (kPa)	Mid-length anchor deflection		Mid-length anchor force	
								$(\delta_y)_{exp}$ (mm)	$(\delta_x)_{exp}$ (mm)	$(V_{ay})_{exp}$ (kN)	$(V_{ax})_{exp}$ (kN)
C1	1	4.5+4.5+5	Wet	250	2(5+5)=20	90	28	14.3	8.2	1.1	0.7
C2							69	15.3	12.3	1.2	1.0
C3	1	5	Wet	250	2(5+5)=20	90	28	21.8	21	1.7	1.6
C4							69	25.4	24.8	2	1.9
C5	3	6+6	Mech.@ Long:83 Short:75	Long:250 Short:225	2(7+3)=20	90	28	24.4	11.5	2	0.9
C6							69	31.1	12.3	2.5	1.0
C7	1	4.5+4.5+5	Mech.@ 125	500	2(3+3)=12	90	28	21.4	-	1.7	-
C8							69	43.7	-	-	-
C9	1	4.5+4.5+5	Mech.@ 100	400	2(4+4)=16	125	28	-	-	-	-
C10							69	32.5	-	2.6	-
C11	3	4.5+4.5+5	Mech.@ Long:125 Short:113	Long:500 Short:225	2(4+3)=14	125	28	18.4	15.4	1.1	1.0
C12							69	73.5	19.5	1.4	1.2
C13	3	4.5+4.5+5	Mech.@ Long:100 Short:100	Long:400 Short:305	2(4+2)=12	125	28	20.3	12.8	1.9	-
C14							69	-	21.1	2.0	-
S1	3	4.5+4.5+5	Wet	Long:250 Short:225	2(7+3)=20	90	28	14.7	6.5	1.4	0.6
S2							69	16.7	6.9	1.6	0.7
S3	3	5	Wet	Long:250 Short:225	2(7+3)=20	90	28	14.1	5.7	1.4	1.6
S4							69	14.9	6.3	1.4	0.6
S5	1	4.5+4.5+5	Wet	250	2(7+3)=20	90	28	17.2	11.9	1.6	1.1
S6							69	23.4	23	1.7	1.6
S7	1.7	4.5+4.5+5	Wet	Long:250 Short:250	2(7+5)=24	90	28	10.2	6.3	1.0	0.6
S8							69	12.3	7.1	1.2	0.7
S9	1.7	5	Wet	Long:250 Short:250	2(7+5)=24	90	28	9.3	5.5	0.9	0.5
S10							69	10.8	6.7	1.0	0.6
S11	1	4.5+4.5+5	Mech.@ 125	500	2(3+3)=12	90	28	33.0	22.3	2.3	1.6
S12							69	33.0	22.3	2.3	1.6
S13	1	4(4.5)+5	Mech.@ 100	400	2(4+4)=16	90	28	17.4	13.2	2.0	1.60
S14							69	48.9	36.2	2.4	2.0
S15	3	4.5+4.5+5	Mech.@ 125	Long:500 Short:225	2(4+2)=12	90	28	19.8	11.2	2.0	1.4
S16							69	98.2	24.9	2.7	1.7

Note: $(V_{ax})_{exp}$ and $(V_{ay})_{exp}$ are experimental shear forces; $(\delta_x)_{exp}$ and $(\delta_y)_{exp}$ are experimental tip deflections for anchors along window edges in x (horizontal) and y (vertical) directions. The symbol (-) indicates data not available.

(b) Windows on concrete block and stone masonry substrates

Test No.	Aspect ratio	Film thickness (mils)	Glazing type and anchor spacing (mm)	Window retention anchor spacing (mm)	No. of retention anchors	Embed. length (mm)	P_r (kPa)	Mid-length anchor deflection		Mid-length anchor force	
								$(\delta_y)_{exp}$ (mm)	$(\delta_x)_{exp}$ (mm)	$(V_{ay})_{exp}$ (kN)	$(V_{ax})_{exp}$ (kN)
B1 B2	1	4.5+4.5+5	Mech.@ 125	300	2(4+4)=16	125	28 69	13.5 25.5	11.2 17.6	1.2 1.8	1.2 1.4
B3 B4	1	4(4.5)+5	Mech.@ 125	300	2(4+4)=16	125	28 69	- -	- -	0.7 1.4	0.6 1.3
B5 B6	3	4.5+4.5+5	Mech.@ 125	Long:400 Short:305	2(4+2)=12	125	28 69	10.9 19.5	6.2 11.2	1.8 1.9	- -
B7 B8	3	4.5+4.5+5	Mech.@ 125	Long:500 Short:305	2(4+2)=12	125	28 69	13.1 -	8.3 15.4	1.3 1.4	- -
B9 B10	3	4.5+4.5+5	Mech.@ 125	Long:600 Short:305	2(3+2)=10	125	28 69	12.5 30.5	7.6 12.6	1.9 1.9	- -
ST1 ST2	1	4.5+4.5+5	Mech.@ 125	300	2(4+4)=16	125	28 69	9.1 15.3	7.2 12.7	1.1 1.5	1.1 1.3
ST3 ST4	3	4.5+4.5+5	Mech.@ 125	Long:400 Short:305	2(4+2)=12	125	28 69	11.5 12.9	7.9 10.4	1.6 1.6	0.8 0.9
ST5 ST6	3	4.5+4.5+5	Mech.@ 125	Long:500 Short:305	2(3+2)=10	125	28 69	11.9 23.7	7.6 17	1.4 1.7	- -

Note: $(V_{ax})_{exp}$ and $(V_{ay})_{exp}$ are experimental shear forces; $(\delta_x)_{exp}$ and $(\delta_y)_{exp}$ are experimental tip deflections for anchors along window edges in x (horizontal) and y (vertical) directions. The symbol (-) indicates data not available.

Table 3.2: Summary of widow test results

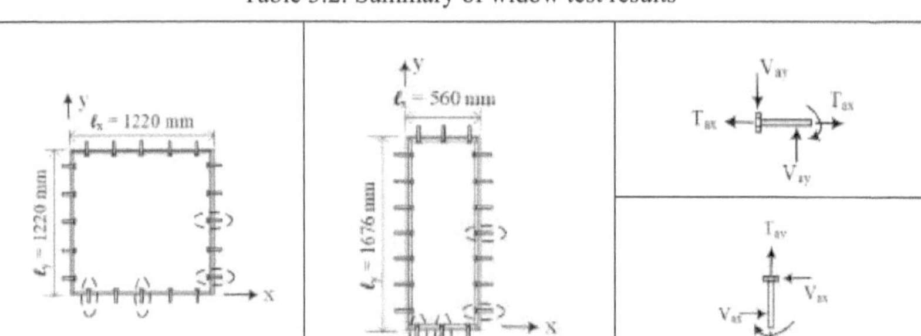

Test No. $(\frac{\ell_y}{\ell_x})$	Mid-length anchor force (kN)		End-anchor force (kN)		Test No. $(\frac{\ell_y}{\ell_x})$	Mid-length anchor force (kN)		End-anchor force (kN)	
	$(V_{ay})_{exp}$ $(T_{ax})_{exp}$	$(V_{ax})_{exp}$ $(T_{ay})_{exp}$	$(V_{ay})_{exp}$ $(T_{ax})_{exp}$	$(V_{ax})_{exp}$ $(T_{ay})_{exp}$		$(V_{ay})_{exp}$ $(T_{ax})_{exp}$	$(V_{ax})_{exp}$ $(T_{ay})_{exp}$	$(V_{ay})_{exp}$ $(T_{ax})_{exp}$	$(V_{ax})_{exp}$ $(T_{ay})_{exp}$
C11 (3)	1.1 1.3	1.0 2.0	1.0 2.7	0.5 2.0	B4 (1)	1.4 3.7	1.3 3.2	1.3 3.4	1.2 1.0
C12 (3)	1.4 7.8	1.2 3.9	1.2 2.9	1.1 3.9	B5 (3)	1.8 7.8	- -	1.5 3.9	1.0 3.2
C13 (3)	1.9 8.2	- -	1.8 2.7	1.3 2.0	B6 (3)	1.9 11.3	- -	1.7 7.9	1.6 5.2
C14 (3)	2 12.3	- -	1.9 10.2	1.4 3.9	B7 (3)	1.3 5.3	- -	1.0 2.0	0.4 1.8
S11 (1)	2.3 7.5	1.6 6.1	1.4 1.9	0.7 2.5	B8 (3)	1.4 6.9	- -	1.3 3.2	1.2 2.0
S12 (1)	2.3 7.5	1.6 6.1	1.4 1.9	0.7 2.5	B9 (3)	1.9 18.2	- -	1.6 6.2	1.6 3.8
S13 (1)	2 5.1	1.6 3.5	1.8 3.4	1.4 2.8	B10 (3)	1.9 19.2	- -	1.8 9.1	1.6 5.4
S14 (1)	2.4 10.7	2.0 9.3	2.3 10.5	1.8 8.6	ST1 (1)	1.1 4.7	1.1 2.2	1.0 3.3	0.8 1.9
S15 (3)	2.0 8.5	1.4 4.6	1.8 3.6	0.2 2.1	ST2 (1)	1.5 8.7	1.3 6.9	1.4 6.1	1.2 5.5
S16 (3)	2.7 14.1	1.7 5.2	2.1 12.1	1.5 4.5	ST3 (3)	1.6 1.7	- -	1.4 1.5	0.8 1.1
B1 (1)	1.2 5.2	1.2 2.8	1.1 3.8	0.9 2.5	ST4 (3)	1.6 3.6	- -	1.5 3.1	0.9 2.0
B2 (1)	1.8 8.9	1.4 7.8	1.4 6.9	1.3 4.9	ST5 (3)	1.4 6.8	- -	1.2 5.1	1.1 2.9
B3 (1)	0.7 1.9	0.6 0.9	0.6 1.9	0.5 0.7	ST6 (3)	1.7 14.6	- -	1.6 6.8	1.5 3.9

Note: $(V_{ax})_{exp}$ and $(V_{ay})_{exp}$ are out of plane anchor shear forces recorded experimentally along the window frame elements in x and y directions. $(T_{ax})_{exp}$ and $(T_{ay})_{exp}$ are axial tension forces recorded experimentally in x and y directions. The symbol (-) indicates data not available.

Table 3.3: Comparisons of experimentally recorded and analytically computed shear and axial tension forces per anchor along two orthogonal directions

Test No $(\frac{\ell_y}{\ell_x})$	Analytically computed values							Experiments	
	t_d (ms)	T (ms)	$(DLF)_{max}$	F (kN)	R (kN)	$(V_{ay})_{anal}$ $(V_{ax})_{anal}$ (kN)	$(T_{ax})_{anal}$ $(T_{ay})_{anal}$ (kN)	$(V_{ay})_{exp}$ $(V_{ax})_{exp}$ (kN)	$(T_{ax})_{exp}$ $(T_{ay})_{exp}$ (kN)
C7 (1)	11.7	41	0.86	41.7	35.8	7.2 7.2	14.1 16.2	6.7 -	- -
C8 (1)	12.7	75	0.47	102.7	47.9	8.9 8.9	34.4 40.5	- -	- -
C13 (3)	13.8	36	1	26.2	26.2	7.8 2.4	4.4 22.3	7.3 2.7	4.0 21.8
C14 (3)	10.2	52	0.24	64.6	15.7	8.4 2.9	8.2 46.6	7.9 2.9	7.8 45
S13 (1)	11.8	32	0.98	41.7	40.6	7.3 7.3	14.3 18.2	7.5 6.1	13 17.1
S14 (1)	10.2	48	0.23	102.7	23.1	9.9 9.9	36.7 42.9	9.4 7.6	36 42.5
S15 (3)	14.4	39	1.03	26.2	26.9	7.9 2.6	13.8 24.8	7.7 2.0	13.4 24.2
S16 (3)	13.4	51	0.26	64.6	16.8	9.2 3.9	19.7 52.9	9.7 4.7	19.4 52.4
B1 (1)	10.2	45	0.55	41.7	22.6	5 5	11.7 18.4	4.6 4.2	11.0 18.0
B2 (1)	11.3	75.5	0.19	102.7	19.5	6.2 6.2	26.8 31.2	6.5 6.5	26.0 31.6
B5 (3)	12.8	46.6	0.74	26.2	19.1	6.3 2.2	6.8 23.1	6.7 2.1	6.5 23.5
B6 (3)	14.6	79.9	0.15	64.6	9.9	7.1 2.7	10.2 37.9	7.3 3.2	10.5 38.4
ST1 (1)	12.1	53.6	0.46	41.7	18.9	4.9 4.9	8.7 16.3	4.3 4.0	8.5 16.0
ST2 (1)	11.6	83.4	0.18	102.7	18.2	6.1 6.1	25.3 30.8	5.9 5.9	25 30
ST3 (3)	13.6	43.6	0.68	26.2	17.7	5.8 2.1	2.8 7.6	5.3 1.7	2.5 7.0
ST4 (3)	15.3	80.2	0.14	64.6	8.8	6.6 2.4	3.8 13.9	6.2 1.8	3.9 13.5

Notes: V_{ax} and V_{ay} are average out-of-plane shear forces per anchor along window frame elements in x and y directions. T_{ax} and T_{ay} are average axial force per anchor in x and y directions. Subscripts "anal" and "exp" refer to analytically computed and experimentally measured values. Symbol (-) indicates no data.

a) Shock tube driver section and expansion chamber

b) Shock tube end frame

Figure 3.1: University of Ottawa shock tube

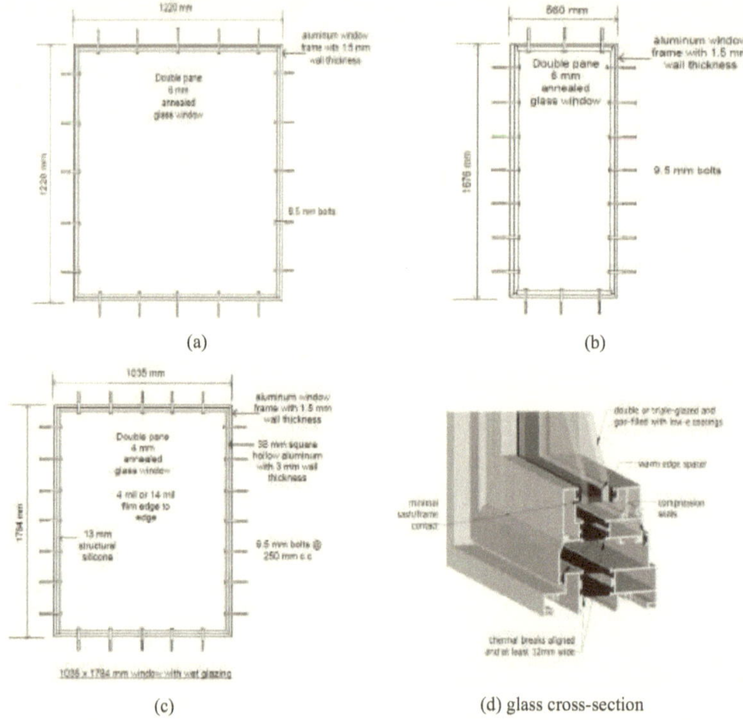

(a)

(b)

(c)

(d) glass cross-section

Figure 3.2: Dimensions and details of typical test windows

(a) Wet-glazing

(b) Mechanical glazing

Figure 3.3: Window glazing

Figure 3.4: Drop-in anchors

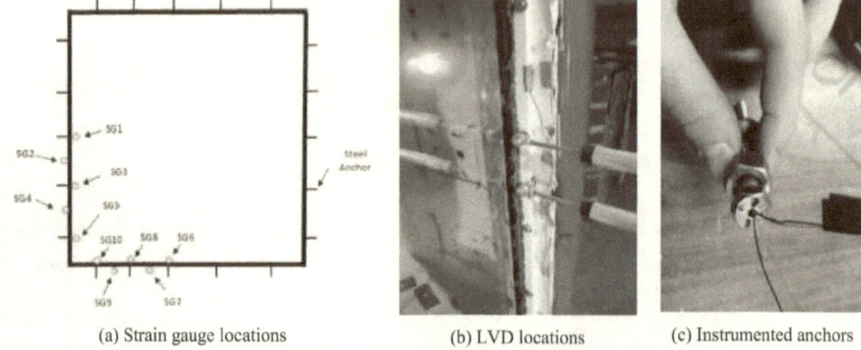

(a) Strain gauge locations   (b) LVD locations   (c) Instrumented anchors

Figure 3.5: Instrumentation

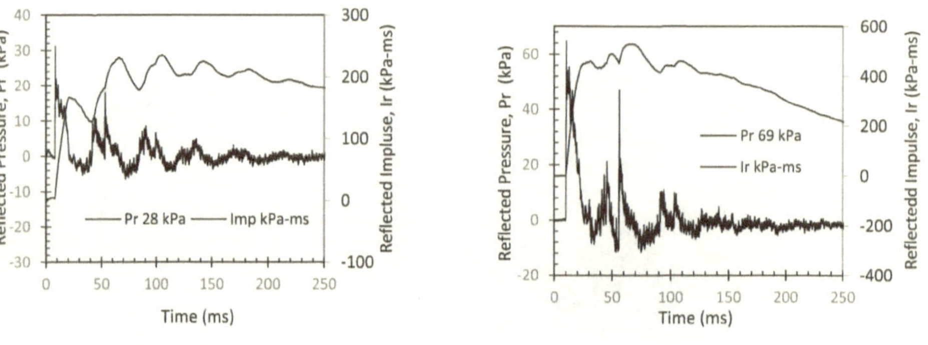

Figure 3.6: Typical reflected pressures and impulses

Figure 3.7: Failure of unprotected outer glass

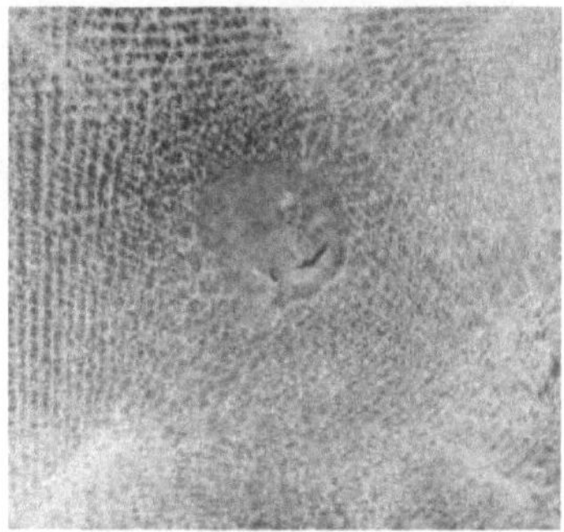

Figure 3.8: Failure of protective film

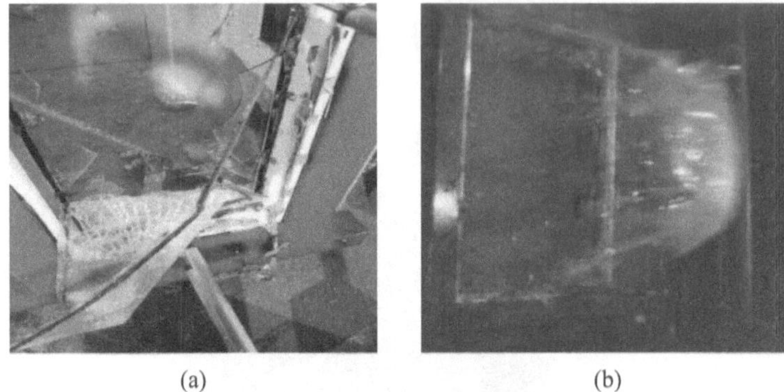

(a)   (b)

Figure 3.9: Failure of wet-glazing

Figure 3.10: Successful performance of a glazed window

Figure 3.11: Failure of a window frame

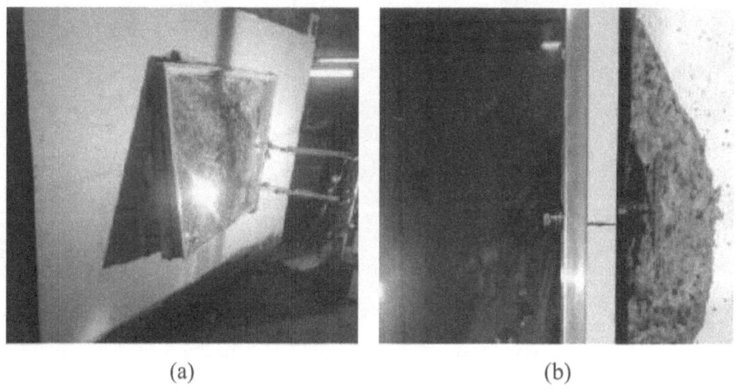

(a)   (b)

Figure 3.12: Failure of reinforced concrete substrate in anchorage zones

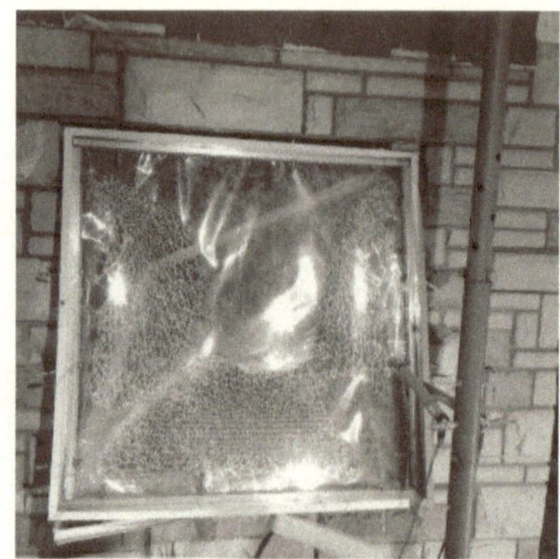

Figure 3.13: Square window on stone masonry after the application of 69 kPa

(a) Concrete block after test B4

(b) Stone wall after test ST2

Figure 3.14: Observed damage on stone masonry substrate

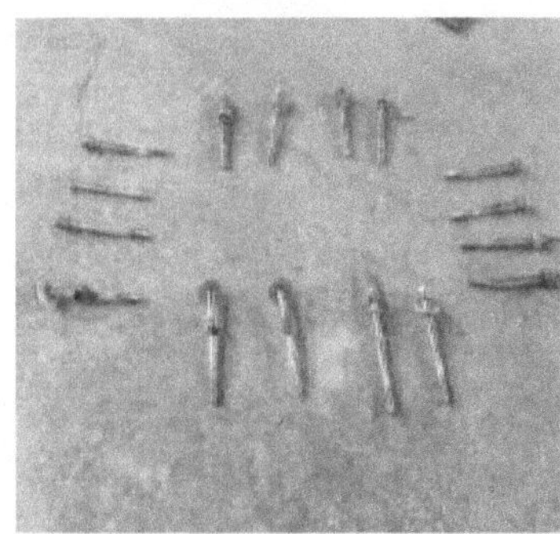

Figure 3.15: Deformed window retention anchors after test

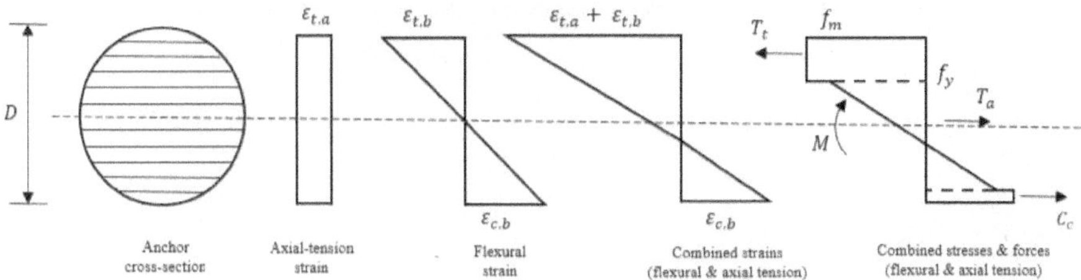

Figure 3.16: Stress-strain profiles for retention anchors

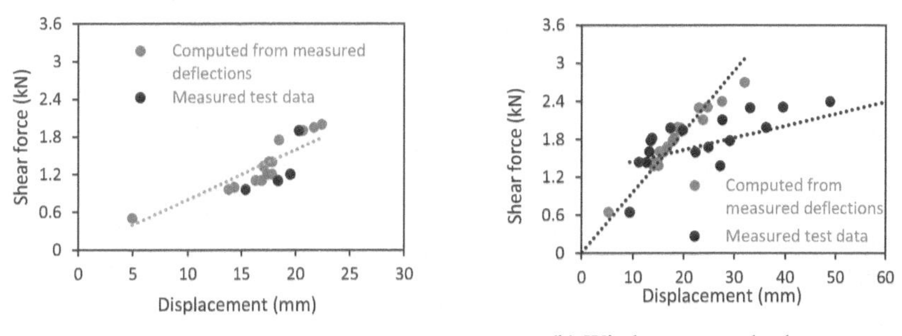

(a) Windows on reinforced concrete substrate

(b) Windows on steel substrates

Figure 3.17: Anchor shear force variation with anchor tip deflection

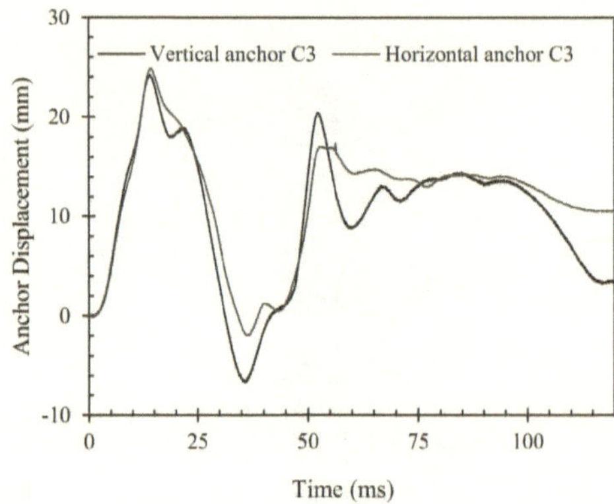

Figure 3.18: Measured mid-length anchor displacements along vertical and horizontal sides of a square window (ℓ_y/ℓ_x =1) on reinforced concrete substrate

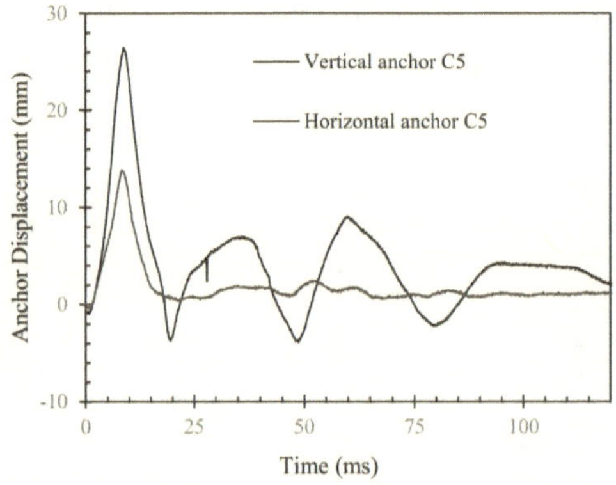

Figure 3.19: Measured mid-length anchor displacements along vertical (long) and horizontal (short) sides of a rectangular window ($\ell_y/\ell_x = 3$) on reinforced concrete substrate

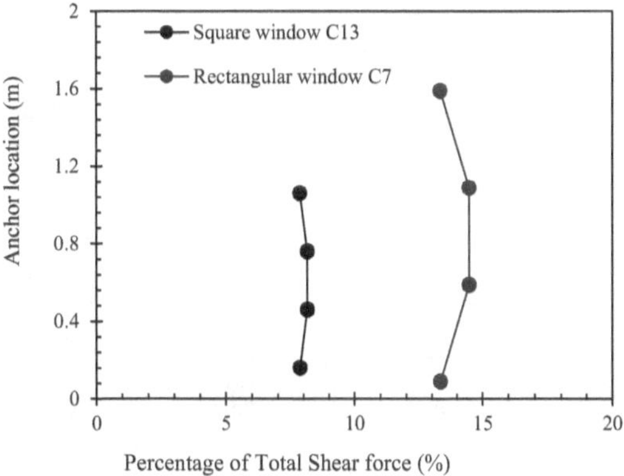

Figure 3.20: Percentage of total anchor shear forces assigned to each anchor
in vertical direction

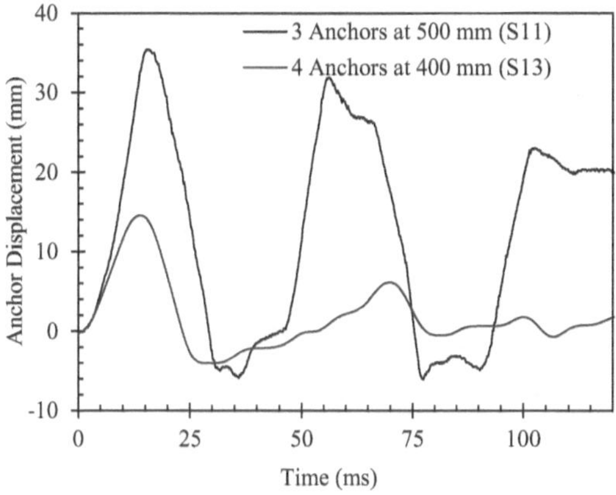

Figure 3.21: Effect of anchor spacing/number of anchors on
central anchor displacement in square windows

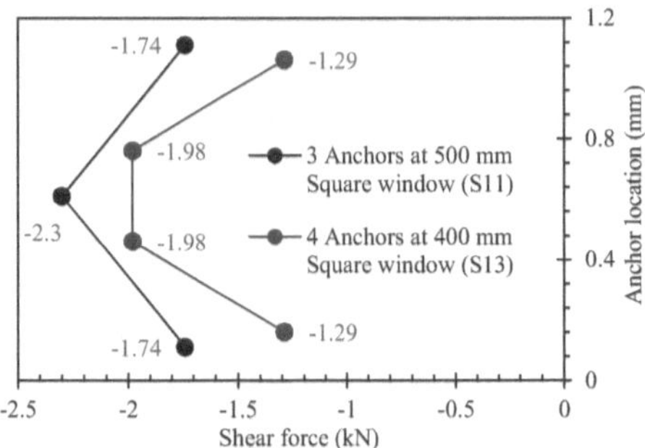

Figure 3.22: Effect of number of anchors/anchor spacing on anchor forces

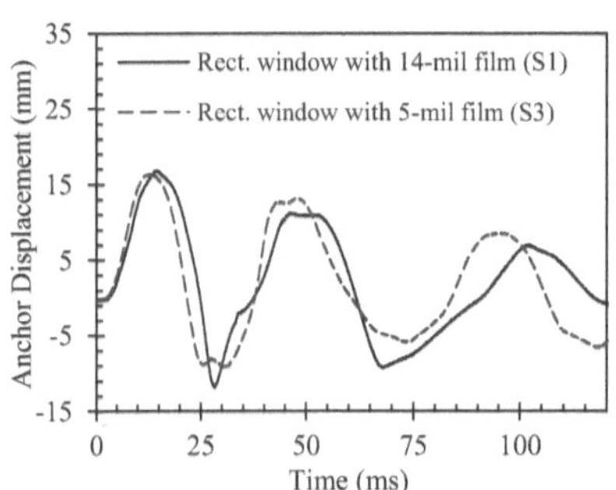

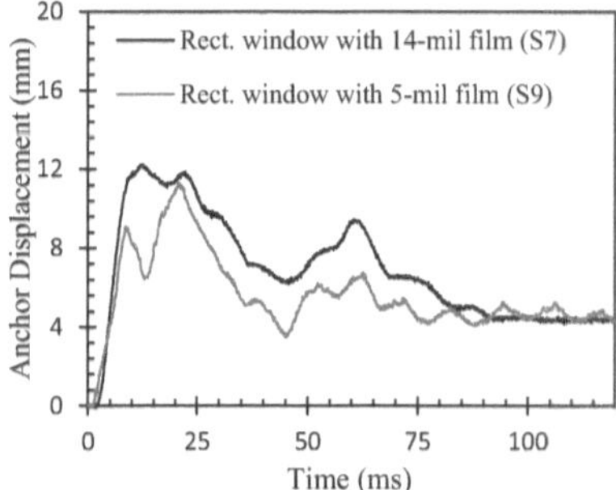

(a) Windows with an aspect ratio of 3.0   (b) Windows with an aspect ratio of 1.7

Figure 3.23: Rectangular windows with different film thickness subjected to 28 kPa

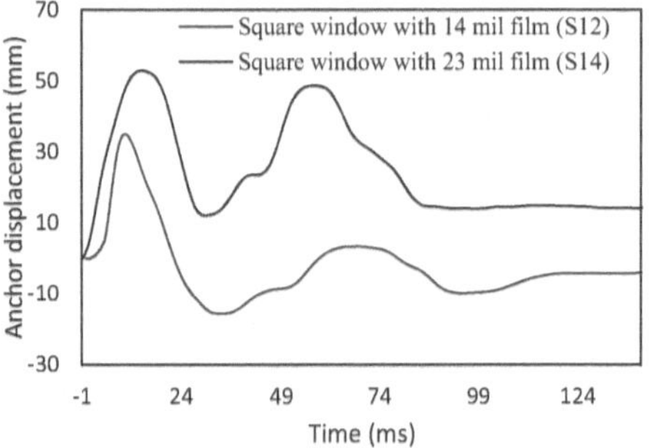

Figure 3.24: Square windows with different film thickness subjected to 69 kPa

102

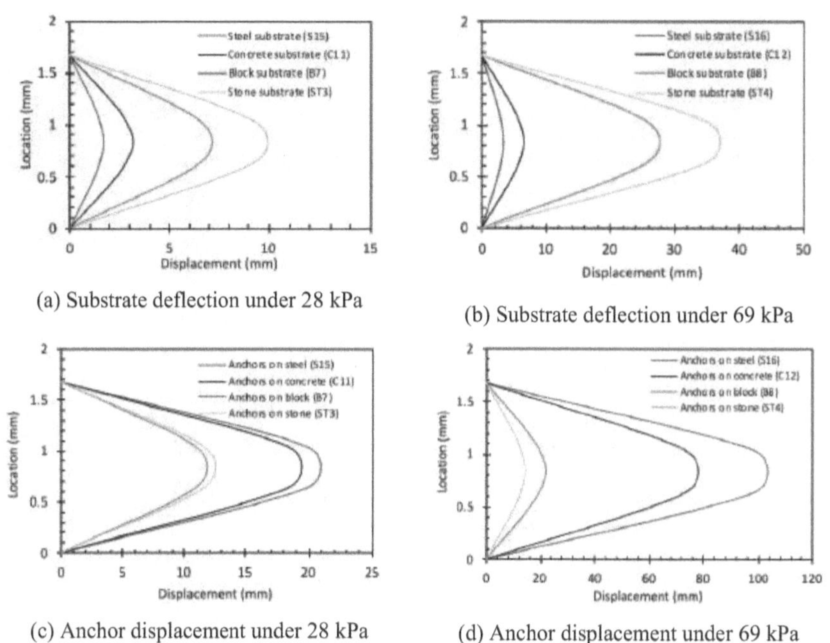

(a) Substrate deflection under 28 kPa

(b) Substrate deflection under 69 kPa

(c) Anchor displacement under 28 kPa

(d) Anchor displacement under 69 kPa

Figure 3.25: The effect of substrate type on anchor response

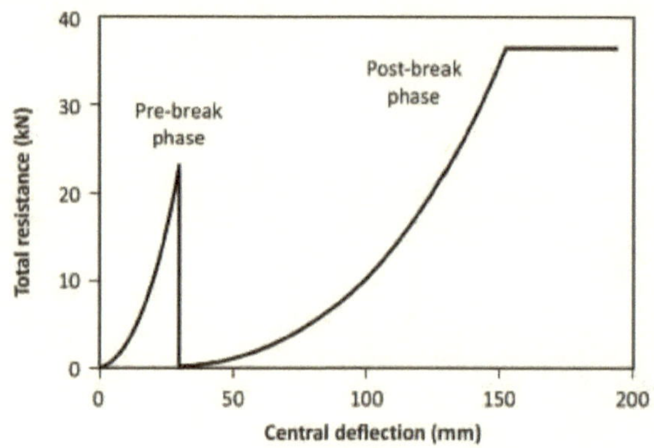

Figure 3.26: Resistance curve for a window exhibiting pre-break
and post-break phases of response (CSA 852-18 2018)

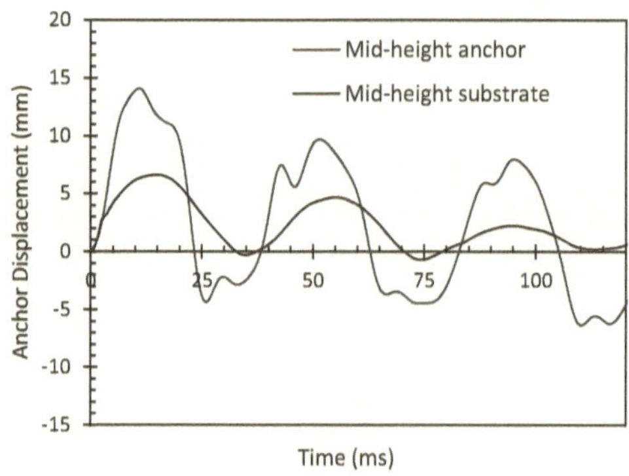

Figure 3.27: Typical substrate and anchor response to blast pressure (Test B5)

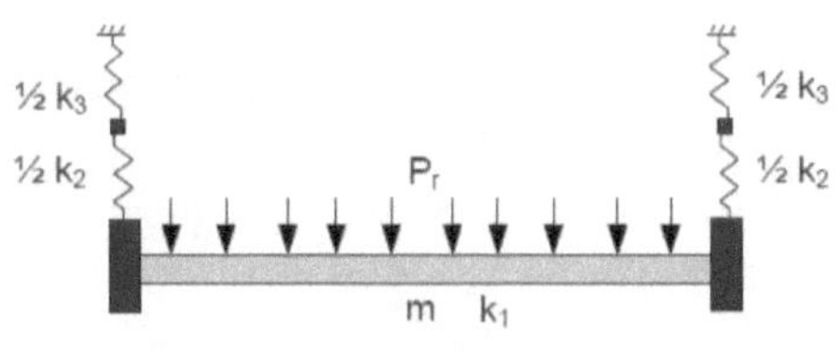

k_1: Flexural/membrane stiffness of window
 pane(s)
k_2: Flexural stiffness of window anchors
k_3: Flexural stiffness of substrate
k_e: Total equivalent stiffness of window

$$u_1 = \frac{F}{k_1} \qquad u_2 = \frac{F}{k_2} \qquad u_3 = \frac{F}{k_3}$$

$$u = \frac{F}{k_1} + \frac{F}{k_2} + \frac{F}{k_3} \qquad k_e = \frac{F}{u}$$

$$\frac{1}{k_e} = \frac{1}{k_1} + \frac{1}{k_2} + \frac{1}{k_3}$$

Figure 3.28: SDOF model with springs in series

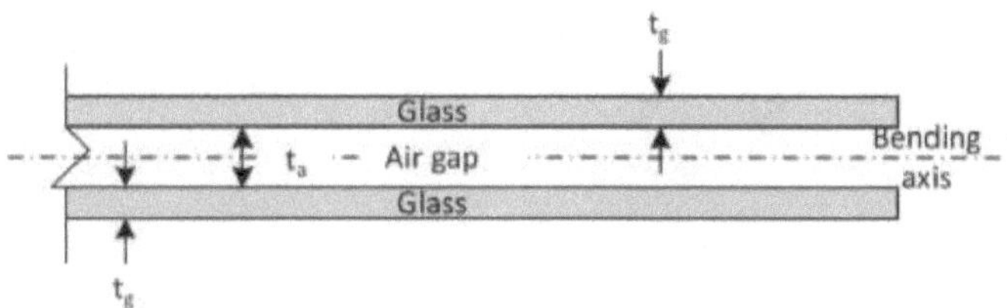

Figure 3.29: Cross-section of a typical IGU (CSA 852-18 2018)

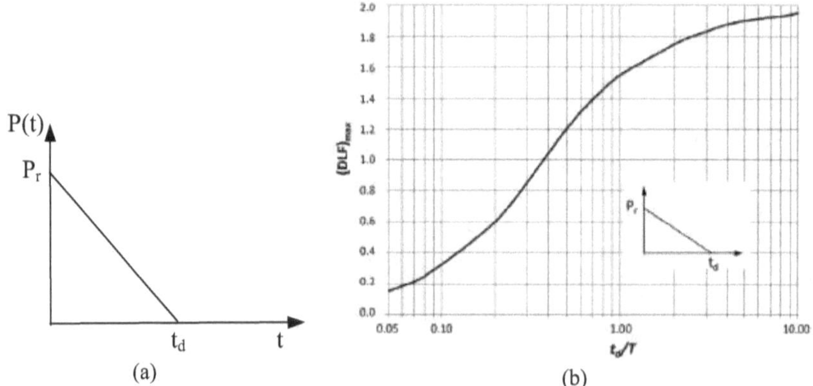

Figure 3.30: a) Idealized reflected pressure (P_r) vs. time (t) relationship, and
b) maximum dynamic load factor $(DLF)_{max}$ (CSA 852-18 2018)

Part III

Analytical Research

CHAPTER 4. Numerical Investigation of Blast-Resistant Window Anchors

4.1 Introduction

Civilian bomb attacks and accidental explosions pose significant threat to buildings and their occupants. Windows form one of the most critical elements of building envelope. Previous bomb attacks, such as the attack on the Australian Embassy in Jakarta in 2004, the accidental gas explosion of 1986 in Texas, the Oklahoma City Bombing of 1995, the Oslo Regjeringskvartalet Bombing of 2011, and the 2015 Mexico City Hospital gas explosion illustrate the vulnerability of windows to blast threats. Their failure results in casualties and injuries due to the flying broken glass shards followed by the penetration of blast shock waves into the building. Therefore, windows, including curtain walls are one of the first elements considered in vulnerability assessment of critical building infrastructure.

Different techniques and materials are used to safeguard windows against blast loads. (Lin et al. 2004) presented a detailed review of blast risk mitigation practices. Security film is one of the most effective measures. The films are typically in the form of polyester layers with a thickness ranging between 0.2 to 0.6 mm (0.007 and 0.024 in) applied to the interior pane of window glass. They are attached to the interior surface by adhesion, forming a clear and transparent surface, maintaining the functionality of glass while keeping the pieces of cracked/ broken glass intact after a bomb blast, reducing the potential for lacerations caused by glass fragmentation. The most common types of film application include the daylight application without anchorage to window frames and anchored applications as wet glazing by means of structural silicon or mechanical glazing using aluminum or steel sections for connecting the film to the window frame. The protective films can be applied on new, as well as existing windows for blast retrofitting. A similar protective functionality is provided in new blast-resistant windows by means of an interlayer of similar materials that ensure post-break integrity of the windows.

Several design guidelines have been developed for blast-resistant windows. The U.S. Department of Defence (DoD) document (UFC 4-010-01 2003) provides empirical and prescriptive design information for windows. The design loads are specified in (ASTM F2248 2009) and the methodology for computing window resistance is outlined in (ASTM E1300 2003). (UFC 4-010-01 2003), (AAMA 510-06 2006) and DFATD Design Guide (CERL 2015) provide limited design information for window retention anchors. A simplified design procedure is described for window anchor design in the Manual for Counter Terrorist Protective Security Measures (MCTPSM) of the UK using an equivalent static load approach (Mays et al. 2003). Anchor designs based on equivalent static loads may result in a conservative solution that lead to the use of too many anchors, which may compromise the performance of window frame (Ward et al. 2006). Recently the Canadian Standards Association developed a design standard for anchor design as part of the current investigation (Alameer et al. 2020).

Previous research on blast-resistant windows is summarized by (Saatcioglu et al. 2015) and (Alameer et al. 2020). It included live or laboratory tests, analytical derivations, and finite element analysis of window performance. Limited research was conducted specifically on window retention anchor (Saatcioglu et al. 2015). Most of the previous numerical studies concentrated on the use of laminated glass. (Oda et al. 1997) incorporated discrete element method (DEM) to simulate laminated glass fractured by steel ball impact. (Sun et al. 2005) analyzed insulated glass units (IGU) with polyvinyl butyral (PVB) interlaminates by modelling the glass panes with shell elements and the PVB interlayer with solid elements. Other researchers proposed the use of three-dimensional solid elements (Larcher 2012; Zhang 2011; Flocker 1997). A layered laminated glass model was used by (Timmel et al. 2007) for investigating windshield impact. The previous research indicated that 3D models gave the best agreement with experimental data. Also, the use of smeared models was more appropriate for predicting small panel displacements (Zhang et al. 2013a). It was also reported that the layered models resulted in acceptable results. Some of the previous analytical research involved the use of single-degree-of-freedom (SDOF) analysis. However, the limitation of SDOF was that it could only be used to obtain the total window displacement without giving the sequence and nature of the mechanism of failure in windows.

A detailed finite element analysis was conducted in the current research project to expand the experimental results obtained earlier as part of the same research program, reported in the companion paper (Alameer et al. 2020). The commonly used commercial software LS-DYNA was employed for this purpose. The window parameters considered in the numerical study included window aspect ratio, film thickness, window frame rigidity, and the arrangement of window retention anchors (number and spacing). The emphasis in the numerical investigation was placed on window anchor response, especially on anchor forces and their distributions. An analytical model was developed first and validated against the results of extensive shock tube testing conducted by the authors (Alameer et al. 2020).

4.2 Numerical Models

4.2.1 Window Details

The windows analyzed in the current investigation was of the same type of punched windows tested in the experimental program reported in the companion paper (Alameer et al. 2020). The experimental project focused on double-pane insulated glass units (IGU) with window aspect ratios of 1.0 and 3.0. The rationale for the selection of these two aspect ratios was to investigate performance of two-way and one-way modes of deformation. They were supported by four different types of substrates; reinforced concrete, structural steel, concrete block masonry, and stone masonry. The windows were secured on substrates by means of Grade 8 steel anchors. Figure 4.1 shows the overall geometry of a square and a rectangular window tested. A square and a rectangular window from each substrate category were selected for numerical analysis. Table 4.1 provides a list of windows that were selected from the experimental program and analyzed using LS-DYNA software. The numerical analysis was extended to include additional windows on reinforced concrete substrates with aspect ratios of 1.0, 1.5, 2.0, and 3.0. The analysis was further extended to include windows with rigid steel window frames, as well as windows with different number and spacing of retention anchors. Table 4.2 shows the properties of additional windows considered in the numerical analysis.

4.2.2 Element Modelling and Finite Element Discretization

An important step in FEM analysis is the selection of appropriate element models and the generation of FEM mesh. Figure 4.2 shows a typical FEM model used for a square window with loading and support boundary conditions. The window geometry was defined by specifying L, B, d_g, d_a and d_f for window length, window width, top and bottom glass thicknesses, air-gap, and protective film thickness, respectively. The glass was modelled using three-dimensional solid mesh elements (***SECTION_SOLID**) included in LS-DYNA. This involved the use of eight-node hexahedron solid mesh elements. A wide range of solid element formulations is available in LS-DYNA for modeling glass. These elements can have one or more volume integration points. It is generally recommended to use fully integrated elements to control zero energy modes (LS-DYNA 2007). According to (Larcher 2012), the use of 3D solid element models for glass yields accurate numerical solutions, hence the reason for selecting this element in the current investigation. Figure 4.2 shows solid mesh elements for the inner glazed glass pane and the outer unprotected glass. A mesh-size sensitivity analysis was conducted to obtain the optimized element size for the glass. The number of elements across the thickness of the glass was maintained the same to ensure appropriate stress variation across the thickness. Six different mesh sizes, varying between 40 mm and 15 mm with an increment of 5 mm were used. The maximum tip anchor displacement was selected for the convergence criterion. Figure 4.3 indicates that a mesh size of 20 mm x 20 mm x 3 mm provided acceptable convergence. The use of finer mesh would increase the computational time substantially without improving the accuracy in a meaningful manner. Similar sensitivity analyses were conducted for the retention anchors, the window frame, and the protective film, with resulting mesh sizes of 0.5 mm, 2.0 mm, and 20 mm, respectively.

The IGU glass unit contains compressed air in between the two glass panes. ***SIMPLE_AIRBAG_MODEL** was used to simulate the thermodynamic behavior of gas entrained between the glass panes. The air was enclosed by six surfaces, which consisted of the upper surface of the inner glazed pane, bottom surface of the outer unglazed pane and four surfaces of an assumed edge glass, as depicted in Figure 4.2.

Two-dimensional beam mesh elements were used to model the anchors and the frame. (***SECTION_BEAM**) Hughes-Liu element (Hughes et al 1981a; 1981b) was used to model the anchors as circular members and the window frame as rectangular members having the same rigidity (stiffness) as the aluminum sections. This type of element utilizes a cross-section integration beam element formulation with 2 x 2 Guess integration points. The mesh size for the beam element was 0.5 mm and 2 mm for the anchors and the frames, respectively. The anchor bolts had a circular cross-section with a diameter of 8.54 mm within the threaded segment. They were 67 mm long for steel substrates and 105 mm long for all other substrates, simulating the actual length used in the experimental program. The protective film was modeled by using two-dimensional shell elements. The default shell element formulation was used to model the films as proposed by Belytschko-Tsay (Belytschko et al. 1989; 1992). This element had two integration points through the film thickness. It was discretized to shell elements of size 20 mm x 20 mm. Five plies of film were used for the square window models with a thickness of 23 mils (0.73 mm). Three plies of films were used for the rectangular window models with a thickness of 14 mils (0.375mm).

Substrates were introduced as supporting elements for the anchors with support flexibility introduced as measured during the tests. FEM modelling of the entire substrate would increase the computational time substantially and make the analyses extremely cumbersome, as a large number of numerical simulations were conducted, each taking approximately 2 to 3 weeks. Discrete two-node elastic spring elements with translational spring/damper systems were used to introduce the experimentally recorded substrate displacements in the direction of blast loading. The comparison between the substrate experimental displacements and those calculated using the simple beam theory for a simply supported wall strip showed excellent agreement for the maximum displacements under the two levels of pressures applied during the tests (28 kPa and 69 kPa).

Damping was considered in dynamic analysis. The damping value reported in the literature varies between 1% and 5%. The software WINGARD (ARA 2005) for window analysis considers 2% of critical damping. The 2% value is also commonly used by other researchers (Andersson et al. 2012; Carlsson et al. 2012; Rezaei 2011; Kyei 2014; PEC et al. 2008; ARA 2005) and has been adopted in the current investigation after conducting a sensitivity analysis. The results indicated that the use of 2% of critical damping improved the correlation of analysis results with experimental data, especially when the response waveforms are compared.

4.2.3 Material Constitutive Modelling

The IGUs analyzed in the current investigation consisted of two annealed glass panes with an air-gap in between. Annealed glass typically behaves in a brittle manner under blast loads with very little post-peak strain increase prior to failure (Zhang et al. 2013). Researchers in the past reported a wide range of variation in glass strength, ranging between 30 MPa and 120 MPa depending on the type of glass (Moore 1980; ARA 2005; Zhang et al. 2013a; 2013b)). (Moore 1980) conducted extensive testing of annealed glass and showed that the static capacity of this type of glass varied approximately between 25 MPa and 30 MPa. It was observed in the experimental phase of the current investigation that the glass strength of 28 MPa represented window performance accurately during the tests.

There is considerable controversy in the literature on the significance of strain rate effects on glass. (Zhang 2013); Holmquist et al. 1995) adopted Johnson Holmquist Ceramic constitutive model

(JH2) which considers the effect of high strain rate on glass. The use of (JH2) and other dynamic glass material models have not been validated experimentally (Zhang et al. 2013a; 2013b), and the effect of high strain rate on glass was not well-justified. Therefore, most of the previous FEM studies on dynamic response of glass incorporated static material models (Larcher 2012; Peroni 2011). The same approach was adopted in the current investigation with ***MAT003-PLASTIC_KINEMATIC** model simulating glass behavior with the static glass strength. Table 4.3 shows the parameters that were assigned to the glass material model in LS-DYNA.

The air between the two glass panes was modelled using ***SIMPLE_AIRBAG_MODEL** that is available in LS-DYNA for the glass temperature at approximately 27°C. Table 4.3 provides the parameters that were used to define the material model for the air gap between two glass panes.

The material properties for the frame, the protective film and the window retention anchor bolts were introduced through ***MAT003-PLASTIC_KINEMATIC** model in LS-DYNA. The stress-strain characteristics of the window frame were established through coupon tests of aluminum samples under static loading. The dynamic increase factor for the aluminum was taken as 1.0, as recommended by (CSA S850 2012). Standard tension tests were also conducted for the steel anchors to establish their stress-strain characteristics, listed in Table 4.3. The dynamic increase factor of 1.1 was applied to the steel strength as per (CSA S850 2012). The properties for the protective film were adopted from the WINGARD Manual (ARA 2005). The material properties for the film are listed in Table 4.3.

The elastic springs used to model the substrate movement as support flexibility were simulated by using ***MAS01-SPRING_ELASTIC** model in LS-Dyna. The spring coefficient used for each window was obtained from the test data so that the same substrate deflections as those recorded during the tests could be obtained. These deflections compared favorably with those computed based on the one-way beam theory.

4.2.4 Modelling of Contacts

An important step in the FEM model was the selection of contact models. The analysis of windows involved the transmission of applied blast loads to window anchors through different types of materials. This requires the introduction of various contact types in the numerical model. A special consideration was given to the contacts between the protective film and the interior glass pane and the properties of the adhesive glue used between the two materials. The film should be perfectly bonded to the glass to allow for synchronous deformations. This was ensured by specifying ***Eroding_SURFACE_TO_SURFACE** contact option, which is recommended in the (LS-DYNA Manual 2007). The contact type specified is especially applicable to simulate the behavior of a protective film that maintains its contact upon the failure of the glass. However, it was necessary to define the erosion criteria in the model to avoid premature deletion of elements. The erosion concept is a numerical manipulation that simulates the deletion of an element, as in the case of glass failure, or film rupturing that may be encountered during response. However, the deleted elements should maintain their mass during the simulation (Zhang et al. 2013b). Erosion is also used for modeling contacts for solid elements to ensure that the glass keeps its contact with the remaining elements upon failure. This mimics the actual behavior of window response observed in the tests, as the broken glass fragments remained attached to the protective film. It was confirmed by previous researchers that the numerical simulation with erosion yields favourable results (Sun 2005; Timmel 2007; Zhang 2013a; Bois 2003). The film was attached to the window frame using

***TIED_SHELL_EDGE_SUFACE_BEAM** contact that is typically used for surfaces that are normal or orthogonal to the direction of the load.

4.2.5   Loading

The blast load was applied in LS-DYNA as pressure along the top segment of the outer unglazed pane. This was done by specifying ***LOAD-SEGMENT_SET** keyword; and the pressure was specified using ***DEFINE-CURVE** keyword. The curve that was used during model validation was the actual recorded pressure time relationship obtained from tests. Figure 4.4 shows typical reflected pressure-time relationships recorded during the tests. An idealized forcing function was used for the numerical simulations of windows in the parametric study, representing only the positive phase of loading as a triangular impulsive forcing function.

4.3   Validation of Numerical Model

Numerical simulations were conducted to validate the analytical model presented in the preceding section. Because the focus of the experimental program was on anchor performance, selected anchors were instrumented to measure anchor tip deflection. This quantity was used to validate the analytical model. The anchors in the numerical model were connected to the springs that simulated substrate flexibility. The boundary conditions at the anchor-spring connection were of significance. The anchor bolts of test windows were secured into the substrates either by means of tightened nuts in the case of steel substrates, or by means of drop-in-anchors in the case of reinforced concrete, block masonry and stone masonry substrates. During response to blast loads, especially under higher pressures, the initial anchor fixity could not be maintained, and the support condition changed from fixed to partially fixed boundary condition. This was especially true for steel substrates where the holes opened in the substrates to accommodate the anchor bolts were of slightly larger diameter than the bolts. In steel substrates the behavior approached to simply supported condition shortly after loading. In the case of other substrates, the behavior was closer to fixed support under lower levels of blast shots and experienced partial fixity under increased pressures. In certain cases, the anchors suffered from partial pull-out, experiencing relaxation, not only in rotational restraints but also in longitudinal and transverse constraints at the supports, resulting in a visible partial pull-out. This is illustrated in Figures 4.5. For this reason, the simulations were made twice for each case, first with pin supports at the ends of anchors and second with full fixity. Figures 4.6 and 4.7 shows comparisons of selected central window anchor tip deflections on steel, reinforced concrete, concrete block masonry and stone masonry substrates, subjected to two levels of pressure-impulse combinations. The same Figure also contains the results of two analyses for each case with either pin or fixed supports at the substrate ends of anchors. The results indicate that the measured displacement response falls between the two computed responses having pin and fixed anchor supports. The comparisons given for a rectangular window on reinforced concrete substrate indicates that the anchors during Test C13 under 28 kPa maximum pressure maintained their fixity and the computed response for fixed anchor supports approached to the experimental response. This is illustrated in Figure 4.6 (a). The same window, when subjected to the higher pressure of 69 kPa (Test C14), indicated closer correlation with the simulation based on pin ended anchors. This observation indicates the relaxation of anchor ends in the substrate under higher levels of pressure-impulse combination. At this level of loading the anchors performed in the inelastic range of deformations and experienced some degree of loss in bond and end fixity conditions though they maintained their functions, keeping the window attached to the substrate. Beyond 15 m-sec of response, the anchors experienced further loss off their end restraints inside the substrate, developing partial pull-out and higher out-of-plane displacements. The experimental displacements started showing divergence from the computed response. The anchors in the numerical model had boundary conditions that constrained longitudinal and transverse movements in all cases. The models did not simulate the partial loss of displacement constraint and associated loss of bond and partial pull-out, hence divergence beyond the peak response. The second set of comparisons shown in Figures 4.6(c) and 4.6(d) are for square windows on steel substrates. As was indicated earlier, the pre-drilled holes along the window opening in steel substrates had slightly larger diameters for easy installation of anchor bolts, which were fixed at their ends by means of tightened nuts. This way of securing anchor bolts resulted in full fixity at the beginning of response, but very quickly lost their rotational fixity and showed response closer to pin-supported anchor model in the numerical simulation (in both Tests S13 and S14). In fact, under the higher level of blast loading (Test S14) the anchors became loose in the pre-drilled holes and started showing higher displacements. This is evident in Figure 4.6(d). The other window responses that are compared in Figures 4.7 for block and stone masonry substrates indicate similar trends as those for reinforced concrete substrates. The emphasis in the current research project was placed on maximum anchor forces and anchor force distributions along the frame for use in design. Therefore, the comparisons of experimental and numerical results were of significance up to the peak displacement and peak load and not the entire time history. These peak resistance values obtained from numerical simulations were used to explain the significance of each parameter.

Maximum numerical and experimental anchor displacements and forces (both shear force and axial tension) are compared in Table 4.4 for selected test windows. The selected cases considered included one rectangular and one square window on each substrate, subjected to two levels of pressure-impulse combinations. Their properties are shown in Table 4.1. The results shown in Table 4.4 are for all the instrumented anchors along the window height and length in two orthogonal directions. Two anchors were instrumented in each direction in the majority of the window tests (Alameer et al. 2020). The anchors were placed at mid-height (along the vertical direction) and mid-length (along the horizontal direction) of one side of the window frame, as well as near the end of the frame in each direction (near corners). The results indicate that the measured anchor forces were consistently in between the pin-ended and fixed anchor simulations, approaching pin-ended anchor behavior in the majority of cases.

4.4   Parametric Investigation

A parametric investigation was carried out through numerical simulation of window response to expand the experimental observations reported on anchor behavior by (Alameer et al. 2020). The emphasis in the parametric investigation was placed on anchor shear and axial force levels and the distribution of anchor forces along the window frame. The effects of the following parameters were investigated numerically:

- Effect of substrate flexibility.

- Effect of anchor fixity in the substrate.

- Window size and aspect ratio.

- Rigidity of window frame.

- Number of anchors and anchor spacing.

- Level of blast pressure-impulse combination.

The effects of the first two parameters indicated above were assessed using the analysis of test windows. The effects of the remaining four parameters were investigated using numerical window models on reinforced concrete substrate, which was selected as a reference substrate because it has a flexibility between the two extremes among the substrates considered. i.e., the rigid steel and flexible masonry substrates. The anchors were modelled to have pin supports in the substrate. This support condition provided a closer representation of the majority of the window tests, especially under higher levels of blast pressure-impulse combinations.

4.4.1 Effect of Substrate Flexibility

The four different substrate types, consisting of reinforced concrete, steel, block masonry and stone masonry, were modelled to assess the effects of substrate flexibility on anchor forces. A rectangular and a square window on each of the four substrates were analyzed under two pressure-impulse combinations. The results for rectangular windows (560X1676 mm) modeled on each substrate are shown in Figure 4.8. They are consistent with the measured response reported by (Alameer et al. 2020). As the substrate stiffness increases, the mid-height substrate deformation decreases as expected. This is accompanied by an increase in anchor displacements relative to those for the substrate at anchor locations, resulting in higher anchor forces on more rigid substrates. Anchors secured on the most rigid steel substrate developed the highest displacement and force response, whereas those placed on the most flexible stone masonry substrate developed the least response for the same pressure-impulse combinations, indicating a significant influence of substrate type on anchor response. Indeed, during the experiments the only anchors that failed or developed excessive inelastic deformations were those square windows that were placed on rigid steel substrates (Alameer et al. 2020).

4.4.2 Effect of Anchor Fixity in Substrates

Window tests indicated that the anchor fixity in substrates varied during dynamic response between initially fixed and pin supports, experiencing relaxation in support fixity. The measured response was in-between the numerical simulations with these two rotational restraint limits. This is illustrated in Figure 4.6 and 4.7 and discussed under "Validation of Numerical Model." Depending on the level of end fixity that could be attained during blast response, the anchor forces approached to one of the two numerical results. Therefore, the significance of anchor end condition was assessed by conducting numerical simulations with fixed and pinned anchors. Response time histories are compared in Figures 4.6 and 4.7. The maximum anchor shear and axial tension forces are 25% (under 28 kPa) to 45% (under 69 kPa) and 55% (under 69 kPa) to 85% (28 kPa) higher when the anchors were fully fixed, relative to those that had pin supports for windows on steel/reinforced concrete and concrete block/stone masonry substrates, respectively. Another observation was the change in the frequency characteristics of anchor response. Figures 4.7 indicate that the frequency of response was higher when fully fixated anchors were used, indicating potentially significant effect on dynamic load factors and the anchor design force requirements.

4.4.3 Window Size and Aspect Ratio

The dimensions of windows in practice vary substantially as they form part of a building envelop. The effect of window dimensions is twofold; affecting window surface area and associated blast loads applied on the window, and the window aspect ratio defined as the ratio of longer to shorter dimensions of window, affecting window performance in terms of bending action in two orthogonal directions. Four window sizes with aluminum frames having four different aspect ratios were modelled on reinforced concrete substrates to investigate the effect of window size and window aspect ratio numerically on the magnitude and distribution of anchor forces. The window sizes and properties selected are presented in Table 4.2, resulting in window aspect ratios of 1.0, 1.5, 2.0, and 3.0. All the windows had the same width (short side) of 1220 mm and a variable height (long side). The same thickness of protective film was used in 5 plies, resulting in a total film thickness of 23 mils. This film thickness was found to be sufficient to prevent premature rupturing of the film. Figure 4.9 shows the variation of anchor forces with window aspect ratio. Accordingly, the ratio of anchor forces along the long and short sides is equal to 1.0 when the window aspect ratio is 1.0, as expected, perfectly indicating two way-bending. The behavior changes to pre-dominantly one-way bending as the aspect ratio increases to 3.0 with higher forces along the longer sides of window as the applied load is distributed in the short direction, with 40% and 60% higher anchor forces when the aspect ratio is increased to 1.5 and 3.0, respectively. The Figure indicates that one-way action prevails beyond an aspect ratio of approximately 1.5 with the longer side forces asymptotically approaching 2.8 times the shorter side anchor forces.

Windows with larger surface area resulted in higher anchor forces. Figure 4.10 shows the comparison of anchor shear and axial tension forces for windows having a constant width and variable height. Windows with longer heights (vertical dimensions) had larger surface areas and were exposed to higher blast loads under the same reflected pressure. These windows developed higher anchor forces, almost in proportion to the increase in surface area. The windows analyzed in the current investigation fall into the quasi-static range of dynamic window response, rather than the impulsive range. Analyses of windows under the impulsive range of response by (Mutalip et al. 2010) showed no effect of window size on window resistance. This was explained by the proportional increase in inertia resistance of window mass with increasing surface area, effectively cancelling the effects of higher applied pressures on larger windows. Figure 4.10 also shows the distribution of anchor forces along the frame elements. The middle anchors showed about 15% to 30% higher forces than the anchors near the corners.

4.4.4 Rigidity of Window Frames

Windows are usually fabricated using flexible frames made from aluminum or wood. Blast-resistant windows are often manufactured using rigid steel frames. The rigidity of window frames has a direct bearing on the distribution of anchor forces. Infinitely rigid frames result in uniform distribution of anchor forces along the frame elements, whereas flexible frames result in non-uniform force distribution with higher anchor forces near the mid-length of frame elements. The effect of frame rigidity on anchor force distribution was investigated by comparing windows with aluminum and steel frames. Numerical models were configured to represent two windows geometry; 1220 mm x 1220 mm with an aspect ratio of 1.0, and 560 mm x 1676 mm with an aspect ratio of 3.0. Four anchors were placed along the long side of frames and two along the short side. Figure 4.11 confirms the expected trend, showing more uniform distribution of anchor forces on rigid steel frames. The difference between the anchor forces near the corners and those at mid-frame lengths of steel frames was approximately 5% and 10% under 28kPa and 69 kPa blast loads, respectively. The rigid steel frames also contributed to the magnitude of anchor forces, resulting in slight increases in shear forces. It was also observed that the steel frames restrained the in-plane action, resulting in reduced anchor tension forces relative to those of aluminum frames. The aluminum frames exhibited significant out-of-plane and in-plane deformations. Therefore, mid-frame anchors experienced 30% higher forces in comparison with those near the corners. The flexibility of aluminum frames led to lower magnitudes of shear forces and larger in-plane deformations (membrane action) resulting in higher axial tension.

4.4.5　Number of Anchors and Anchor Spacing

One of the important parameters investigated numerically was the number of anchors per side and associated anchor spacing. Five different numbers of anchors with five different anchor spacings were modelled using a window size of 1240 mm X 1840 mm with aspect ratio of 1.5. The window was subjected to pressure-impulse combinations of 28 kPa; 207 kPa-ms (4 psi; 30 psi-ms) and 69 kPa; 621 kPa-ms (10 psi; 90 psi-ms) . The anchors were distributed using two patterns; i) odd number anchors had an anchor placed at mid-length and equally spaced, and ii) even number anchors had two anchors placed in the mid-length region, one on either side of the frame centerline, having equal anchor spacing. Anchor shear and axial tension forces are plotted in Figure 4.12. The anchor forces were higher per anchor when fewer anchors were used, as expected. Of significance is the effect of the distribution of anchors along the length of the frames. The anchor forces peaked at the center. Avoiding the center point as anchor location improve the distribution of forces, resulting in more uniform anchor shear and axial tension forces. It can be seen that the use of a minimum of 4 anchors per side, while avoiding the frame center as the anchor location result in reasonably uniform anchor forces, with higher forces near the central portion of the frame.

4.4.6　Level of Blast Pressure-Impulse Combination

The effect of the use of different reflected pressure-reflected impulse combinations was investigated by analyzing a square window with 1220 mm x 1220 mm dimensions and an aluminum frame secured on a reinforced concrete substrate. The window selected was the same window that was tested earlier in the experimental phase of the current investigation (Alameer et al. (2020). Four different pressure-impulse combinations were applied. The first two were adopted from GSA standard test procedure (GSA 2003) and consisted of 28 kPa; 207 kPa-ms (4 psi; 30 psi-ms) and 69 kPa; 621 kPa-ms (10 psi; 90 psi-ms), as shown in Figures 4.4. The other pressure-impulse combinations consisted of 103.4 kPa; 577 kPa-ms (15 psi; 84 psi-ms) and 138 kPa; 760 kPa-ms (20 psi; 110 kPa-ms). The latter two forcing functions were established as idealized forcing functions obtained from two assumed threat levels. Anchor shear and axial tension forces are plotted in Figure 4.13. The results indicated that the anchors performed elastically under 28 kPa and developed lower anchor forces. An increase of 35% in average anchor forces was observed when the load was increased to 69 kPa. The anchors exhibited inelastic behavior at this level of loading. Further increase in blast pressures to 103.4 kPa and 138 kPa resulted in 12% to 15% increase in average anchor forces in each increment of pressure increase. The reduced incremental increase in anchor forces can be attributed to the post-yield behavior of anchors, with little increase in resistance within the strain hardening range. However, the anchors at these stages of loading experienced increased inelastic deformations, as shown in Figure 4.13. It was also noticed that the natural period vibration of the windows increased during the post-yield response, also resulting in reduced dynamic load factor.

4.5   Magnitude and Distribution of Anchor Forces

The parametric investigation reported in the preceding section shows that a number of parameters play important roles on anchor forces. The primary parameters that affect the magnitude of the anchor forces are window surface area and the threat level (pressure-impulse combination). Large size windows with larger surface areas are subjected to higher blast loads under the same pressure-impulse combination. This is true for the windows considered in the current investigation, which performed in the quasi-static range of dynamic response, rather than the impulsive range. Other researchers reported that windows in the impulsive range of dynamic response would not be sensitive to the increase in window surface area, because the effects of increased surface area would be offset by the proportional increase in inertia resistance (Mutalip et al. 2010). The other principle parameter that has an effect on the magnitude of anchor forces is the threat level. While anchor forces increase with the threat level, yielding of anchors may limit the increase in anchor forces. Other parameters that affect anchor forces are the window aspect ratio, substrate type, and the end fixity condition of anchors. The anchor forces on vertical and horizontal frame elements indicated that those with an aspect ratio of 1.0 show equal forces on orthogonal frame elements, whereas the ratio of forces on the long to short side increase up to 2.8 as the window aspect ratio increases to 3.0 due to the one-way action, as depicted in Figure 4.9. Windows on flexible substrates develop smaller anchor displacements relative substrates, developing smaller forces than those on rigid substrates. Also, anchors that maintained their fixity in substrates attract higher levels of anchor forces as indicated in Table 4.4.

Anchor shear forces in the pre-break phase of glass panes result from the bending of glass. In this range of deformations, the membrane action and the anchor axial tension is very small. In the post-break phase, the protective film performs as a membrane, generating in-plane forces that produce axial tension and shear forces in anchors. The membrane forces increase as the protective film experiences plastic behavior under high levels of blast loads, increasing both the axial tension and shear forces in anchors. In this range of response axial tension becomes higher than the anchor shear forces. This is illustrated in Figures 4.10 to 4.13 and in Table 4.4. The average anchor shear forces computed numerically were approximately 15-30% of the average axial tension forces as indicated in Table 4.4. The magnitude of anchor forces must be established through dynamic analysis, which captures all the parameters discussed in the preceding section. This may be the type of numerical finite element analysis conducted in the current investigation, or approximately a single degree-of-freedom (SDOF) analysis that can be conducted as a design tool. The companion paper presents a SDOF analysis technique that can be used for the glazed windows considered (Alameer et al. 2020).

Based on the anchor force distributions indicated by the experimental investigation (Alameer et al. 2020) and the current numerical simulations, a parabolic or a half sine distribution can be considered as also suggested by (TM5-1300 1990) for flexible frames. The following distribution of anchor shear and tension forces can be used in design.

$$q = q_o \sin \theta \qquad\qquad 4.1$$

$$\theta = \frac{x}{L}.\pi \qquad\qquad 4.2$$

q = variable edge shear or axial tension force depends on anchor location (x)

q_o = average edge shear or axial tension force

θ = angle of force distribution in radians

x = anchor location along window edge

L = window edge length

It should be noted that the rigidity of window frames plays a significant role on anchor force distribution. Rigid steel frames, as typically used in blast-resistant windows develop uniform or near-uniform force distribution, depending on the rigidity of window frames.

4.6   Summary and Conclusions

Numerical investigation of blast-resistant windows was conducted with emphasis on window retention anchors. Analytical models for software LS-DYNA were generated and validated against test data. An analytical parametric investigation was conducted to assess the significance of design parameter. The following are the conclusions obtained from this investigation.

- The behaviour of glazed window systems secured on different types of substrates with different force-deformation characteristics can be modelled using LS_DYNA software fairly accurately. The numerical model can be simplified substantially for the purpose of obtaining anchor design forces by incorporating the effects of substrates as anchor support flexibilities in the numerical model. This simplification can be justified in view of experimental observations where the substrate and the window responded in phase, especially during initial response when the maximum anchor forces were developed, reaching their design force levels.

- Substrate flexibility affects anchor design force levels. Windows on rigid substrates, as in the case of structural steel, develop high anchor forces. Windows on flexible substrates, such as masonry walls develop smaller anchor forces. This is attributed to the relative anchor deformations. Window anchors secured in flexible substrates deform less relative to the substrate when compared with those on rigid substrates where the substrate deforms less and the anchors deform more, attracting higher forces.

- Anchors in reinforced concrete and masonry substrates develop full fixity in drop-in anchors as observed under 28 kPa reflected pressure but may develop plastic deformations and anchorage slippage under higher blast pressures as observed under 69 kPa. Anchors on steel substrate may become loose early in response if they are attached by means of bolt heads or nuts.

- Square windows with an aspect ratio of 1.0 develop two-way action, with anchor forces equally distributed in two orthogonal directions, while higher forces are observed near the mid-length of each frame component. Rectangular windows exhibit predominantly one-way behaviour in short direction with 40% and 60% higher anchor forces along the long edges when the aspect ratio is increased to 1.5 and 3.0, respectively. The one-way action prevails beyond an aspect ratio of approximately 1.5 with the longer side forces asymptotically approaching 1.6 times the shorter side anchor forces.

- Windows with rigid frames show near uniform anchor force distribution. Windows with flexible aluminum frames develop parabolic force distribution along window edges, which can be estimated by a half sine curve.

- Anchor shear forces are higher than axial tensile forces in the pre-break phase of response. Upon breakage, membrane forces become significant, decreasing the ratio of anchor shear force to axial tension force. For the blast pressures considered in the current investigation, anchor shear forces in the post-break range varied between 15% to 30 % of axial tension.

Table 4.1: Properties of windows

Test NO.	Aspect Ratio	Film Thickness (mils)	Glazing Anchor Spacing (mm)	Retention Anchor Spacing (mm)	No. of Anchors	Embed. Length (mm)	Pr (kPa)
C7 C8	1	4.5+4.5+5	Mech.@ 125	500	2(3+3)=12	90	28 69
C13 C14	3	4.5+4.5+5	Mech.@ Long:100 Short:100	Long:400 Short:305	2(4+2)=12	125	28 69
S13 S14	1	4(4.5)+5	Mech.@ 100	400	2(4+2)=12	90	28 69
S15 S16	3	4.5+4.5+5	Mech.@ 125	Long:500 Short:225	2(4+2)=12	90	28 69
B1 B2	1	4.5+4.5+5	Mech.@ 125	300	2(4+4)=16	125	28 69
B5 B6	3	4.5+4.5+5	Mech.@ 125	Long:400 Short:305	2(4+2)=12	125	28 69
ST1 ST2	1	4.5+4.5+5	Mech.@ 125	300	2(4+4)=16	125	28 69
ST3 ST4	3	4.5+4.5+5	Mech.@ 125	Long:400 Short:305	2(4+2)=12	125	28 69

Table 4.2: Window details used for the parametric study

Model No.	Aspect Ratio	Dimension (mm)	Retention Anchor Spacing (mm)	No. of Anchors	Embed. Length (mm)
1	1	1220X1220	Long:300 Short:300	2(4+4)=16	125
2	1.5	1220X1840	Long:500 Short:300	2(4+4)=16	125
3	2	1220X2440	Long:700 Short:300	2(4+4)=16	125
4	3	1220X3680	Long:1100 Short:300	2(4+4)=16	125

Table 4.3: Material properties used in the model

Mat	Density, (kg/m^3)	Yield Stress (MPa)	Elastic Modules (MPa)	Passion's Ratio	Rupture Strain (%)
Frame	2,700	305	70,000	0.33	0.012
Film	1,390	157	4,140	0.25	1.3
Anchor	7,800	1,050	200,000	0.3	0.15
Glass					
Density (kg/m^3)	Elastic Modulus (MPa)	Passion's Ratio		Breakage Strength (MPa)	
2500	42,000	0.22		28	
Air					
Heat Capacity at Constant Volume (kJ/(kg.K))			0.717		
Heat Capacity at Constant Pressure (kJ/(kg.K))			1.04		
Temperature (K)			300		
Ambient Pressure (MPa)			0.1		
Ambient Density (kg/m^3)			1.184		

Table 4.4: Comparisons of experimental and numerical results for windows on reinforced concrete and steel substrates

Model		Anchor displacement			Shear forces			Axial tension force		
		δ_P (mm)	δ_F (mm)	δ_E (mm)	V_P (kN)	V_F (kN)	V_E (kN)	T_P (kN)	T_F (kN)	T_E (kN)
C7	M-H	29.1	17.8	21.4	1.35	1.98	1.7	7.6	11.2	-
	C-H	27.96	17.1	20.6	1.22	1.92	1.64	6.83	10.4	-
Variation (%)					23.1	16.8		-	-	-
C8	M-H	32	24.1	43.7	2.29	2.45	Missed	12.6	13.8	-
	C-H	27.8	22.7	29.9	1.9	2.03	Missed	10.7	11.5	-
Variation (%)					-	-		-	-	-
C13	M-H	27.63	16.87	20.3	1.45	2.11	1.9	7.4	10.8	8.2
	C-H				1.32	1.92	1.75	2.3	4.6	2.7
	C-L	17.4	10.57	12.81	1.04	1.82	1.326	1.8	2.7	2
Variation (%)					23.3	17.5		34.9	14.6	
C14	M-H	32	20.5	-	1.85	2.28	2	10.9	14.6	12.3
	C-H				1.79	2.19	1.95	9.3	11.7	10.2
	C-L	23.26	16.1	21.1	1.19	1.92	1.402	3.22	5.9	3.873
Variation (%)					10.5	22.9		11.3	23.4	
S13	M-H	15.33	7.27	13.19	1.83	2.3	1.98	3.9	8.1	5.1
	C-H	9.8	5.9	12.6	1.61	2.05	1.78	1.36	5.7	3.43
	M-L	10.2	6.4	17.35	1.47	2.1	1.607	2.91	5.3	3.49
	C-L	15.8	7.9	13.4	1.28	1.89	1.434	2.1	3.98	2.82
Variation (%)					16.6	45		15.9	46.1	
S14	M-H	33.6	22.4	48.9	2.21	2.8	2.4	9.2	14.8	10.7
	C-H	24.6	18.3	39.53	2.13	2.63	2.31	8.9	14.1	10.5
	M-L	28.3	20.2	36.2	1.78	2.6	1.99	7.98	14.0	9.31
	C-L	18.7	14.6	29.14	1.54	2.35	1.78	6.8	12.3	8.58
Variation (%)					3.8	34.5		3.5	33.7	
S15	M-H	23.5	9.7	19.8	1.77	2.38	1.95	7.1	11.4	8.5
	C-H	15.4	6.2	13.7	1.54	2.12	1.82	2.2	6.1	3.6
	M-L	17.9	7.8	N/A	1.29	1.93	1.44	3.4	6.7	4.6
	C-L	14.3	5.8	11.15	0.16	0.72	0.204	1.2	3.5	2.1
Variation (%)					16.6	44.5		15.9	44.2	
S16	M-H	38.3	17.3	98.16	2.6	3.65	2.7	13.6	19.1	14.1
	C-H	32	14.1	27.6	2.04	2.81	2.11	11.7	16.3	12.1
	M-L	25.3	11.9	N/A	1.62	2.25	1.68	5.02	6.96	5.2
	C-L	21.1	10.3	24.85	1.46	2.03	1.51	4.36	6.05	4.5
Variation (%)					3.5	34.2		3.3	34.6	

Table 4.5: Comparisons of experimental and numerical results for windows on concrete block and stone masonry substrates

Model		δ_P (mm)	δ_F (mm)	δ_E (mm)	V_P (kN)	V_F (kN)	V_E (kN)	T_P (kN)	T_F (kN)	T_E (kN)
		Anchor displacement			Shear forces			Axial tension force		
B1	M-H	19.2	10.9	13.5	0.87	1.45	1.2	3.4	6.3	5.2
	C-H	-	-	-	0.72	1.32	1.097	2.48	4.57	3.8
	M-L	15.2	8.92	11.2	0.79	1.43	1.18	1.85	3.35	2.8
	C-L	-	-	-	0.59	1.08	0.89	1.63	2.97	2.48
Variation (%)					34	20.9		34.4	20.2	
B2	M-H	32.1	15.6	25.5	1.36	2.51	1.78	6.72	12.5	8.9
	C-H	-	-	-	1.08	2.05	1.43	5.21	9.48	6.9
	M-L	21.81	10.84	17.56	1.04	1.94	1.38	5.93	10.8	7.8
	C-L	-	-	-	0.95	1.73	1.25	3.75	6.83	4.9
Variation (%)					24.2	40.8		24.1	38.9	
B5	M-H	15.9	8.1	10.88	1.12	2.2	1.82	4.91	9.43	7.81
	C-H	-	-	-	0.91	1.81	1.49	2.27	4.7	3.91
	C-L	8.91	4.9	6.2	0.63	1.25	1.02	1.95	3.92	3.23
Variation (%)					38.5	21.6		39.6	20.8	
B6	C-L	26.3	11.81	19.5	1.46	2.71	1.91	8.62	15.9	11.3
	M-H	-	-	-	1.32	2.39	1.74	6.01	11.1	7.88
	C-H	14.51	6.65	11.22	1.21	2.23	1.58	4.1	7.41	5.24
Variation (%)					23.7	40.1		23.1	41	
ST1	M-H	12.82	8.52	9.1	0.68	1.21	1.087	2.91	5.11	4.7
	C-H	-	-	-	0.62	1.13	1.02	2.02	3.72	3.3
	M-L	10.1	6.73	7.2	0.66	1.17	1.06	1.31	2.42	2.2
	C-L	-	-	-	0.49	0.91	0.82	1.22	2.13	1.92
Variation (%)					38.7	10.9		38.5	10.6	
ST2	M-H	16.97	9.97	15.3	1.37	2.09	1.54	7.69	11.7	8.65
	C-H	-	-	-	1.24	1.87	1.38	5.51	8.3	6.1
	M-L	13.91	8.18	12.7	1.13	1.73	1.32	6.2	9.6	6.9
	C-L	-	-	-	1.05	1.64	1.23	5.04	7.48	5.5
Variation (%)					12.6	33.9		9.8	36.6	
ST3	M-H	16.1	10.71	11.52	0.98	1.78	1.6	1.08	1.91	1.74
	C-H	-	-	-	0.87	1.52	1.4	0.97	1.67	1.52
	C-L	11.04	7.26	7.94	0.53	0.92	0.84	0.7	1.24	1.12
Variation (%)					37.8	9.8		37.2	10.1	
ST4	M-H	18.5	10.9	16.85	1.44	2.21	1.62	3.34	5.09	3.75
	C-H	-	-	-	1.29	1.97	1.45	2.81	4.3	3.1
	C-L	11.83	6.81	10.44	0.8	1.26	0.89	1.76	2.67	1.95
Variation (%)					10.8	38		10	37.1	

Notes: (M-H), (C-H), (M-L), and (C-L) are the mid-height, corner height, mid-length, and corner length anchors, respectively. (δ_P), (δ_F) and (δ_E) are numerical pinned and fixed displacements, and experimental tip deflections for anchors. (V_P) and (V_F) are out of plane anchor shear forces recorded numerically for pinned and fixed cases, respectively. (T_P) and (T_F) are axial tension forces recorded numerically for pinned and fixed cases, respectively. (V_E) and (T_E) are the experimental shear and axial tension forces. The symbol (-) indicates data not available.

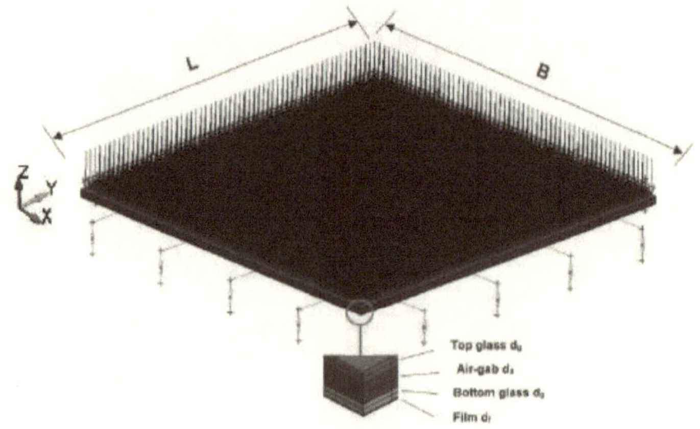

Figure 4.1: Model geometry and load application

(a) Top View

(b) Bottom View

Figure 4.2: Full geometry of FEM model

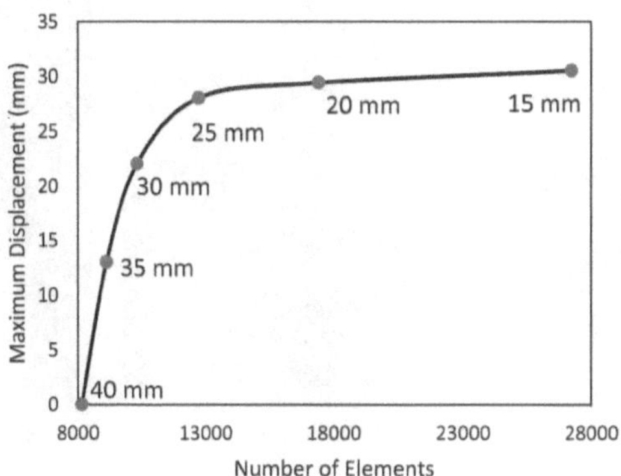

Figure 4.3: Convergence study

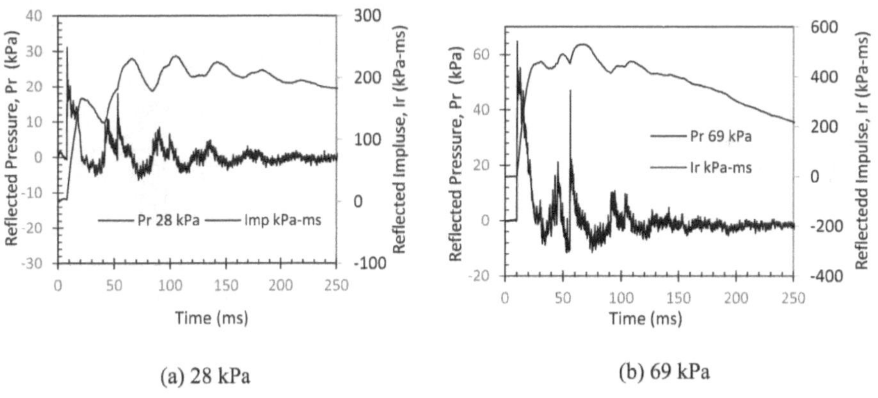

(a) 28 kPa   (b) 69 kPa

Figure 4.4: Typical reflected pressures and impulses

Figure 4.5: Anchorage pull-out during tests

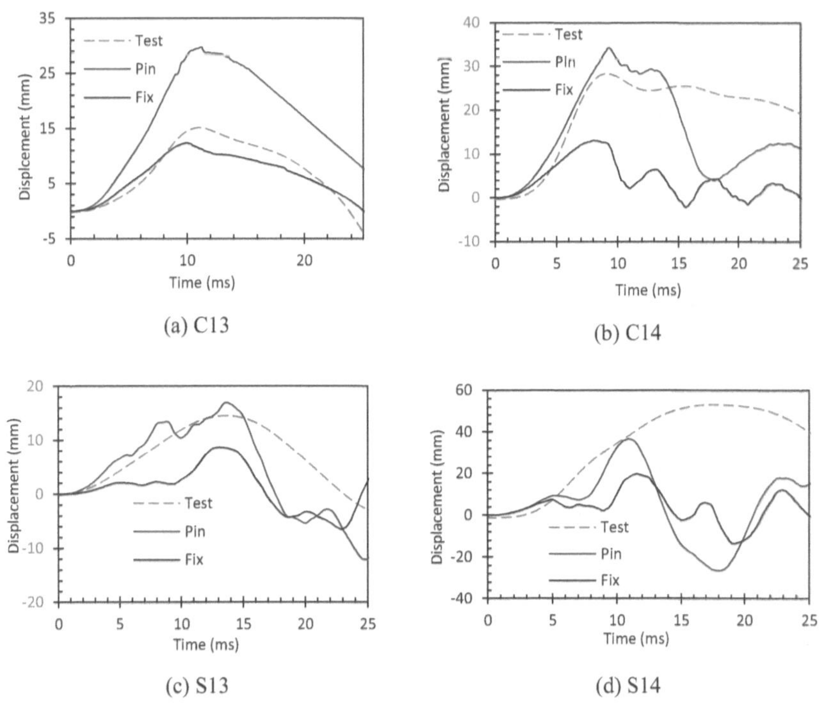

(a) C13

(b) C14

(c) S13

(d) S14

Figure 4.6: Experimental response vs. numerical response for selected cases

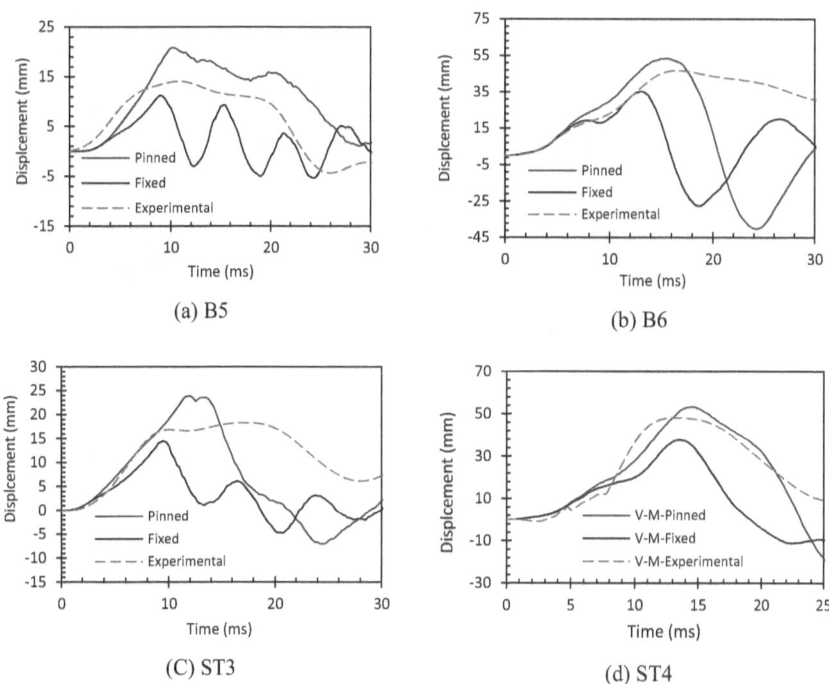

Figure 4.7: Comparisons between the experimental and numerical response for selected cases

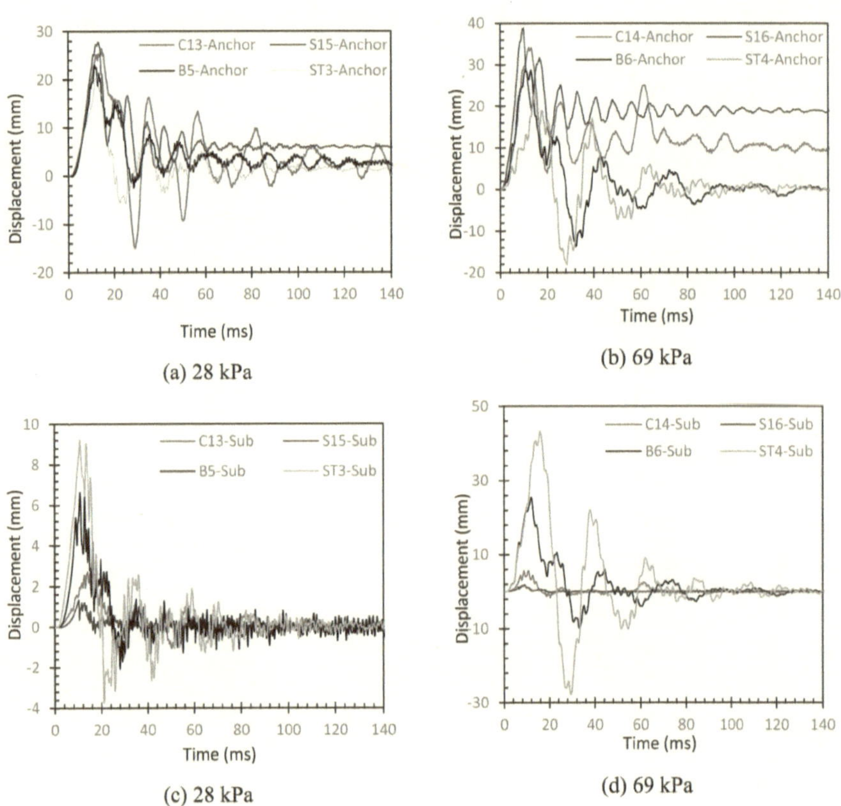

Figure 4.8: Numerical mid-height anchor tip/substrate displacements

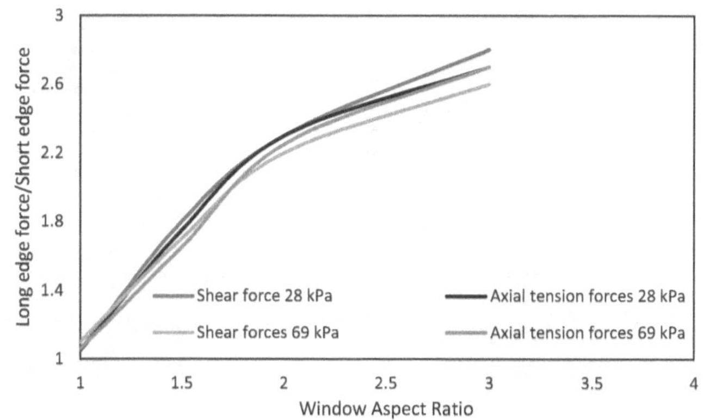

Figure 4.9: Effect of window aspect ratio

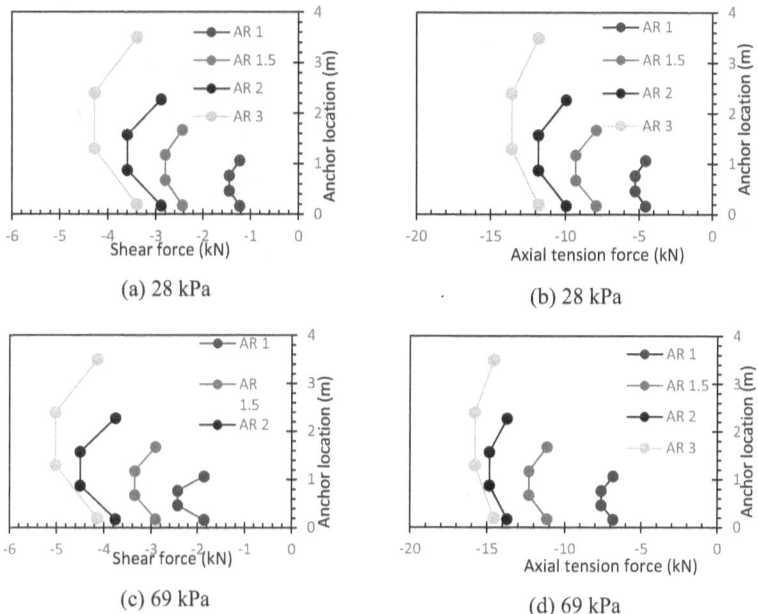

(a) 28 kPa

(b) 28 kPa

(c) 69 kPa

(d) 69 kPa

Figure 4.10: Force distribution as affected by aspect ratio

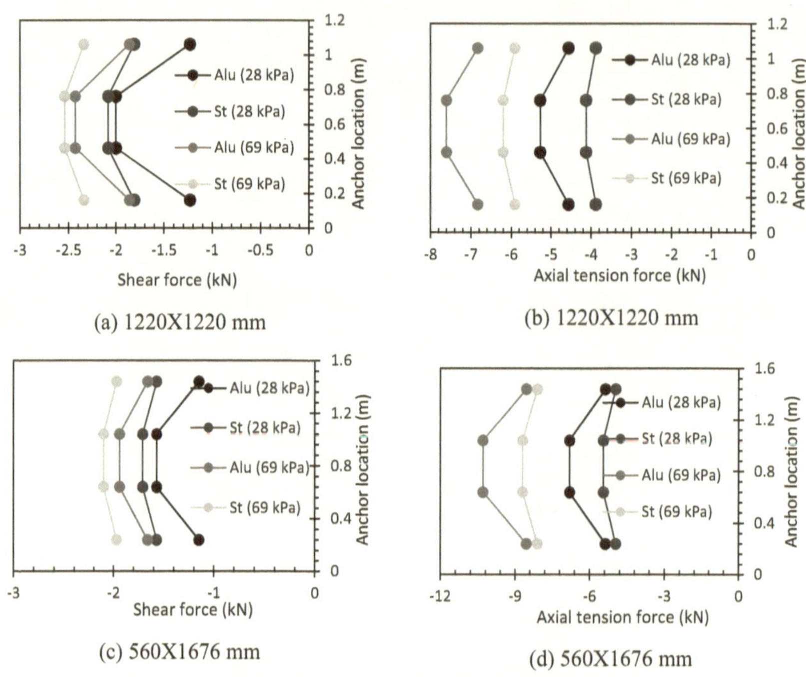

(a) 1220X1220 mm

(b) 1220X1220 mm

(c) 560X1676 mm

(d) 560X1676 mm

Figure 4.11: Effect of frame rigidity

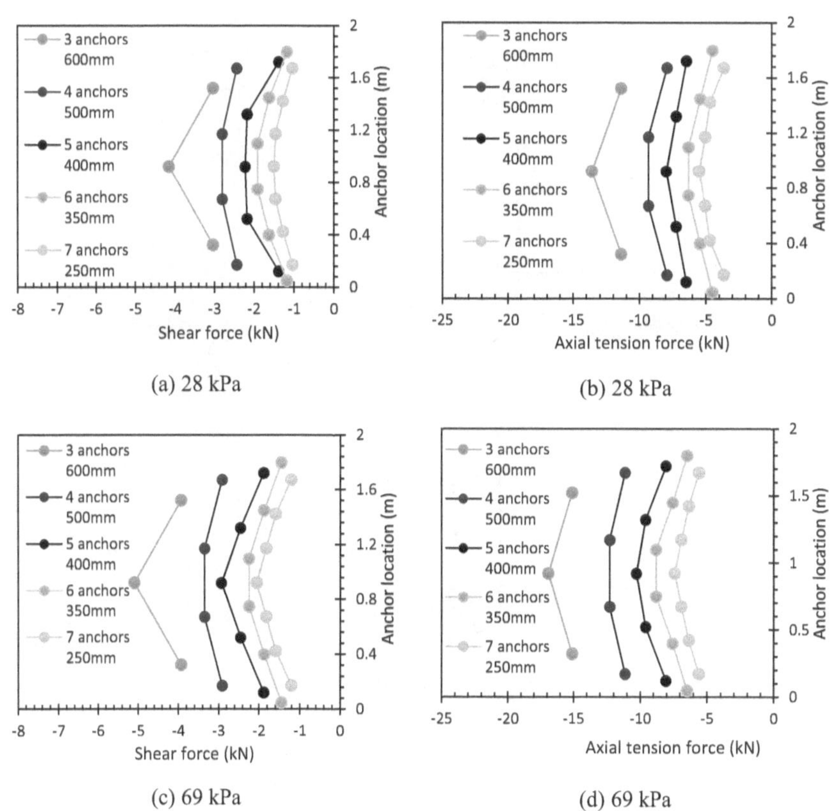

(a) 28 kPa

(b) 28 kPa

(c) 69 kPa

(d) 69 kPa

Figure 4.12: Effect of anchor spacing

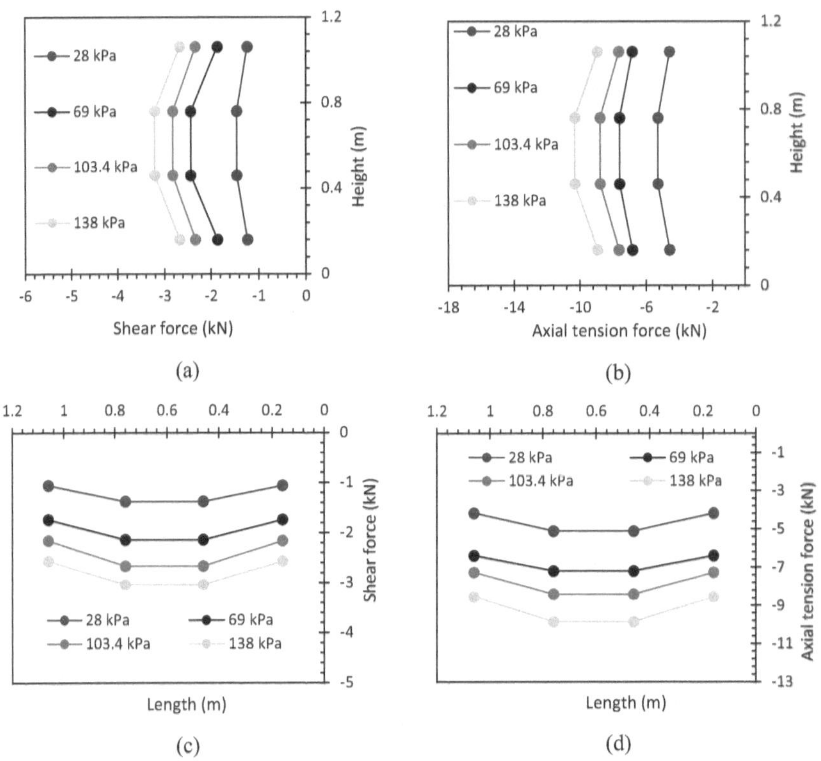

Figure 4.13: Effect of increased blast pressure

CHAPTER 5. SDOF Analysis for Anchorage Design of Blast-Resistant Windows

5.1   Introduction

Blast injuries caused by flying window debris after an explosion account for a considerable number of casualties during blast events (Fryberg 2002). After the Oklahoma City bombing, the glass-related injures reached 48 % of total human injuries reported (Norville et al. 1999). The 2011 Oslo bombing resulted in extensive damage to the windows of government buildings in Central Oslo, with glass debris covering the streets of the entire area, causing extensive injuries. It is clear that glass windows are the most vulnerable building components in the event of an explosion. A significant effort was made in recent years to protect windows against maliciously intended civilian bomb attacks. The review of previous research indicates that the focus has been placed on window glazing methodologies, including the application of protective films and the use of blast resisting laminated windows (Saatcioglu et al. 2015; Alameer et al. 2020). The design of window retention anchors received limited attention, increasing the risk of complete failure of window systems as a whole, potentially resulting in serious consequences. A comprehensive experimental and numerical research program was conducted by the authors at the University of Ottawa to investigate the performance of window retention anchors. The experimental research included 46 window tests on four different types of substrates, using a shock tube (Alameer et al. 2020a). The substrates consisted of reinforced concrete, structural steel, concrete block masonry, and stone masonry panels. The test parameters considered were; window aspect ratio, threat level (reflected pressure-impulse combination), substrate type, glazing type, protective film thickness, and anchor pattern/spacing. The numerical research included Finite Element Method (FEM) of analysis using software LS-Dyna (Alameer et al 2020b). The numerical window models were established and validated against the experimental data. An analytical parametric study was conducted to expand the results of the shock tube tests by further investigating the significance of window size, window aspect ratio, threat level, window frame rigidity and anchor pattern and spacing (Alameer et al. 2020b). The research program provided significant input into the development of the Canadian Standard (CSA S852 2018); "Blast-resistant window anchor systems." The standard includes two analysis procedures for establishing window anchor forces. The first procedure involves a two-degree-of freedom (TDOF) dynamic analysis, with the mass and the stiffness of the window and the substrate forming a TDOF system. Software BRADS was developed as part of the same overall research program for window anchor analysis and design (Jacques 2018), which is referenced in the standard. The second procedure in (CSA S852 2018) is the equivalent static load procedure, which is based on a single-degree-of-freedom (SDOF) window response. The latter approach is intended for manual design calculations. The flexibility of the window system, including the flexibilities of the attached anchors and the substrate are modelled as springs in series, leading to an equivalent stiffness for SDOF response of the entire system. The resistance function for windows is considered in two parts as pre-break (elastic) and post-break (membrane resistance). The anchor design forces are computed from support reactions, consisting of the combination of out-of-plane shear forces, in-plane tension forces and the resulting bending moments. The objective of the current paper is to introduce refinements to the SDOF-based window anchor design procedure by performing non-linear analysis of window systems during pre-break and post-break phases of response while introducing the effects of anchor flexibility and the substrate rigidity into the analysis. The computation of window resistance functions during the initial flexural response of unbroken glass, followed by the membrane action of glazed window in the post-break phase of response is illustrated. The resistance functions developed for windows with different aspect ratios and protective film thicknesses are validated against the computer software WINGARD (ARA 2005) and the anchor design forces computed by the nonlinear SDOF analysis are validated against the extensive test data obtained from shock tube tests conducted by the authors.

5.2   SDOF Representation and Dynamic Analysis of Windows

5.2.1   SDOF Model

Figure 5.1 illustrates the equivalent SDOF model that represents a window system subjected to uniform blast pressure. M_e in the model represents a lumped mass equivalent to the distributed mass of the window, K_e represents a spring constant equivalent to the stiffness of the window system, and $F_e(t)$ represents a concentrated force equivalent to the uniform blast pressure applied on the window. The equivalent SDOF system is selected such that the deflection "u" of the equivalent lumped mass M_e is equal to the maximum deflection of the window pane. The deflection anywhere on the window can then be computed as a function of the maximum deflection if window shape function $\phi(x,y)$ is known. Because the time scale is not changed, the response of the window in terms of displacement and time remains exactly the same as that of the equivalent SDOF model. Hence the use of SDOF model gives a convenient solution of window response for design purposes. The shape function is often taken as the deflected shape under an equivalent static load, which in this case can be taken as uniformly distributed load.

The equation of motion for the SDOF spring-mass model shown in Figure 5.1 can be expressed as shown below:

$$M_e \ddot{u}(t) + K_e u(t) = F_e(t)$$

5.1

Where, $u(t)$ is the displacement of the lumped mass under blast load and $\ddot{u}(t)$ is the acceleration of the lumped mass. $M_e \ddot{u}(t)$ is inertia resistance and $K_e u(t)$ is restoring force, also known as window resistance. Window resistance is an important component of the above equation incorporating the parameters of window design related to strength and stiffness. The construction of window resistance function is discussed in the next section for pre-break and post-break inelastic phases of response. The latter includes the membrane action associated with the security film or the interlayer of the glass for protection against blast loads.

An important step in the above SDOF analysis is the computation of equivalent mass M_e, equivalent stiffness K_e, and equivalent force $F_e(t)$. This can be achieved through the use of energy principles. The kinetic energy of the actual window system with distributed mass is set equal to that of the equivalent lumped mass. Similarly, the strain energy associated with window stiffness is set equal to the spring energy of the SDOF model. The work done by applied blast pressure is set equal to the work done by the concentrated force on the lumped mass. Equating energy/work expressions for the actual window to those of the equivalent mass-spring model, one can derive expressions for equivalent mass, equivalent stiffness and equivalent force as shown below:

$$M_e = \iint m\phi^2\,(x, y)dxdy \qquad\qquad 5.2$$

$$K_e = \iint EI\,[\phi''\,(x, y)]^2\,dxdy \qquad\qquad 5.3$$

$$F_e(t) = \iint p\,(x, y)\phi(x, y)dxdy \qquad\qquad 5.4$$

It is convenient to develop transformation factors that can be expressed as the ratio of the above equivalent quantities to the actual quantities for the window. The transformation factor for mass "C_M" is expressed below.

$$C_M = \frac{M_e}{M_t} \qquad\qquad 5.5$$

$$M_t = mA \qquad\qquad 5.6$$

Where; m is the uniform mass of the window pane per unit area, and A is the surface area of the window pane. Similarly, the transformation factor for load C_L can be found as;

$$C_L = \frac{F_e}{F_e(t)} \qquad\qquad 5.7$$

$$F_t(t) = p(t)A \qquad\qquad 5.8$$

The stiffness term relates to the restoring force, which is equal to stiffness "k" times deflection "u," and restores the mass from its loaded and deformed shape to its undeformed position. Hence it is directly related to the applied load. Therefore, the ratio of the restoring force to that of the equivalent system is the same as the ratio of the actual applied force to that for the equivalent system. Hence, the transformation factor for stiffness is equal to the transformation factor for load, i.e., $C_K = C_L$.

$$C_K = \frac{K_e}{k} = \frac{K_e u}{ku} = C_L \qquad\qquad 5.9$$

The equation of motion can be re-written in terms of the transformation factors, as illustrated below:

$$C_M M_t \ddot{u}(t) + C_L ku(t) = C_L p(t)A \qquad\qquad 5.10$$

Dividing both sides by C_L gives the equation of motion in terms of load-mass factor, C_{LM}, where; $\quad C_{LM} = C_M/C_L$.

$$C_{LM} M_t \ddot{u}(t) + ku(t) = p(t)A \qquad\qquad 5.11$$

Transformation factors were derived by (Biggs 1964; Morrison 2007) for one-way and two-way members having different support conditions. Damping may be neglected during the forced vibration response because of the short duration of loading, though it may have to be considered during the subsequent free vibration phase. Damping is often specified to be 2% of the critical damping for blast load analysis (ARA 2005; Morrison 2007).

During non-linear response, the stiffness of the window system may change continuously. This can be introduced by considering incremental dynamic analysis, where the stiffness can be updated during each time increment. The following equation represents incremental equation of motion with the damping term included, where viscous damping as combination of mass and stiffness terms may be used.

$$C_{LM} M_t \Delta\ddot{u}(t) + c(t)\Delta\dot{u} + k(t)\Delta u(t) = \Delta p(t)A \qquad\qquad 5.12$$

Where, $\Delta\ddot{u}(t)$, $\Delta\dot{u}(t)$ and $\Delta u(t)$ represent incremental acceleration, incremental velocity, and incremental displacement. The stiffness term k(t) and the damping term c(t) represent tangential slopes of force-displacement resistance function and the damping force-velocity curve, respectively at the beginning of each time step. Incremental pressure $\Delta p(t)$ is the difference in pressure between the end and the beginning of a time step. Eq (5.12) can be solved numerically. In this paper, step-by-step linear acceleration method was adopted for numerical solution, where the response acceleration is assumed to vary linearly within each time step.

5.2.2 Blast Loads

Figure 5.2(a) illustrates a blast pressure time history caused by an external surface burst explosion and associated hemispherical shock wave. The incident blast overpressure increases sharply at the arrival of shock wave, which reflects upon interaction with a target structure, increasing its intensity. The shock wave has a positive phase, followed by a much less intense negative phase, which is often neglected in blast load analysis. The reflected pressure-impulse combination used for window analysis can be idealized as a triangular pressure-time relationship shown in Figure 5.2(b). Design loads for blast-resistant windows can be computed from the threat level established by the authorized security personnel, in the case of a terrorist bomb threat, and the engineer in charge of the design of an industrial facility, in the case of an accidental explosion. The pressure-impulse combination associated with a potential explosion is used to determine the design load. Sometimes, the infrastructure owners or authorities having jurisdiction over the target infrastructure define the pressure-impulse combinations for use in design based on the use and occupancy of the building or the facility and the consequence of damage. As an example, the US General Services Administration (GSA) provides design pressure-impulse combinations for US government buildings (GSA 1997; ISC 2001).   Similarly, the International Organization for Standardization (ISO) provides recommendations for pressure impulse combinations for vehicle bombs and hand carried satchel bombs to be used in arena testing (ISO16934 2006) and for shock tube testing (ISO16933 2006).

The design strength required by CSA Standard (S852 2018; CSA S850 2012) for blast-resistant window anchors is based on a balanced approach among the window components. Accordingly, the window retention anchors should be designed to be 50 % stronger than the resistance provided by other components of the window system (glazed glass panes, window frame and mullions if any). Therefore, the pressure-impulse combination required for anchor design can be taken as that corresponding to the capacity of the weakest element of the window system. The resulting anchor forces can then be increased by a safety factor, which is recommended as 1.5 by CSA S850 and CSA S852.

5.3   Window Resistance

Window resistance is based on the stiffness of the window during elastic and inelastic response to blast loading. The use of correct stiffness during each time step of dynamic analysis is paramount for the accuracy of results as the window undergoes different phases of response. A window pane supported by its frame develops one-way or two-way deformations, depending on the window aspect ratio, when subjected to uniform blast pressure. The end restraints provided by the frame and the window stops prevent out-of-plane translation of the glass pane during blast loading. The aluminum window frames used in the experimental phase of research were stiffened by replacing the window stops with aluminum HSS sections as illustrated in Figure 5.3 (Alameer et al. 2020a) and provided sufficient restraints against out-of-plane translation. Blast-resistant window frames should be supported by sufficiently closely spaced window anchors that promote continuous support to the window panes without significant bending of the window frames between the anchors. Therefore, the edge support conditions for the window panes were assumed to be continuous simple supports as also assumed by previous researchers (Morrison 2007; ARA 2005).

The window frame is secured to the substrate through the window retention anchors. Depending on the anchor geometry, their fixity conditions and the intensity of the blast load, the anchors may flex and relax the window supports in the out-of-plane direction. This is especially true if the anchors experience inelastic deformations. Figure 5.4 shows bent window anchors after a test, indicating the development of out-of-plane translations of window frames. Therefore, the anchor flexibility should be considered in computing the overall window stiffness. Furthermore, the substrate flexibility also contributes towards the window support flexibility. The experimental phase of research involved punched windows placed on four different substrates, consisting of structural steel, reinforced concrete, concrete block masonry and stone masonry panels, having different substrate rigidities as shown in Figure 5.5 (Alameer et al. 2020a). The most rigid substrates were structural steel panels with little out-of-plane deflections, resulting in the highest anchor displacements relative to the substrates, generating highest anchor forces. In contrast, the stone masonry walls had the lowest rigidity, developing cracks along the mortar joints and deflecting the most. This is illustrated in Figure 5.6. Anchors on flexible substrates deflected along with the substrates, developing smaller relative anchor deflections and smaller anchor forces (Alameer et al., 2020a; 2020b). Therefore, the substrate rigidity is a factor to be considered in establishing the overall window stiffness. The experimental research also indicated that the window, the anchor and the substrate deflections were in phase during the initial cycles of response when the displacements were the highest, as depicted in Figure 5.7, permitting the use of these three rigidities, i.e., those of the window pane, retention anchors and the substrate to be lumped together as springs in series. Figure 5.8 shows the SDOF simplification for a window system in which the flexibilities of the anchors and the substrate serve as support flexibilities for the window.

5.3.1 Resistance Function for Window Panes

Blast resistant windows, whether in the form of a single pane, a multi-pane insulated glass units (IGU), or laminated or filmed glass have physical properties that dictate their dynamic response to air blast loads. The resistance function for window panes traces the window stiffness during the many phases of dynamic response under blast loads. Figure 5.9 illustrates a typical resistance function for a glazed window glass pane. The first phase of response is the "Pre-break phase" and provides glass resistance up to the glass breakage. Upon breakage, the load resistance drops sharply to zero, only to continue picking up resistance provided by the protective film or the interlayer as the blast load continues acting on the window. The second phase is the "Post-break phase," during which the window behaves in the membrane mode provided by the protective film or the interlayer. When incremental dynamic analysis is conducted, the stiffness of window pane is obtained as tangential stiffness from the resistance function during each time step.

Pre-break phase:

The glass units exhibit flexural behaviour initially when subjected to blast loading. The flexural stiffness intended for structural members, such as one-way and two-way slabs, given by (Biggs 1964) may be used in the small deflection range up-to a deflection of approximately half the panel thickness (Moore 1980; Morrison 2007). (Moore 1980) conducted non-linear analysis of glass panes while incorporating geometric nonlinearities to account for the effects of large deflections on panel behaviour. The researcher indicated that the membrane stresses start providing a portion of the window resistance beyond a deflection of 50% of the glass pane thickness. He developed relationships between the applied load and mid-panel deflection, as well as the applied load and glass stress. Figure 5.10 shows non-dimensional relationships ($L_{nd} = pb^4/Dt$ versus h/t, and L_{nd} versus

$S_{nd} = sig * t * b^2/D$) for window panes that are simply supported along four edges, where $D = \frac{Et^3}{12(1-v^2)}$ with E and v equal to the Young's modulus and Poisson's ratio of glass, respectively; and

h/t equals to the ratio of mid-panel deflection to window thickness. Each curve in Figure 5.10 was developed for a glass pane having a specific aspect ratio of "a/b" where "a" is the long side of a window pane and "b" is the short side. These relationships can be used to establish the glazed window resistance up to the breakage, defining window pane stiffness for each time step of the SDOF analysis. The breakage point is obtained by setting the term "sig" to the capacity of the glass. (Moore 1980) conducted an extensive study of the glazing capacity under static loading and recommended a static glass design strength of 27.6 MPa for annealed glass corresponding to the probability of failure of 1 to 8 breaks per thousand windows. The US Army Corps of Engineers recommended that the breakage strength of the annealed glass under dynamic loading can be taken as 100.7 MPa with a probability of failure of 750 breaks per thousand windows. The increased strength value given by the Corps of Engineers is believed to reflect the dynamic increase factor, as well as the increased probability of failure. This quantity was adopted in the current research program for verification against the test data generated in the experimental phase, which consisted of windows with annealed glass. The plots in Figure 5.10 were also adopted by (Morrison 2007) and the Applied Research Associates Inc. (2005) in developing WINGARD software for window glazing design.

Post-break phase:

The second phase in window response is the post-break phase that follows the breakage of glazed glass. The window pane in this range responds in the membrane mode with the protective film or the interlayer developing membrane stresses. The membrane theory for thin plates was developed by Timoshenko in 1940 for simply supported square and rectangular plates. He also recommended coefficients to simplify the membrane analysis for square plates. Others also worked on membrane theory and its applications. (Vallabhan 1983) developed a simplified expression for in-plane membrane stresses based on Timoshenko's membrane theory. (Mansfield 1989) indicated that an elastic plate (film) under membrane stresses displaces in proportion to the cube root of the applied force. The Applied Research Associates Inc. (ARA 2005) developed a membrane resistance model for GSA (General Services Administration) by balancing the strain energy in the membrane with the work done by the applied uniform static pressure and incorporated the model in WINGARD software (GSA 2005). Their model accommodates four-sided, two-way membranes for both elastic and elasto-plastic failure modes. It is intended for use with different protective materials, including surface mounted films or interlayers that have different material characteristics. The GSA membrane model was adopted in current research with the resistance function defined in Eq. (13), where p_o is the resistance and w_o is the centre deflection of the two-way membrane.

$$p_o = \frac{E.t.w_o^3.\pi^2}{73728} \cdot \frac{\left[4.\left(\frac{a}{2}\right)^6.C_1.C_2^2.\left(\frac{b}{2}\right)^6 - \left(\frac{a}{2}\right)^6.C_4^2.C_2.\left(\frac{b}{2}\right)^4 - \left(\frac{a}{2}\right)^4.C_3^2.C_2.\left(\frac{b}{2}\right)^6 + C_4.C_5.C_3.\left(\frac{b}{2}\right)^2.\left(\frac{a}{2}\right)^2 - C_1.C_5^2\right]}{\left\{\left(\frac{a}{2}\right)^4.\left(\frac{b}{2}\right)^4.(1-v^2).\left(4.\left(\frac{b}{2}\right)^6.\left(\frac{a}{2}\right)^6.C2_2^2 - C_5^2\right)\right\}}$$
5.13

Where:

E = Modulus of elasticity of the protective film or laminate

t = Membrane thickness

v = Poisson's ratio

a = the short dimension of window

b = the long dimension of window

w_o = maximum window deflection at the center of the window

$C_1, C_2, C_3, C_4, and\ C_5$ are coefficient that can be calculated using the expression given below:

$$C_1 = \left(18.\left(\tfrac{b}{2}\right)^2.\left(\tfrac{a}{2}\right)^2 + 81.\left(\tfrac{b}{2}\right)^4 + 81.\left(\tfrac{a}{2}\right)^4\right).\pi^4 \qquad \text{5.14 (a)}$$

$$C_2 = (10368 - 1152.v).\pi^2 \qquad \text{5.14 (b)}$$

$$C_3 = \left(-3072.\left(\tfrac{a}{2}\right)^3 + 768.v.\left(\tfrac{b}{2}\right).\left(\tfrac{a}{2}\right)^2 - 768.\left(\tfrac{b}{2}\right).\left(\tfrac{a}{2}\right)^2 + 1536.v.\left(\tfrac{b}{2}\right)^2.\left(\tfrac{a}{2}\right)\right).\pi^2 \qquad \text{5.14 (c)}$$

$$C_4 = \left(-3072.\left(\tfrac{b}{2}\right)^3 + 768.v.\left(\tfrac{b}{2}\right)^2.\left(\tfrac{a}{2}\right) - 768.\left(\tfrac{b}{2}\right)^2\left(\tfrac{a}{2}\right) + 1536.v.\left(\tfrac{b}{2}\right).\left(\tfrac{a}{2}\right)^2\right).\pi^2 \qquad \text{5.14 (d)}$$

$$C_5 = (16384v + 16384).\left(\left(\tfrac{b}{2}\right)^3.\left(\tfrac{a}{2}\right)^3\right) \qquad \text{5.14 (e)}$$

5.3.2 Support Flexibility

The window frame provides support to the window panes. The frames are mounted on the substrate through anchorage, which may in the form of steel bolts secured in the substrate either mechanically (by mean of drop-in-anchors or nuts in the case of steel substrates) or through adhesion (adhesive anchors). The anchors develop out-of-plane bending when the window is subjected to blast pressures, resulting in flexibility of window supports at frame-substrate connections. This flexibility depends on the rigidity of the retention anchors, the anchor spacing and the unsupported anchor length between the frame end, where the blast load is applied, and the point of fixity in the substrate (shear span). This is illustrated in Figure 5.11. The anchors are also subjected to axial tension associated with membrane forces, but the effect of axial tension on out-of-plane bending is small and may be neglected. Similarly, anchor shear deformations are also negligible and can be neglected in computing the support flexibility introduced by the anchors. However, the anchor bending may be more significant if the anchors are allowed to yield. The bending stiffness of anchors in cantilever mode of deformation can be written as shown in Eq. (15) and can be used in place of the spring coefficient k_2 shown Figure 5.8.

$$k_2 = \sum_1^n \frac{3EI}{x_v^3}$$

5.15

Where x_v is the average anchor shear span, EI is the flexural rigidity of each anchor and "n" is the total number of anchors around all four sides. Anchors are designed to remain elastic and the above elastic flexural rigidity is sufficient to model the support flexibility, unless inelastic anchor behaviour is sought, in which case elasto-plastic flexural stiffness may be specified.

The second component of potential support flexibility is associated with the flexibility of the substrate. The wall panel, forming the building envelop deflects under blast loads, which provides further flexibility to the window supports in the out-of-plane direction. This deflection can be computed by considering the geometry and the boundary conditions of the wall panel, as well as its flexural rigidity. The average of wall deflection at window level can be used to compute the spring coefficient k_3 in the SDOF simplification shown in Figure 5.8. The window tests conducted as part of the experimental phase of research consisted of punched windows on wall panels that were representative of wall segments providing tributary areas to the windows tested. The panels were attached to the floor slabs above and below by simple supports, deflecting in one-way mode. For the test windows used to validate the resistance functions presented in the next section, three fifth of the mid-height wall deflection was used as representative of the average parabolic deflected shape.

$$\delta_{wall} = \frac{5L^3 F_{wall}}{384EI}$$
5.16

$$k_3 = \frac{5F_{window}}{3\delta_{wall}}$$
5.17

Where, F_{wall} and F_{window} are blast loads applied on the total wall surface (including the window surface area which is supported by the wall) and on the window, respectively. EI is the effective elastic flexural rigidity of the wall substrate, and L is the span within which the wall is deforming in one-way flexural mode.

5.3.3 Sample Resistance Functions

The resistance functions for selected windows with aspect ratios of 1.0 and 3.0, tested on different types of substrates, were generated for use in SDOF analysis. Details of the selected windows are presented in Table 5.1. The material properties used during the analysis are shown in Table 5.2. The resistance curves were obtained by following the procedure outlined in the preceding section for pre-break and post break phases. Figure 5.12 illustrates resistance functions for unprotected exterior pane and protected interior pane. These are the resistance curves used in conducting SDOF analyses, results of which are validated against experimentally obtained anchor forces presented under "Validation of SDOF Analysis." It is noteworthy that the resistance curves presented in Figure 5.12 are for the window systems, including the resistances of window panes, retention anchors and the substrate wall panels. The contribution of each components to overall stiffness varies with the substrate type. For example, the anchors in reinforced concrete substrate, well anchored into the concrete, are stressed more and deform more, having higher contribution to window flexibility than those anchored to masonry walls. On the other hand, unreinforced masonry walls deflect more relative to steel and reinforced concrete substrates and have higher contributions to window flexibility.

The initial response up to the first peak (breakage point) represents the resistance function of the unprotected exterior pane. During the pre-break phase it is assumed that the protected interior glass pane behaves the same as the unprotected exterior glass pane. Upon breakage, indicated by a sudden drop in resistance, the membrane action of the protective film provides resistance to the broken interior glass pane until the film yielding. These resistance functions define change in stiffness during many phases of dynamic response.

5.4   Window Reactions and Anchor Design Forces

5.4.1   Window Edge Reactions

The computation of window edge reactions is based on the applied load and the inertia resistance. They cannot be computed directly from the lumped mass SDOF analysis under concentrated blast loads. The distributions of mass and the applied pressure, as well as the variation of accelerations along the window need to be considered. The applied blast load is uniformly distributed. The inertia force is related to the acceleration of the mass. Though the mass is distributed uniformly, the acceleration of each point on the window follows the deflected shape. (Biggs 1964) provided expressions to compute edge support reactions based on the assumed distribution of inertia forces for relatively thick concrete slabs with small deflections (Biggs 1964). (US Army Corps of Engineers 1957; Morrison 2003) indicated that the expressions provided for concrete slabs are not representative of glazed windows with much higher deflections. (Morison 2007) conducted extensive FEM analysis to develop expressions for dynamic reactions of thin plates with simple supports as boundary conditions. These expressions are given below for computing out-of-plane shear forces as support reactions.

$$V_A(t) = C_{FA}F(t) + C_{RA}R(t) \qquad\qquad 5.18$$

$$V_B(t) = C_{FB}F(t) + C_{RB}R(t) \qquad\qquad 5.19$$

Where C_{FA} and C_{RA} are coefficients for the applied load and window resistance along the short side of the window panel, respectively, whereas coefficients C_{FB} and C_{RB} are for the long side. These coefficients can be obtained from Figure 5.13 for different window aspect ratios as a function of non-dimensional deflection, $ND = \frac{\delta_m}{t_p}$, where δ_m is the central window deflection and t_p is the pane thickness. $F(t)$ is the blast load applied statically on the window and can be computed by multiplying the reflected pressure by the total window surface area. $R(t)$ is the total window resistance.

Windows subjected to blast forces perpendicular to the plane of the window also develop concentrated corner forces that tend to lift up the corners (UFC-3-240 2002). The distribution of reactive forces on window frame is shown in Figure 5.15, with equal and opposite forces acting on the frame as edge reactions. The corner forces can be obtained from uniformly loaded Navier solution. Such solution is provided by the Applied Research Associates Inc. (ARA 2005) in the form of reaction factors for simply supported rectangular plates with different aspect ratios, which are tabulated in Table 5.3. Total reactive shear forces computed by using Eqs. (5.18) and (5.19) along all four sides of a window frame can be multiplied by the reaction factors to find edge shear and corner forces, where the corner forces act in the opposite direction to edge shear forces.

The in-plane support edge reactions for window panes can be computed from the membrane forces. Membrane forces developed in the protective film or laminate pull on the edge supports, generating tensile reactive forces. The maximum membrane force in window panels occur near the central deflection region and can be computed from the membrane model adopted from the Applied Research Associates Inc. (ARA 2005), as given below:

$$T_x = \frac{Et}{1 - v^2} \left(\varepsilon_x + v\varepsilon_y \right) \tag{5.20}$$

$$T_y = \frac{Et}{1 - v^2} \left(\varepsilon_y + v\varepsilon_x \right) \tag{5.21}$$

$$\varepsilon_x = \frac{du}{dx} + \frac{1}{2}\left(\frac{dw}{dx}\right)^2 = \frac{u_0\pi}{b/2} = \frac{-(\frac{a}{2}).\pi.\left(2.C_3.(\frac{b}{2})^4.(\frac{a}{2})^2.C_2 - C_5.C_4\right)}{4.(\frac{b}{2})^6.(\frac{a}{2})^6.C_2^2 - C_5^2}.w_0^2 \tag{5.22}$$

$$\varepsilon_y = \frac{dv}{dy} + \frac{1}{2}\left(\frac{dw}{dy}\right)^2 = \frac{v_0\pi}{a/2} = \frac{-(\frac{b}{2}).\pi.\left(2.C_4.(\frac{b}{2})^2.(\frac{a}{2})^4.C_2 - C_5.C_3\right)}{4.(\frac{b}{2})^6.(\frac{a}{2})^6.C_2^2 - C_5^2}.w_0^2 \tag{5.23}$$

Where;

T_x =Maximum axial tension force per unit length in x direction

T_y =Maximum axial tension force per unit length in y direction

The nomenclature used in the above equations are the same as those given for Eq. (5.13) with coefficients C_2 through C_5 specified in Eq. (5.14). The distribution of membrane forces across the window can be obtained from the observations made during the window tests conducted by the authors (Alameer et al 2020a). Figure 5.14 shows pictures of deformed glazed window panes with aspect ratios of 1.0 and 3.0 at or near yielding of the protective film indicating yield lines, drawn with 45-degree inclination from each corner, that can be used to identify the segments of window that transfer the membrane forces to window edges. Accordingly, the maximum membrane forces T_x and

T_y represent the intensity of membrane forces per unit length at maximum deflection points. The average tensile edge support reaction can be found by setting the area under each segment to the average (uniformly distributed) reactive force. For a square panel with triangular panel segments per edge, this becomes:

$$(T_{av})_x \ell_y = T_x \ell_y / 2 \qquad\qquad 5.24$$

$$(T_{av})_x = T_x / 2 \qquad\qquad 5.25$$

Where; $(T_{av})_x$ is the average edge tension for per unit length in the x direction and ℓ_y is the window dimension in the y direction. Similarly, for rectangular windows, the area under the trapezoid along the long side and the triangle along the short side can be set equal to rectangular reactive tensile force distributions along the long and short sides to find the average reactive tension force per unit length.

5.4.2 Anchor Forces

Window retention anchors are subjected to out-of-plane shear forces and in-plane tension forces. These forces also generate bending of the anchors in their critical regions, where they are anchored to the substrate, developing high flexural stresses at the point of fixity. Figure 5.16 illustrates forces acting on a typical window retention anchor. During the pre-break stage flexural deformations dominate response, with negligible effect of the membrane action. Hence, the anchors are subjected to shear and bending, as illustrated in Figure 5.16(b), with maximum values corresponding to glass breakage. In the post-break stage membrane forces dominate response. In this case both shear, axial tension and bending moment become significant. The shear forces for both pre-break and post-break phases of response can be obtained from maximum dynamic response and associated out-of-plane displacement. The axial tension forces during the post-break phase can be obtained from the maximum membrane force that is tangent to the deflected membrane, providing maximum axial tensile force per unit length, which is distributed along the window edge support. The computation of window edge reactions is discussed in the previous sub-section. Anchor forces are obtained from average edge reactions by distributing them among the anchors on each edge. This is done by following a parabolic or a half-sine distribution obtained through experimental and analytical observations (Alameer et al. 2020a; 2020b), as illustrated in Figure 5.17. Accordingly, the anchor forces are computed by multiplying the average edge reactive force per unit length by the spacing of the anchors.

Based on the anchor force distributions indicated by the experimental investigation (Alameer et al. 2020) and the current numerical simulations, a parabolic or a half sine distribution can be considered as also suggested by (TM5-1300 1990) for flexible frames. The following distribution of anchor shear and tension forces can be used in design.

$$q = q_o \sin \theta \qquad\qquad 5.26$$

$$\theta = \frac{x}{L}.\pi \qquad\qquad 5.27$$

q = Variable edge shear or axial tension force depends on anchor location (x)

q_o = Average edge shear or axial tension force

θ = angle of force distribution in radians

x = Anchor location along window edge

L = Window edge length

It should be noted that the rigidity of window frames plays a significant role on anchor force distribution. Rigid steel frames, as typically used in blast-resistant windows develop uniform or near-uniform force distribution, depending on the rigidity of window frames.

It is noteworthy that the analysis results provide the resistance of individual window panes separately and undependably. During the post-break response of double pane IGUs it is the inner protected pane that provides resistance and hence the analysis results can be used directly to compute shear and tension forces. During the pre-break phase however, the analysis results give anchor forces per pane and the resistance must be added to compute the edge support reactions. A simplifying assumption was made in the current investigation and assumed that the blast pressure applied on the outer pane is also representative of the pressure applied on the inner pane until breakage. The numerical investigation conducted by the authors using LS-DYNA FEM software indicated that the time lag for the arrival time of the blast pressure to the inner pane varied between 0.3 to 0.33 ms. Furthermore, it was assumed that the air gap between the two panes would directly transfer the applied pressure to the inner pane. WINGARD Software (ARA 2005) considers the interaction of the two panes with the air gap through a fairly sophisticated approach. A typical resistance function for a double pane IGU generated by WINGARD is shown in Figure 5.18, indicating only a minor difference of the interaction of the two panes (plates 1 and 2) with the air gap.

5.5   Validation of SDOF Analysis

The SDOF analysis approach used in the current investigation for glazed windows with uniform mass and support flexibilities has been validated against the available software specifically developed for blast resistant windows, as well as the window tests conducted in the experimental phase of the same research program. The SDOF analysis had full mass of glass assigned to the window panel during the pre-break phase. Beyond breakage, it was assumed that 50% of the broken glass will continue to be present. The following sections describe the validations.

Validation against WINGARD: WINGARD (ARA 2005) was developed for glazed window design and has been in extensive use in industry. The software is intended for design and assessment of window glazing with protective films or internal laminates. It does not incorporate anchor design. However, it does provide edge support forces as out-of-plane shear forces per unit length and in-plane membrane tension forces per unit length. Therefore, the validation against WINGARD was done in terms of window pane resistance functions and central window displacement response of glazed windows. The average edge support reactions are also compared for validation. Two windows with two different window aspect ratios were selected for analysis with the SDOF approach recommended and the WINGARD software. The window geometry was the same as those tested in the experimental phase of research, and they were subjected to the same two pressure-impulse combinations used in the window tests, consisting of 28 kPa (4 psi) – 207 kPa-ms (30 psi-ms) and 69 kPa (10 psi) – 621 kPa-ms (90 psi-ms). The windows consisted of double-pane IGU's with unprotected outer glass pane (threat side) and protected inner glass glazed with 23 mil thick PET protective film installed through mechanical glazing.

Figure 5.19 shows the comparisons of resistance functions established for the two IGU windows. The results indicate perfect correlation between those generated for the proposed SDOF analysis and WINGARD. This is not surprising as the proposed approach used the same methodologies for establishing resistance functions for individual window panes as those for WINGARD. The validation was extended to include displacement time histories during the pre-break and post-break phases of response, as well as comparisons of average anchor shear and axial forces.

Figure 5.20 and 5.21 show the comparisons of response time histories for the same two IGU windows for which the resistance functions are compared in Figure 5.19. The comparisons indicate reasonably good agreement of displacement time histories. This is especially true for the initial wave form when the maximum displacement occurs, based on which anchor forces are computed. Table 5.4 provides comparisons of computed maximum window central deflection at breakage (δ_{cr}) and post-breakage central deflection (w_o), as well as total shear and axial tension edge reactions along long and short sides of window. The comparisons show very good correlations.

Validation against BRADS: Software BRADS was developed as part of the same overall research program as a Two-Degree of Freedom (TDOF) dynamic analysis software for window anchor design (Jacques 2018; Jacques et al. 2018). The software considers the mass of the substrate and the window separately as a TDOF system with separate blast loads applied to the substrate and the window. The interaction between the two panes through the air gap in-between is considered following the same approach as WINGARD. However, WINGARD follows an algorithm for reduction in broken glass mass by computing the velocity of glass fragments whereas BRADS considers a fixed percentage of glass mass beyond breakage.

Figure 5.20 and 5.21 show the comparisons of response time histories for the same two IGU windows for which the resistance functions are compared earlier in Figure 5.19. The comparisons indicate reasonably good agreement of displacement time histories. This is especially true for the initial wave form when the maximum displacement occurs, based on which anchor forces are computed.

Validation against window tests: The SDOF analysis approach presented in the paper was used to calculate window anchor forces in selected windows that were tested in the experimental program.

Two windows with an aspect ratio of 1.0 and 3.0, each placed on structural steel, reinforced concrete, concrete block masonry and stone masonry walls were analyzed for comparison with experimentally recorded anchor forces. The resistance functions for the windows used in the comparison are shown in Figure 5.12. Analytically generated window anchor forces at mid-length of window frames in x and y directions, as well as those near the window corners are compared with experimentally recorded shear and axial tension forces in Table 5.5. The results show very good correlations, confirming the applicability of the SDOF simplification of window systems, consisting of window panes, flexible anchors, and the substrate.

5.6   Summary and Conclusions

SDOF analysis for glazing design of windows under blast loading is widely used. However, the analysis has not been expanded to the design of window anchors. The current paper extends nonlinear SDOF analysis to anchor design while incorporating flexibility of window supports provided by window retention anchors and the substrates to which the windows are secured. The resulting methodology provides simplification of the TDOF window anchor design problem to a SDOF problem, while providing fairly accurate predictions of anchor forces as validated against the available software and the tests conducted by the authors. The analysis procedure includes the computation of inelastic window resistance in the flexure-dominant pre-break phase and the membrane response dominant post-break phase of window response. It can be used conveniently as a design tool for the computation of anchorage design forces.

Table 5.1: Properties of windows on steel (S), reinforced concrete (C), concrete block (B), and stone masonry substrates (ST)

Test NO.	Aspect Ratio	Film Thickness (mils)	Glazing Anchor Spacing (mm)	Retention Anchor Spacing (mm)	No. of Anchors	Embed. Length (mm)	Pr (kPa)
S13 S14	1	4(4.5)+5	Mech.@ 100	400	2(4+2)=12	90	28 69
S15 S16	3	4.5+4.5+5	Mech.@ 125	Long:500 Short:225	2(4+2)=12	90	28 69
C7 C8	1	4.5+4.5+5	Mech.@ 125	500	2(3+3)=12	90	28 69
C13 C14	3	4.5+4.5+5	Mech.@ Long:100 Short:100	Long:400 Short:305	2(4+2)=12	125	28 69
B1 B2	1	4.5+4.5+5	Mech.@ 125	300	2(4+4)=16	125	28 69
B5 B6	3	4.5+4.5+5	Mech.@ 125	Long:400 Short:305	2(4+2)=12	125	28 69
ST1 ST2	1	4.5+4.5+5	Mech.@ 125	300	2(4+4)=16	125	28 69
ST3 ST4	3	4.5+4.5+5	Mech.@ 125	Long:400 Short:305	2(4+2)=12	125	28 69

Table 5.2: Properties of IGU window components

	Density, (kg/m^3)	Yield Stress (MPa)	Elastic Modules (MPa)	Possion's Ratio	Rupture Strain (%)
Frame	2,700	305	70,000	0.33	0.012
Film	1,390	157	4,140	0.25	1.3
Anchor	7,800	1,050	200,000	0.3	0.15

Note: Annealed Glass was used with probability of breaks =750/1000 and dynamic breakage stress=100.7MPa

Table 5.3: Reaction factors; adopted from (ARA 2005)

Aspect Ratio	Factors		
	Corner	Long Edge	Short Edge
1.0	0.0651	0.3149	0.3149
1.1	0.0645	0.3321	0.2968
1.2	0.0633	0.3468	0.2797
1.3	0.0615	0.3593	0.2637
1.4	0.0595	0.3701	0.2488
1.5	0.0573	0.3794	0.2351
1.6	0.0549	0.3874	0.2224
1.7	0.0526	0.3944	0.2108
1.8	0.0504	0.4006	0.2002
1.9	0.0483	0.4061	0.1904
2.0	0.0463	0.4110	0.1815
2.5	0.0377	0.4292	0.1462
3.0	0.0316	0.4411	0.1220
3.5	0.0271	0.4495	0.1046
4.0	0.0237	0.4558	0.0915
4.5	0.0211	0.4607	0.0814
5.0	0.0190	0.4647	0.0732

Table 5.4: SDOF and WINGARD results for windows

Model	$\delta_{cr}(mm)$ $w_0(mm)$	Total Edge Shear (kN)		Total Membrane Tension (kN)	
		Per Long Side	Per Short Side	Per Long Side	Per Short Side
P_r = 28 kPa (Aspect Ratio=1)					
SDOF	29.7 76.4	9.1	9.1	16.9	15.4
WINGARD	29.3 75.8	8.4	8.4	17.7	17.7
P_r = 69 kPa (Aspect Ratio=1)					
SDOF	29.7 170.7	36.8	36.8	71.3	71.3
WINGARD	29.35 169.9	32.6	32.6	71.3	71.3
P_r = 28 kPa (Aspect Ratio=3)					
SDOF	16.0 36.6	10.6	2.9	41.2	7.2
WINGARD	16.0 35.5	10.6	2.3	42.9	6.9
P_r = 69 kPa (Aspect Ratio=3)					
SDOF	16.1 71.8	46.8	8.3	152.7	10.9
WINGARD	16 70.1	47.7	10.5	154	12.8

Table 5.5: SDOF and experimental results for windows

Test No. ($\frac{\ell_y}{\ell_x}$)	Relative displacement	Mid-length anchor force (kN)		End-anchor force (kN)		Mid-length anchor force (kN)		End-anchor force (kN)	
	$\delta_{cr}(mm)$ / $w_0(mm)$	$(V_{ay})_{SDOF}$ / $(T_{ax})_{SDOF}$	$(V_{ax})_{SDOF}$ / $(T_{ay})_{SDOF}$	$(V_{ay})_{SDOF}$ / $(T_{ax})_{SDOF}$	$(V_{ax})_{SDOF}$ / $(T_{ay})_{SDOF}$	$(V_{ay})_{exp}$ / $(T_{ax})_{exp}$	$(V_{ax})_{exp}$ / $(T_{ay})_{exp}$	$(V_{ay})_{exp}$ / $(T_{ax})_{exp}$	$(V_{ax})_{exp}$ / $(T_{ay})_{exp}$
S13 (1)	29.7 / 69.2	2.4 / 5.9	1.9 / 4.3	1.5 / 4.9	1.3 / 3.5	2.0 / 5.1	1.6 / 3.5	1.8 / 3.4	1.4 / 2.8
S14 (1)	29.7 / 124.3	2.8 / 11.8	1.9 / 11.0	2.6 / 11.4	1.7 / 9.4	2.4 / 10.7	2.0 / 9.3	2.3 / 10.5	1.8 / 8.6
S15 (3)	16.0 / 19.2	2.3 / 9.7	1.6 / 6.1	2.1 / 4.4	1.2 / 3.2	2.0 / 8.5	1.4 / 4.6	1.8 / 3.6	0.2 / 2.1
S16 (3)	16.0 / 38	3.3 / 15.3	2.1 / 6.1	2.7 / 13.0	1.4 / 5.2	2.7 / 14.1	1.7 / 5.2	2.1 / 12.1	1.5 / 4.5
C7 (1)	29.7 / 61.8	2.2 / 5.4	1.8 / 4.1	1.5 / 4.3	1.2 / 3.2	1.7 / -	- / -	- / -	- / -
C8 (1)	29.7 / 117.3	2.7 / 11.1	1.7 / 10.7	2.5 / 11.1	1.6 / 9.1	- / -	- / -	- / -	- / -
C13 (3)	16.0 / 18.1	2.3 / 8.7	1.5 / 3.4	2.1 / 3.2	1.6 / 2.4	1.9 / 8.2	- / -	1.8 / 2.7	1.3 / 2.0
C14 (3)	16.0 / 25.8	2.6 / 13.1	1.7 / 4.6	2.4 / 11.5	1.7 / 3.3	2 / 12.3	- / -	1.9 / 10.2	1.4 / 3.9
B1 (1)	29.7 / 60.2	1.5 / 6.1	1.4 / 3.4	1.3 / 4.6	1.2 / 2.9	1.2 / 5.2	1.2 / 2.8	1.1 / 3.8	0.9 / 2.5
B2 (1)	29.7 / 112.5	2.1 / 9.4	1.6 / 8.3	1.5 / 7.3	1.5 / 5.4	1.8 / 8.9	1.4 / 7.8	1.4 / 6.9	1.3 / 4.9
B5 (3)	16.0 / 17.1	2.2 / 8.5	1.7 / 6.5	1.8 / 4.7	1.4 / 4.2	1.8 / 7.8	- / -	1.5 / 3.9	1.0 / 3.2
B6 (3)	16.0 / 23.3	2.4 / 12.1	1.9 / 7.6	2.0 / 8.8	1.7 / 6.1	1.9 / 11.3	- / -	1.7 / 7.9	1.6 / 5.2
ST1 (1)	29.7 / 59.1	1.5 / 5.6	1.4 / 3.9	1.3 / 4.9	1.2 / 2.6	1.1 / 4.7	1.1 / 2.2	1.0 / 3.3	0.8 / 1.9
ST2 (1)	29.7 / 109.3	1.9 / 9.4	1.8 / 7.4	1.9 / 7.5	1.5 / 6.8	1.5 / 8.7	1.3 / 6.9	1.4 / 6.1	1.2 / 5.5
ST3 (3)	16.0 / 16.7	2.2 / 2.9	1.9 / 2.5	2.0 / 2.7	1.3 / 2.6	1.6 / 1.7	- / -	1.4 / 1.5	0.8 / 1.1
ST4 (3)	16.0 / 21.4	2.5 / 5.1	2.1 / 4.4	1.8 / 3.9	1.5 / 3.1	1.6 / 3.6	- / -	1.5 / 3.1	0.9 / 2.0

Note: (V_{ax}), (V_{ay}), (T_{ax}), and (T_{ay}) are shear forces and axial tension forces, respectively; δ_{cr} and w_0 are glass cracking displacement and post-break displacement, respectively. The symbol (-) indicates data not available.

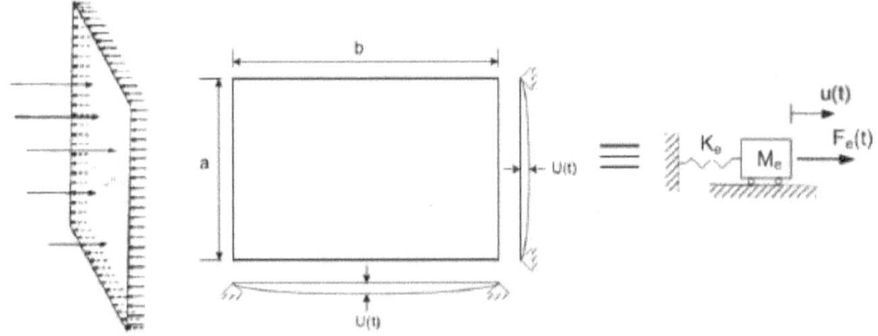

Figure 5.1: Equivalent SDOF mass-spring model

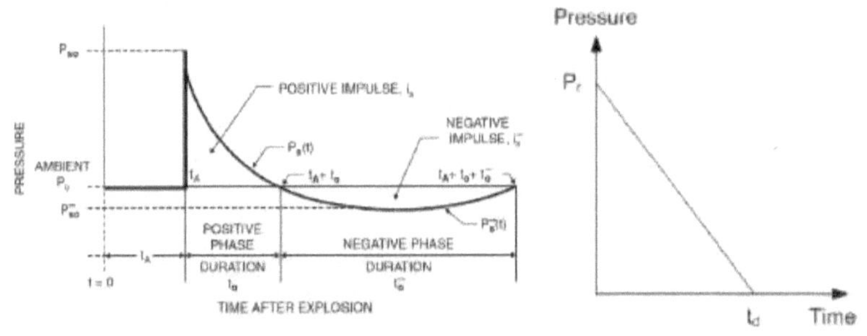

(a) Actual pressure variation   (b) Idealized pressure variation

Figure 5.2: Pressure time relationship generated by external blast shock wave (CSA 852-18 2018)

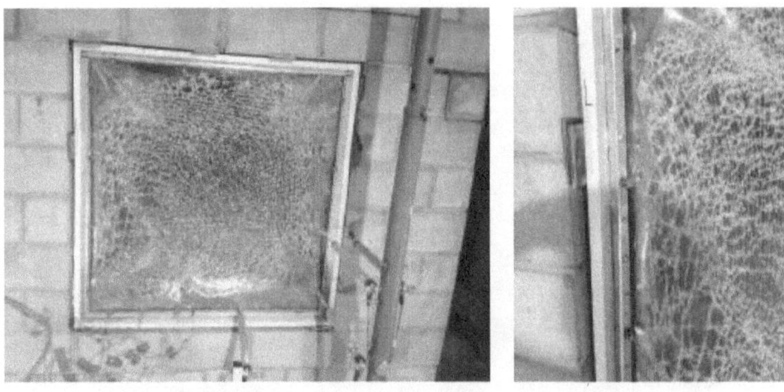

Figure 5.3: Performance of window frame-window stop assembly during blast tests

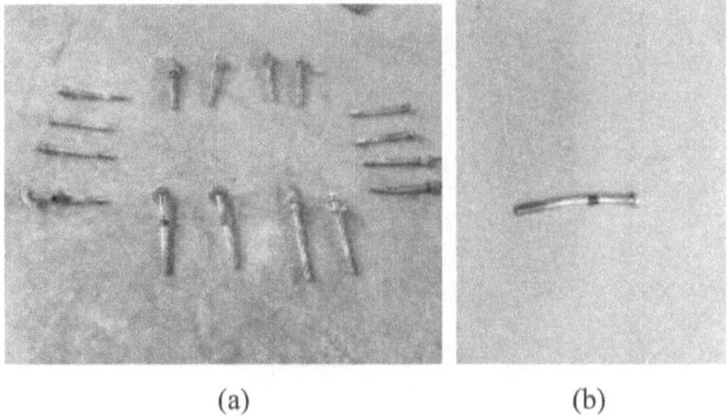

(a)   (b)

Figure 5.4: a) Anchor deformations after a test; (b) close-up view of a deformed anchor

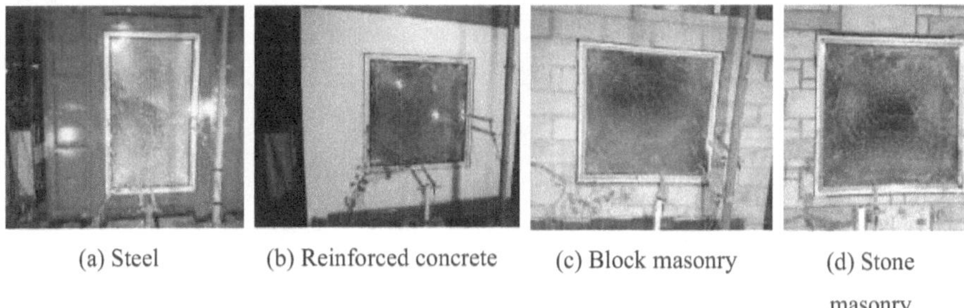

(a) Steel   (b) Reinforced concrete   (c) Block masonry   (d) Stone masonry

Figure 5.5: Window tests with different substrates

175

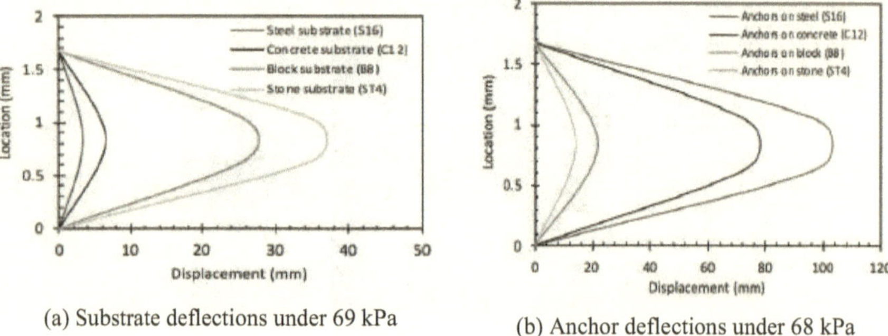

(a) Substrate deflections under 69 kPa   (b) Anchor deflections under 68 kPa

Figure 5.6: Substrate deflections and anchor deflections relative to substrate

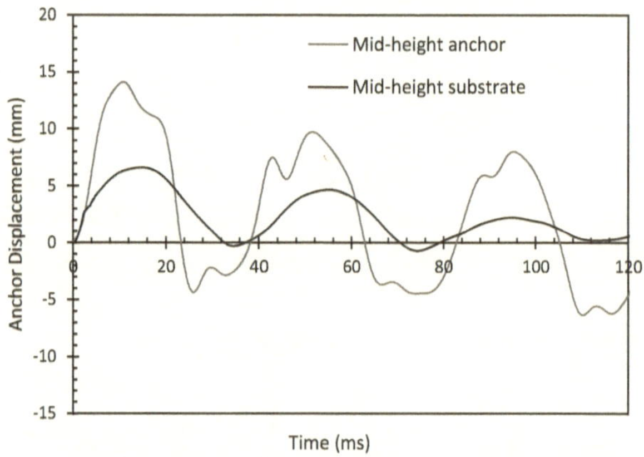

Figure 5.7: Displacement time history of the mid-height anchor and the mid-height concrete block substrate indicating in-phase response

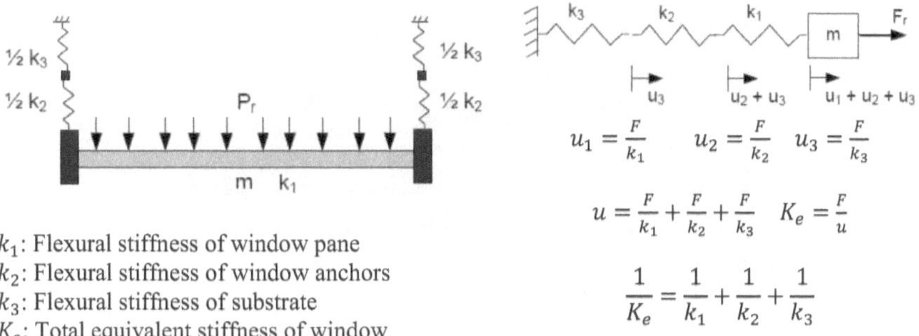

k_1: Flexural stiffness of window pane
k_2: Flexural stiffness of window anchors
k_3: Flexural stiffness of substrate
K_e: Total equivalent stiffness of window

Figure 5.8: Three-spring model incorporating the effects of substrate, retention anchors and window stiffness

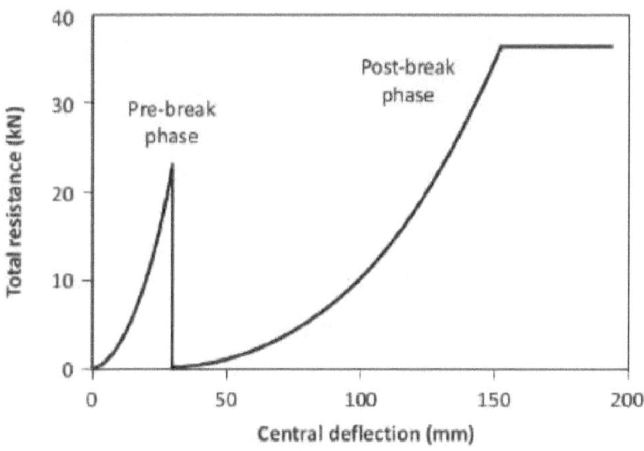

Figure 5.9: Typical resistance function for a glazed window (CSA 852-18 2018)

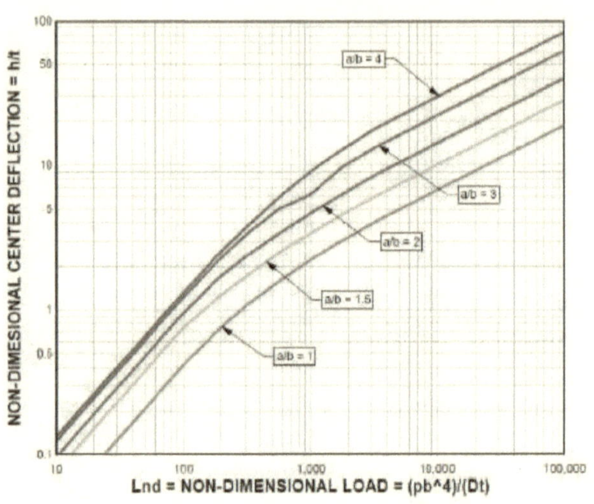

(a) Non-dimensional center deflection versus load

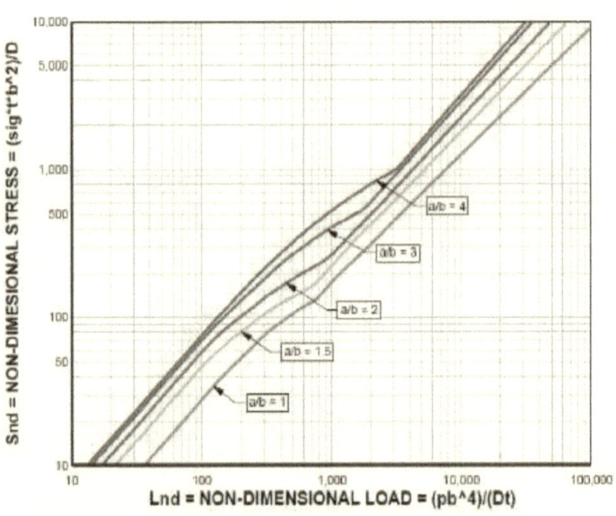

(b) Non-dimensional stress versus load

Figure 5.10: Pre-break glass resistance (Moore 1980)

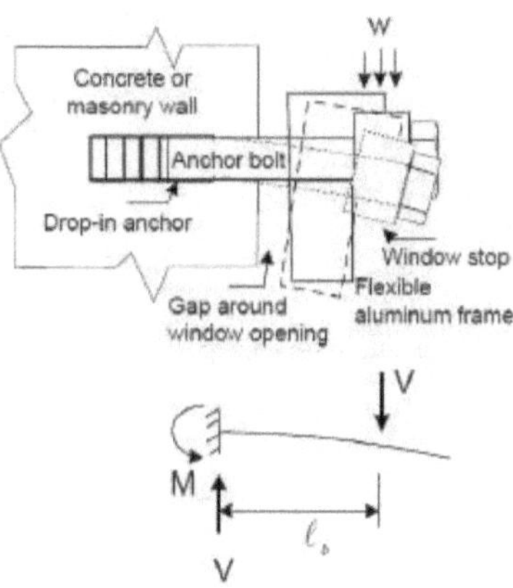

Figure 5.11: Bending of anchors under shear forces generated by blast loads

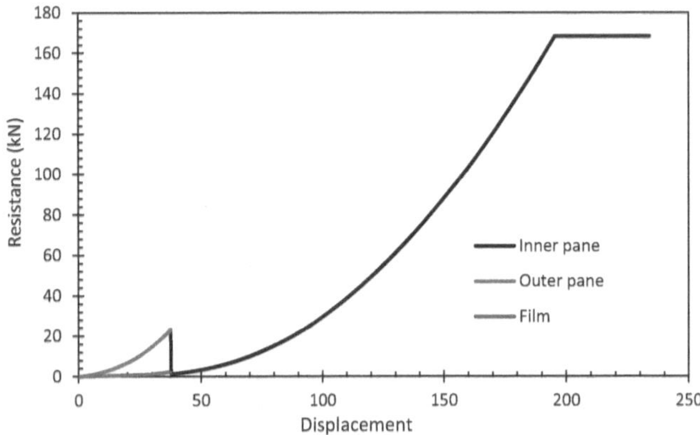

(a) Window on steel substrate with an aspect ratio of 1.0 (for Tests S13 and S14)

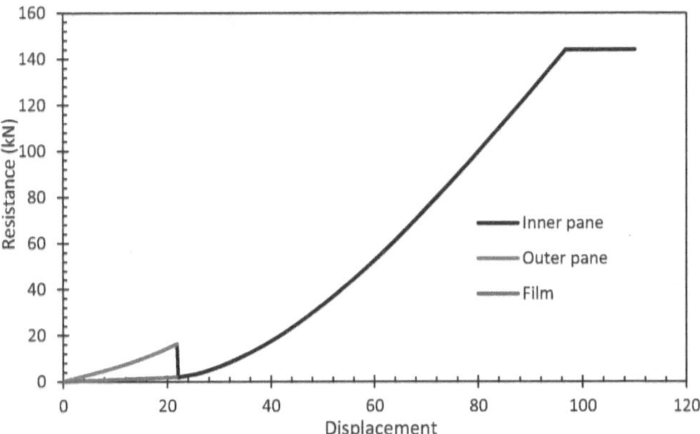

(b) Window on steel substrate with an aspect ratio of 3.0 (for Tests S15 and S16)

Figure 5.12: Resistance functions for each pane of selected test windows

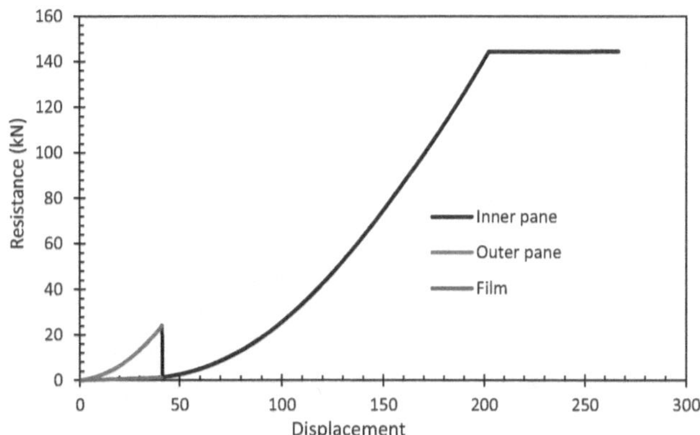

(c) Window on concrete substrate with an aspect ratio of 1.0 (for Tests C7 and C8)

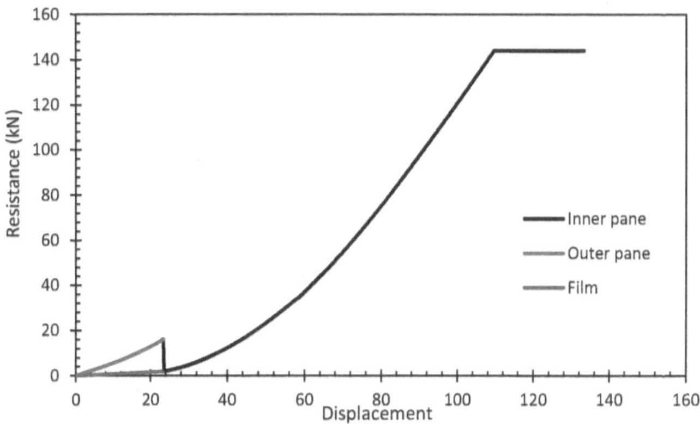

(d) Window on concrete substrate with an aspect ratio of 3.0 (for Tests C13 and C14)

Figure 5.13(Cont'd)

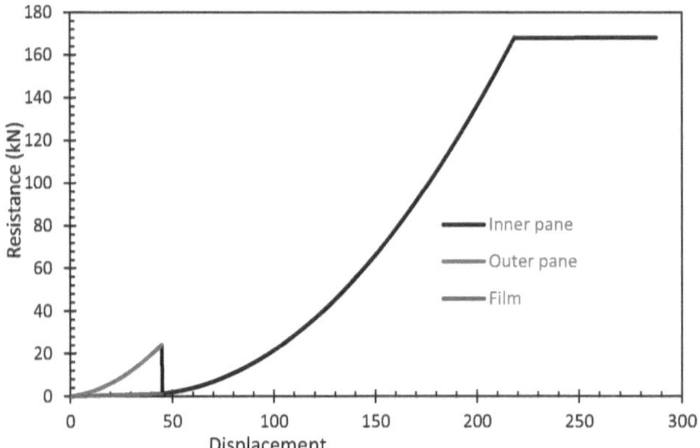

(e) Window on block masonry substrate with an aspect ratio of 1.0 (for Tests B1 and B2)

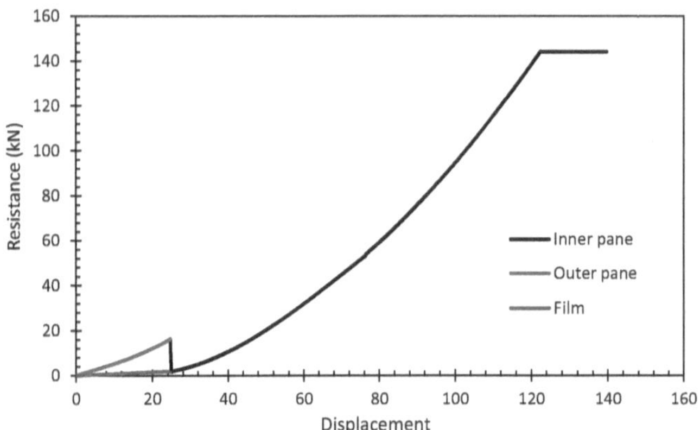

(f) Window on block masonry substrate with an aspect ratio of 3.0 (for Tests B5 and B6)

Figure 5.14(Cont'd)

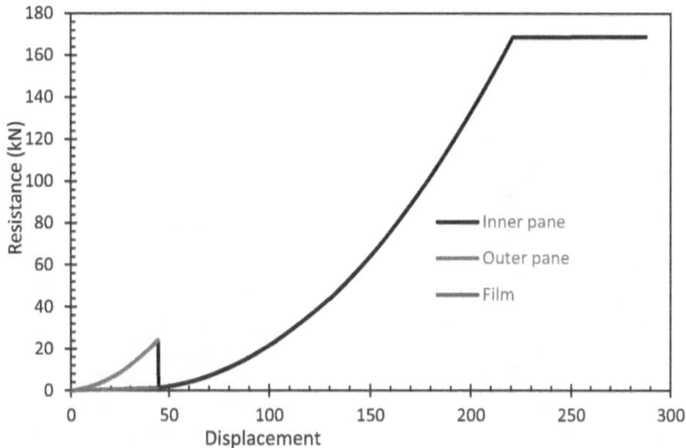

(g) Window on stone masonry substrate with an aspect ratio of 1.0 (for Tests ST1 and ST2)

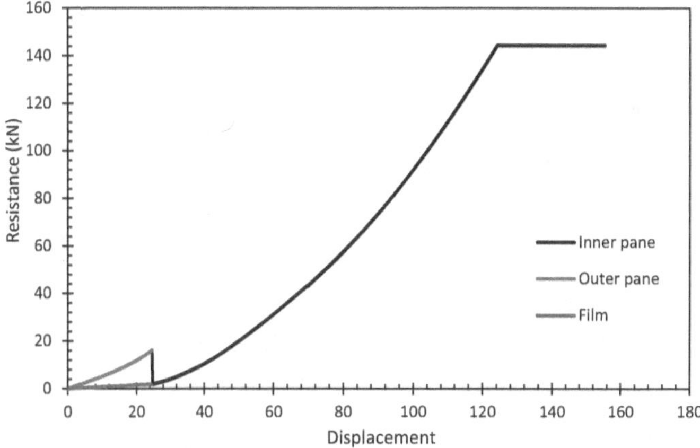

(h) Window on stone masonry substrate with an aspect ratio of 3.0 (for Tests ST3 and ST4)

Figure 5.15(Cont'd)

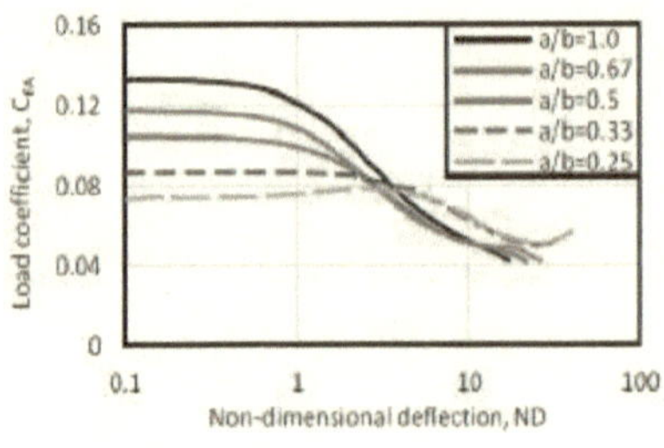

(a) Load coefficient on the short side C_{FA}

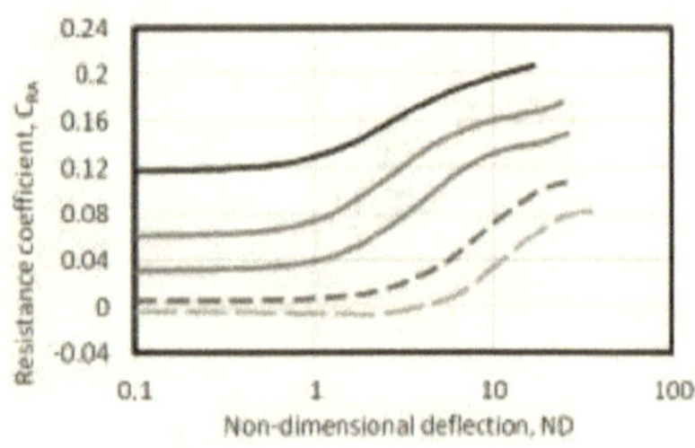

(b) Resistance coefficient on the short side C_{RA}

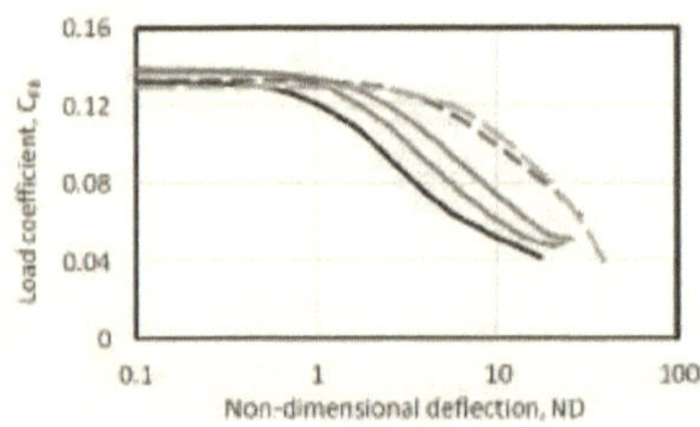

(c) Load coefficient on the long side C_{FB}

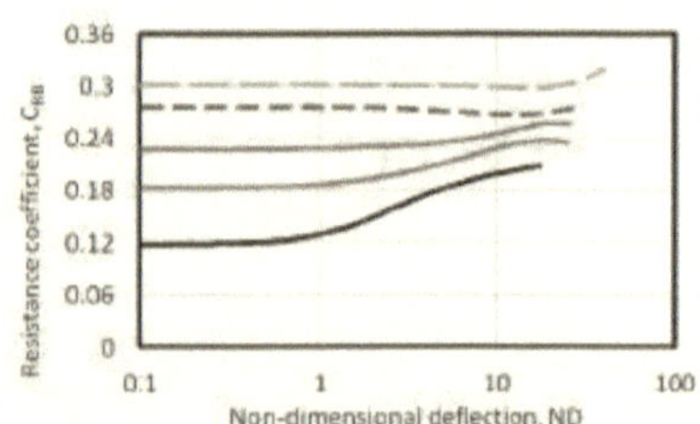

(d) Resistance coefficient on the long side C_{RB}

Figure 5.16: The coefficients C_F and C_R developed by (Morison 2007)

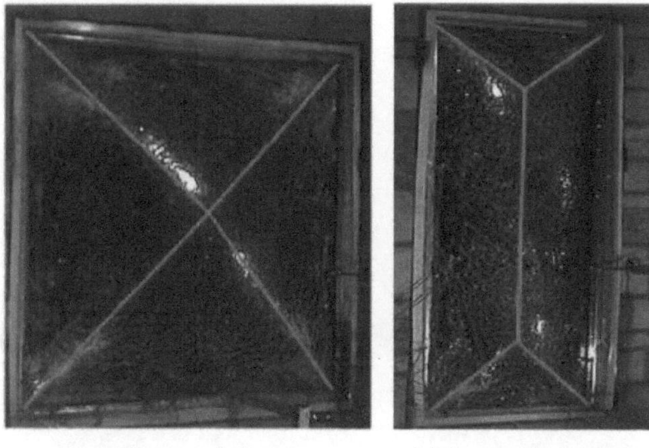

(a) Square window   (b) Rectangular window

Figure 5.17: Yield lines observed during shock tube tests

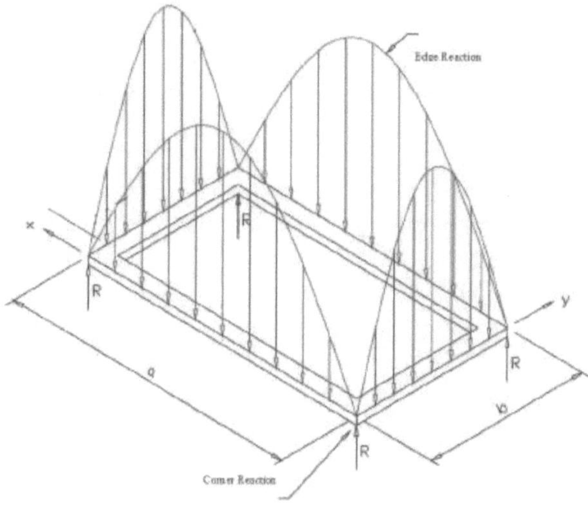

Figure 5.18: Distribution of reactive forces along a typical flexible aluminum window frame under upward blast pressure

185

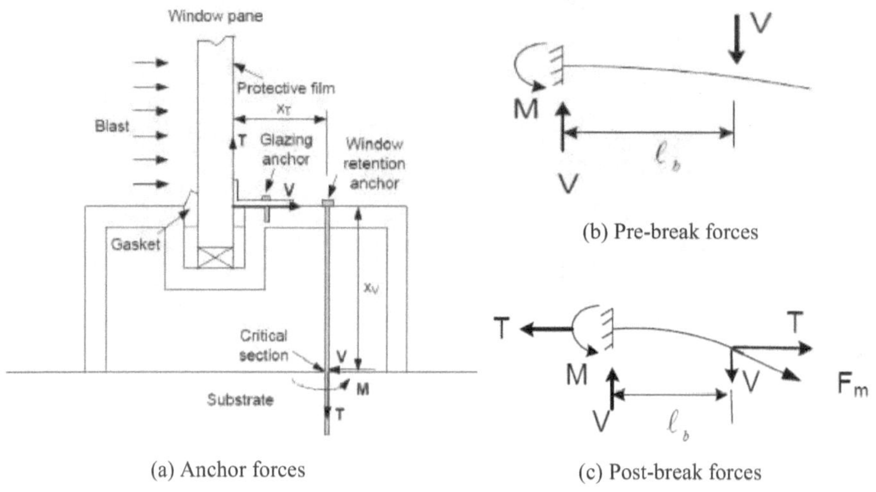

(a) Anchor forces

(c) Post-break forces

Figure 5.19: Anchor forces at critical section

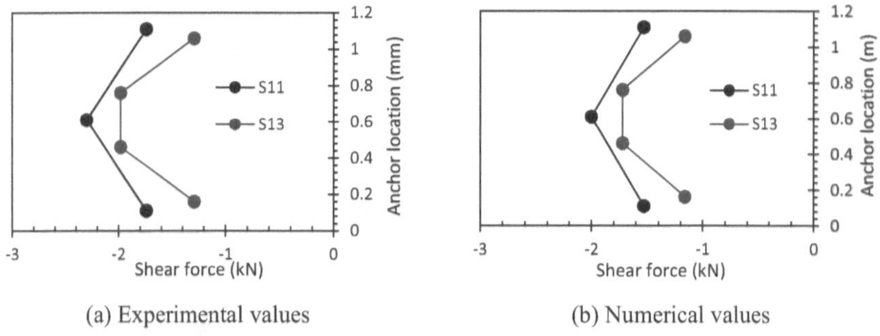

(a) Experimental values

(b) Numerical values

Figure 5.20: Experimental and numerical distribution of anchor shear forces

(Alameer et al 2020a; 2020b)

186

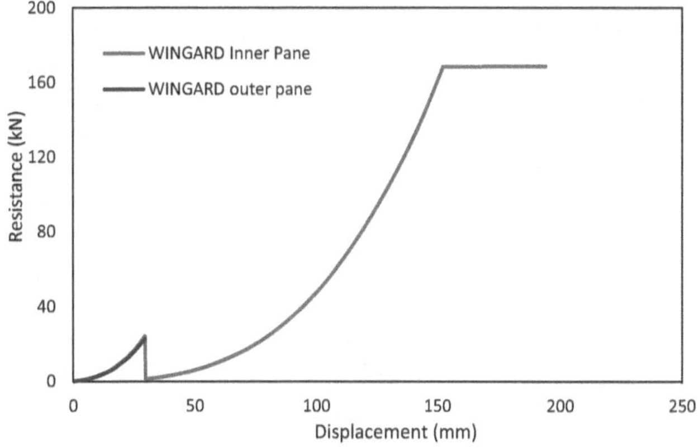

Figure 5.21: An example of (1220x1220 mm) square window resistance function for a double pane IGU generated by WINGARD (ARA 2005)

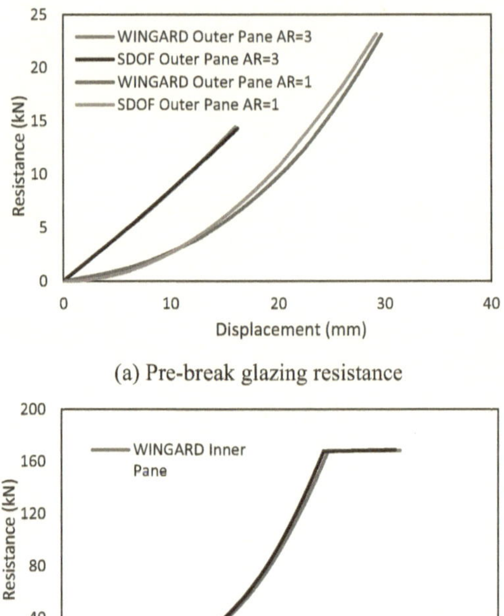

(a) Pre-break glazing resistance

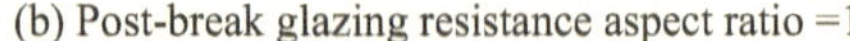

(b) Post-break glazing resistance aspect ratio =1

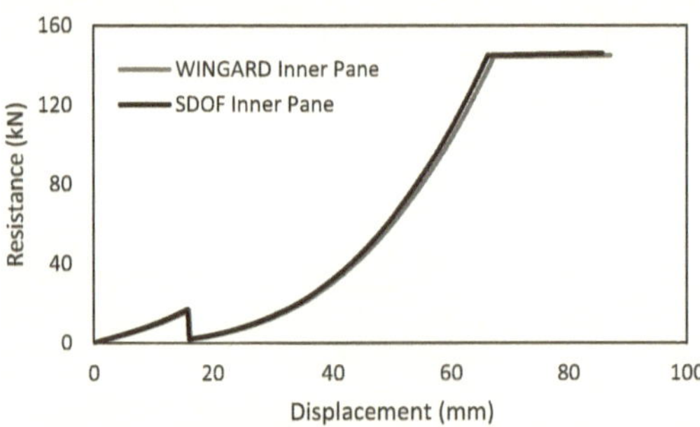

(c) Post-break glazing resistance aspect ratio =3

Figure 5.22: Comparisons of resistance functions; SDOF analysis versus WINGARD

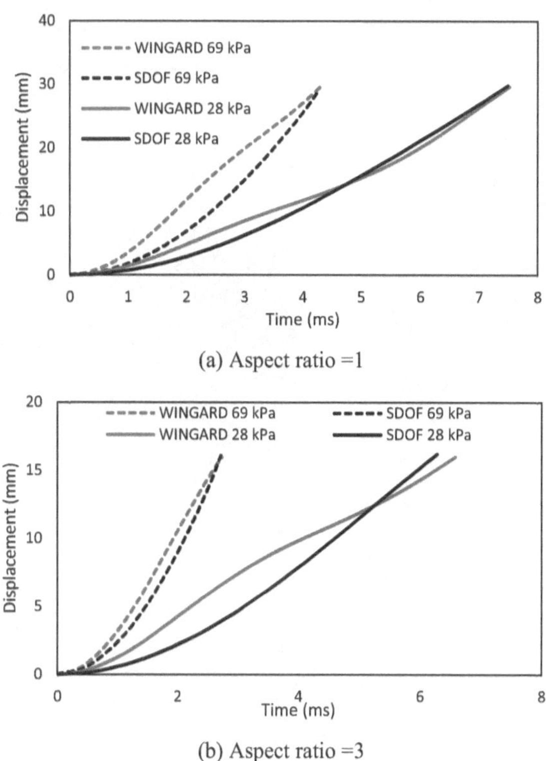

(a) Aspect ratio =1

(b) Aspect ratio =3

Figure 5.23: Central outer glass pane displacement

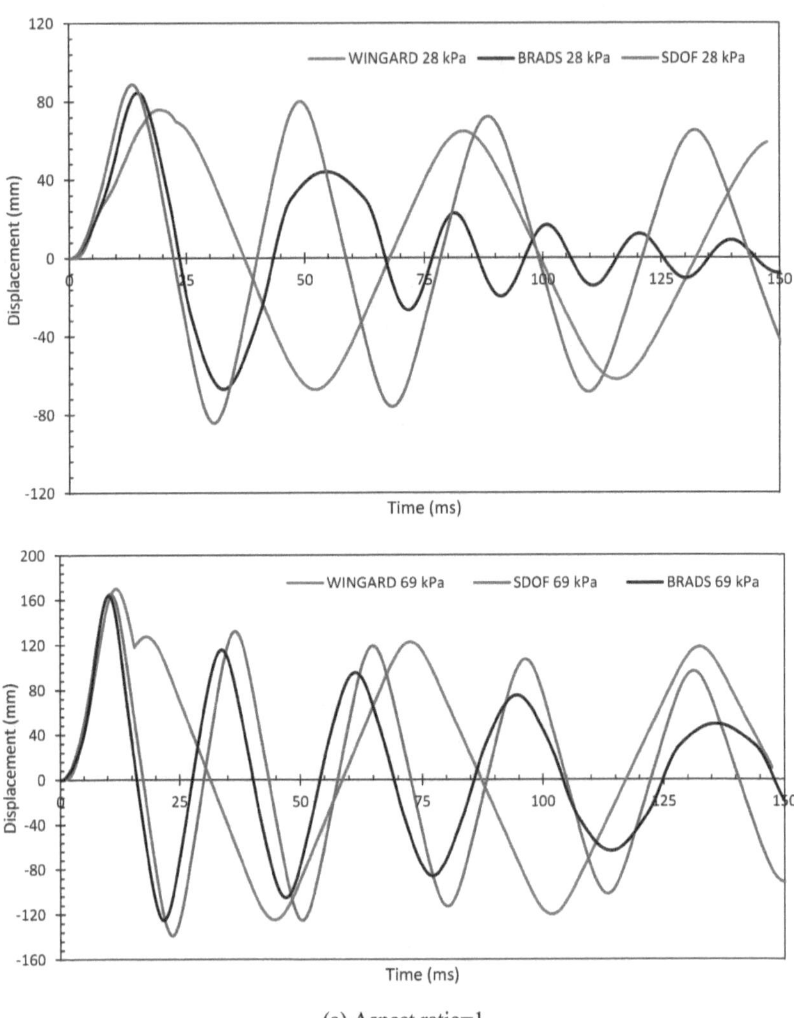

(a) Aspect ratio=1

Figure 5.24: Central inner glass pane displacement

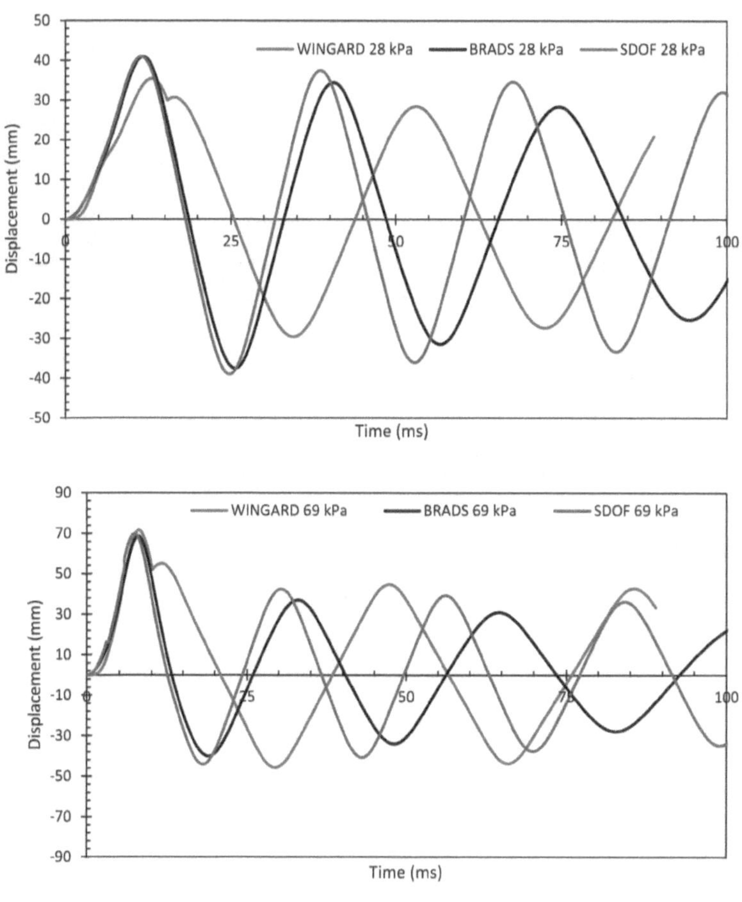

(b) Aspect ratio =3

Figure 5.25 (Cont'd)

Part IV

Conclusions

CHAPTER 6. Summary and Conclusions

6.1   Summary

A combined experimental and analytical research was conducted to investigate the behaviour of window retention anchors for blast-resistant windows. The experimental program involved tests of double pane windows with aluminum frames, retrofitted for blast resistance. A total of 46 tests were conducted on blast-resistant window systems using the University of Ottawa Shock Tube. The windows had different sizes (1220 by 1220 mm; 560 by 1676 mm and 1035 by 1784 mm), different substrates (reinforced concrete; steel; block masonry; stone masonry), different glazing methods (wet or mechanical glazing), different protective film thicknesses (5 mils; 12 mils; 14 mils; 23 mils), different number of retention anchors and anchor spacings. Two pressure-impulse combinations were applied to each window (28 kPa; 207 kPa-msec and 69 kPa; 621 kPa-msec). Hence, each window was tested twice with increasing blast loads. This level of pressure is frequently used by the US General Services Administration (GSA) for window testing.

A numerical investigation was carried out in parallel. Analytical models were generated for the double pane windows tested, and they were subjected to the same blast loads as those used in the experimental program. Selected windows on different substrates were analysed using LS_DYNA software and compared with experimental results. The comparison was conducted on the selected windows for the two applied blast pressures used during tests (28 kPa; 207 kPa-msec and 69 kPa; 621 kPa-msec). The numerical models were first validated against test data. The validated models were then employed to perform a parametric study to evaluate the effects of various key parameters on response and behaviour of retention anchors. These parameters included the effect of substrate flexibility, effect of anchor fixity in the substrate, window size and aspect ratio, frame rigidity, number of anchors and spacing, and level of blast pressure-impulse combination.

The study was extended to propose an anchorage design approach for windows by performing SDOF analysis while incorporating the flexibilities of the anchors and the substrate. The analytical procedure also involved the establishment of window resistance functions for pre-break and post-break phases of response. During the pre-break phase, the flexural glazing resistance was determined from the charts developed by Moore (1980) for glass panels with different aspect ratio. The post-break resistance was resolved by balancing the strain energy in the membrane with work done by the applied uniform static pressure. The model base on this principle and incorporated in WINGARD software was adopted. In addition, the distribution of anchor forces along the window edges were considered on the basis of the observations made during the experimental and numerical phases of research. The procedure provides maximum anchor forces for design.

6.2   Conclusions

The conclusions drawn from the experimental, numerical, and analytical phases of research are presented in different sub-sections, as follows below.

6.2.1   Conclusions from Experimental Phase of Research:

- Wet glazing of protective film, using structural silicon performs well under relatively low levels of blast pressure, whereas mechanical glazing is effective under higher blast pressures. The windows considered in this test program performed well with wet glazing when the pressure-impulse combination was 28 kPa and 207 kPa-ms. The same windows suffered glazing failure when subjected to 69 kPa and 621 kPa-ms unless mechanically glazed. The limitation of glazing type should be considered in design with due considerations given to the window size and the threat level.

- Aluminum HSS sections with a 25 mm square cross-section and a 5 mm wall thickness can be used for mechanical glazing of window panes. The same aluminum sections can replace the existing clip-on window stops for dual role of glazing and supporting window panes against blast pressures.

- Protective films should be designed to have sufficient thickness to remain below the rupturing strength. This can be done by computing the membrane capacity as defined in the Chapter 3 and 5. For the windows tested, 5-mil film thickness was sufficient under 28 kPa-207kPa-ms threat level but did not have sufficient strength against 69 kPa-621kPa-ms. Increasing the film thickness to 14 mils resulted in satisfactory performance under the increased threat level in all rectangular windows with 560 by 1676 mm frame dimensions. The square windows with a larger surface area (1220 mm square) required a film thickness of 23 mils for satisfactory performance in all cases. The effect of film thickness was primarily on strength, though it also affects window membrane stiffness in the post-break phase of response.

- The aluminum window frames with a wall thickness of 1.5 mm can be effective in fulfilling their functions during response to blast threat levels considered, if retrofitted by means of 25 mm hollow aluminum HSS sections with a 5 mm wall thickness used as window stops, as well as mechanical glazing units anchored to the substrates through the frame elements. These window stops helped maintain the connection between the anchor bolts and the frame elements, preventing tearing of the aluminum frame in tension, while providing sufficient bearing strength against the anchors in compression.

- Rigid steel substrates provide increased resistance to blast pressures, while also providing strong anchorage regions for blast-resistant windows. Steel substrates used in the current experimental program, consisting of steel HSS sections provided sufficient strength and stiffness without suffering any damage during testing. These substrates deformed very little (about 1.5 to 3.0 mm depending on the pressure level). They also developed the highest structural frequency (smallest period), interacting with the high-frequency excitations of blast loads, increasing anchor force demands.

- Reinforced concrete substrates can develop sufficient strength and stiffness against blast pressures, while also providing sufficiently strong anchorage zones to accommodate window retention anchors, provided that the anchor embedment lengths extend into the reinforced regions around the window openings with sufficient concrete cover. The reinforced concrete substrates used in the current test program developed maximum mid-span deflections of 2.0 mm and 8.6 mm under 28 kPa-207 kPa-ms; and 69 kP-621 kPa-ms, respectively. There was no damage observed in the wall except for a few hairline cracks under the higher pressure. However, the wall did not develop any permanent deflection. The wall thickness was 150 mm. When the anchors had sufficient embedment length into the 150 mm thick concrete wall panel, as in the case of 125 mm (5 in) anchor bolts, penetrating approximately 90 mm (3.5 in) into the concrete, placed in the centre of the wall thickness for maximum concrete cover, the performance of the anchorage region was satisfactory. However, when shorter bolts (90 mm bolts with 38 mm embedment into concrete) were used, especially when placed with 50 mm (2 in) concrete cover, the concrete around the window opening failed under 69 kPa, triggering the complete failure of the window system.

- Concrete block masonry walls are required to be strengthened around the window openings for sufficient strength in the anchorage zone. The block wall used in the test program were strengthened around the window openings by placing reinforcing steel in grouted cells. The anchorage region performed well at all levels of pressure. When square windows with larger surface area were anchored, the wall developed splitting failures at anchor locations when subjected to 69 kPa pressure at locations away from the reinforced anchorage region. The masonry walls showed flexible behaviour due to the cracking of mortar joints. The maximum wall deflections at mid height were 4.7 mm and 18.0 mm under 28 kPa and 69 kPa, respectively.

- Stone masonry walls may not be suitable for blast-resistant window anchorage unless the walls are strengthened around the window openings. Stone masonry walls tested in the current investigation, with window retention anchors drilled into the stone units were able to sustain 28 kPa, but did not have sufficient strength against 69 psi, developing significant damage both in the main body of the walls, and at the anchor locations. This was true for both rectangular and square windows, though the square window suffered from complete collapse. The maximum substrate deflection recorded at mid-height was 12 mm under 28 kPa. Under 69 kPa pressure, the LVDT attached to the substrate failed at about 250 mm without further reading of wall deflections.

- The embedment depth of drop-in-anchors used in concrete and stone walls must be carefully selected in practical applications to eliminate failures associated with lack of reinforcement in the substrate, sufficient cover, and embedment depth, all of which are required to maintain sufficient anchorage. Drop-in anchors with 38 mm (1.5 in) depth used in the centre of 150 mm walls of the current investigation performed well.

- Rigid substrates increase force demand on anchors (Ex: steel), whereas flexible substrates decrease the force demand (Ex: block and stone masonry). This conclusion can be attributed to the intimate relationship that exists between the frequency of the window system and the frequency of excitation (dynamic blast loading).

- Anchor forces and displacements increase with the spacing between the anchors as expected. In the test program, the 9.5 mm diameter high-strength bolts as anchors with 500 mm spacing developed more than twice the deflection experienced by anchors placed at 400 mm.

- The computation of anchor forces requires dynamic analysis of window systems to account for the intimate relationship that exists between the frequency of the window system and the frequency of excitation (blast shock waves). The anchor forces can be significantly different than those computed by using static analysis.

- The axial tension forces produced by the membrane action in the post-breakage range can be multiple times higher than anchor shear forces. In contrast, axial tension forces in the pre-break range, where the response is dominated by flexural action, can be very small relative to anchor shear forces.

6.2.2 Conclusions from Numerical Phase of Research:

- The behaviour of glazed window systems secured on different types of substrates with different force-deformation characteristics can be modelled using LS_DYNA software fairly accurately. The numerical model can be simplified substantially for the purpose of obtaining anchor design forces by incorporating the effects of substrates as anchor support flexibilities in the numerical model. This simplification can be justified in view of experimental observations where the substrate and the window responded in phase, especially during initial response when the maximum anchor forces were developed, reaching their design force levels.

- Substrate flexibility affects anchor design force levels. Windows on rigid substrates, as in the case of structural steel, develop high anchor forces. Windows on flexible substrates, such as masonry walls develop smaller anchor forces. This is attributed to the relative anchor deformations. Window anchors secured in flexible substrates deform less relative to the substrate when compared with those on rigid substrates where the substrate deforms less and the anchors deform more, attracting higher forces.

- Anchors in reinforced concrete and masonry substrates develop full fixity in drop-in anchors as observed under 28 kPa reflected pressure but may develop plastic deformations and anchorage slippage under higher blast pressures as observed under 69 kPa. Anchors on steel substrate may become loose early in response if they are attached by means of bolt heads or nuts.

- Square windows with an aspect ratio of 1.0 develop two-way action, with anchor forces equally distributed in two orthogonal directions, while higher forces are observed near the mid-length of each frame component. Rectangular windows exhibit predominantly one-way behaviour in short direction with 40% and 60% higher anchor forces along the long edges when the aspect ratio is increased to 1.5 and 3.0, respectively. The one-way action prevails beyond an aspect ratio of approximately 1.5 with the longer side forces asymptotically approaching 1.6 times the shorter side anchor forces.

- Windows with rigid frames show near uniform anchor force distribution. Windows with flexible aluminum frames develop parabolic force distribution along window edges, which can be estimated by a half sine curve.

- Anchor shear forces are higher than axial tensile forces in the pre-break phase of response. Upon breakage, membrane forces become significant, decreasing the ratio of anchor shear force to axial tension force. For the blast pressures considered in the current investigation, anchor shear forces in the post-break range varied between 15% to 30 % of axial tension.

- Consideration of damping in the analysis improves the accuracy of results. While damping may not be significant in blast problems during the initial forced vibration phase, the response wave form, especially during the free vibration mode can be significant. The damping coefficients of 2% from the critical damping for square and rectangular windows respectively, generated reasonable results.

6.2.3   Conclusions from SDOF Analysis Phase:

- The SDOF analysis procedure presented for window retention anchor design generates design forces that correlate well with anchor shear and axial forces recorded during window tests and numerical analyses. The analysis procedure can be used conveniently for the computation of anchorage design forces

- It is possible to simplify the two-degrees of freedom window/substrate system as a SDOF problem for the purpose of computing maximum design forces because of in-phase response of the substrate and the window during the initial maximum displacement response wave form as observed during shock tube tests, and numerical analyses using LS_DYNA. This can be done by introducing the flexibility provided by the substrate and the anchors to the window as support flexibilities. The resulting effective stiffness, obtained by considering three springs in series, generates dynamic response that leads to anchor forces that are in close agreement with experimental and numerical results.

- The resistance functions computed for pre-break and post-break phases of window response, used in the nonlinear SDOF analysis, agree well with those generated by using available techniques in the literature.

6.3 Recommended Anchor Design Procedure

The design of retention anchors for blast-resistant windows involves three primary steps; i) determination of design load/threat level, ii) computation of maximum anchor design forces; iii) proportioning of anchors to withstand the applied forces. The CSA Standard S852 on "Blast-Resistant Window Anchor Systems" requires the supporting substrate to be stronger than the window system and its connections to the substrate. Furthermore, the same standard requires the anchors connecting the window to the substrate to be stronger than the window system by a factor of at least 1.5. This requirement defines the design load for the anchors as the pressure-impulse combination that corresponds to the capacity of the window system. The factor of safety of 1.5 can be applied to the computed anchor design forces before the anchors are proportioned.

The anchor design forces can be computed by following the SDOF dynamic analysis procedure outlined in Chapter 5. The analysis is based on the step-by-step linear acceleration method and associated numerical integration of dynamic inelastic response. The first essential step involves the specification of mass and stiffness of the system. Mass consists of the mass of the window components (glass panes, protective film, and the frame). During the post-break phase of response, the mass of the laminated or filmed window pane reduces substantially. In the absence of a precise estimate of the value of broken glass mass that remains attached to the laminate/film, 25% of the unbroken glass mass may be used. The stiffness involves the computation of three stiffness components; i) stiffness of the substrate incorporating possible softening effects due to cracking (when applicable) and considering substrate support conditions, ii) stiffness of the anchors, usually taken as flexural stiffness based on the deformed shape (cantilever or double curvature), and iii) stiffness of the window. The stiffness of the window can be obtained from window resistance functions in the pre-break and post-break phases of response, established by following the procedure outlined in Chapter 5. The SDOF analysis provides window support reactions at or before the glass breakage and at the end of response beyond the glass breakage, depending on the level of threat and associated reflected pressure and impulse combination. In the pre-break range, flexural behaviour of glass panes governs the behaviour. The support reactions provide average shear forces along the frame elements. In the post-break range, membrane resistance of interlayer or protective film dominates response. The support reactions provide average shear and axial tension forces along the frame elements. These average support reactions are distributed to each anchor, located at pre-defined locations, by following the force distribution patterns specified in Chapters 4 and 5, i.e., uniform forces if a rigid steel frame is used as in the case of blast-resistant window frames, or half sign curve defining force distribution for flexible frames, as in the case of aluminum frames. Anchor spacing is a function of the number of anchors, which is depended on the capacity of each anchor. Trial anchor size and spacing must be specified to be verified against the required strength. Guidance on anchor spacing can be obtained from the experimental results reported in Chapter 3 and the numerical results presented in Chapter 4. Accordingly, a minimum uniform spacing of 400 mm is recommended such that no anchor is placed at mid-length of frames where anchor forces may peak. Placing an anchor at mid frame length results in the highest force being resisted by a single anchor, rather than being shared by two adjacent anchors with additional advantage of providing redundancy against failure.

The anchor forces obtained as described above provide two sets of design forces, one for each phase of response; maximum shear force and associated bending moment in the pre-break region, and maximum shear force, axial tension and the bending moment generated by these two forces at the critical section of the anchor. Figure 6.1 illustrates the design forces acting on a typical window retention anchor. The combined force effects on each anchor is assessed by checking the capacity of each anchor such that they remain elastic, using the combined stress equation of CSA S852, as shown below.

$$\frac{f_{ds}}{\sqrt{\sigma_n^2 + 3\tau^2}} \geq 1.0 \qquad\qquad 6.1$$

$$\sigma_n = \frac{T_{af}}{A_a} + \frac{M_{af}y}{I} \qquad\qquad 6.2$$

$$\tau = \frac{4V_{af}}{3A_a} \qquad\qquad 6.3$$

Where;

f_{ds}: Dynamic design strength of the anchor material; may be taken equal to the tensile strength of material established by static tests f_s, using the dynamic increase factor (DIF) and the strength increase factor (SIF) of unity ($f_{ds} = f_s$ x DIF x SIF).

σ_n: Maximum normal stress in the anchor at the critical section.

τ : Maximum shear stress in the anchor at the critical section.

T_{af}: Factored axial tensile design force applied on the window anchor.

M_{af}: Factored design moment at the critical anchor section.

y : Distance between the anchor centroid and the extreme tension fibre (radius of a circular anchor).

I : Moment of inertia of anchor cross-section.

V_{af}: Factored anchor shear design force at the critical section.

A_a: Cross-sectional area of the window retention anchor.

The above design involves checking pre-defined anchors against two sets of design forces, i.e., those obtained in the pre-break and post break stages. If the anchors pass the requirement of Eq. (6.1) under both sets of design forces, they satisfy the elastic design requirement. Any inelasticity in anchors during response, possibly because of higher threat levels, may provide additional protection associated with the dissipation of blast energy.

6.4   Recommendations for Future Research

The research project reported in this book focused on generating design information for window anchorage under blast loads. All phases of research were limited to punched windows anchored on substrates by means of steel bolts used as mechanical anchors. Additional research is recommended to cover different types of anchors, including adhesive anchors. In addition, further testing with laminated blast-resistant windows and windows glazing along two sides of window frame are recommended to generate more data.

An important gap in the literature is for window anchors of multi-pane windows where each pane is supported by vertical aluminum mullions, anchored to the substrate. It is recommended to undertake a comprehensive window test program, with accompanying numerical research for this type of windows to expand the current research results to other types of windows with multiple lites.

Another area where much research is needed, involves curtain walls. Curtain walls cover large segments of building envelop, with glass panes supported by vertical and horizontal mullions. Anchorage of these mullions to building components, often at floor levels, requires more experimental and analytical research with the objective of developing design guidelines for blast-resistant curtain walls.

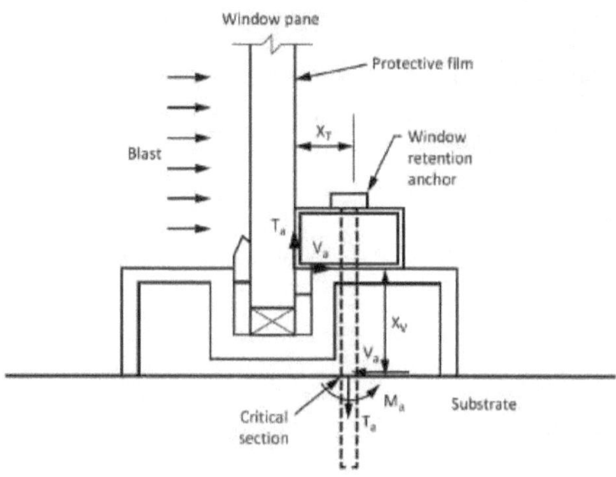

Figure 6. 1: Anchor design forces

REFERENCES

AAMA 510-06. (2006). "American Architectural Manufacturers Association (AAMA) Voluntary Guide Specifications for Blast Hazard Mitigation for Fenestration Windows." http://www.aamanet.org.

AAMA. (2008). "Introduction to Designing Fenestration for Blast Mitigation." American Architectural Manufacturers Association, http://www.aamanet.org.

Abrishami, H.H., and Mitchell, D. (1996). "Analysis of Bond Stress Distributions in Pullout Specimens." J. Struct. Eng., 1996, 122(3): 255-261.

ACI 318-19, (2019). "Building Code Requirements Available for Public Review." American Concrete Institute.

Alameer, A., Elnabelsy, G., Jacques, E., Saatcioglu, M. and Foo, S. "Tests of blast-resistant windows." Research report, Hazard Mitigation and Disaster Management Research Centre, University of Ottawa, Ottawa, Canada, 2017a.

Alameer, A., Jacques, E., and Saatcioglu, M. (2015). "Performance of Glazed Windows Under Blast Loads." The 11th International Conference on Shock & Impact Loads on Structures, Ottawa, Canada.

Amadio C, Bedon, C. (2012a). "Elastoplastic dissipative devices for the mitigation of blast resisting cable-supported glazing facades." Eng Struct: 39:103–15.

Amadio C, Bedon, C. (2012b). "Viscoelastic spider connectors for the mitigation of cable supported facades subjected to air blast loading." Eng Struct: 42:190–200.

Amman, and Walter, J. (1991). "Static and Dynamic Long-Term Behavior of Anchors." Paper SP130-8 in "Anchors in Concrete-Design and Behavior." Edited by George, A. Senkiw, and Harry, B. Lancelot III), Special Publication SP-130, American Concrete Institute, Detroit 1991, pp. 205-220.

Anderson, M., and Dover, D. (2003). "Sealed, Blast-Resistant Windows for Retrofit Protection Against the Terrorist Threat." Proceedings of the 2nd International Conference on Innovation in Architecture, Engineering, and Construction, Lougborough University, UK.

Andersson, S., and Karlsson, H. (2012). "Structural Response of Reinforced Concrete Beams Subjected to Explosions." Masters book, Chalmers University of Technology, Goteborg, Sweden.

ASCE/SEI 59-11, (2011). "Blast Protection of Buildings." American Society of Civil Engineers, USA.

ASTM E1300, (2012). "Standard Practice for Determining Load Resistance of Glass in Buildings." American Society for Testing Materials.

ASTM F1642, (2012). "Standard Test Method for Glazing and Glazing Systems Subject to Airblast Loadings." American Society for Testing Materials.

ASTM F2248, (2012). "Standard Practice for Specifying an Equivalent 3-Second Duration Design Loading for Blast Resistant Glazing Fabricated with Laminated Glass." American Society for Testing Materials.

Bangash, M.Y.H., and Bangash, T. (2006). "Explosion Resistant Buildings." Springer, p. 784.

Barker, D. (1996). "Test Program for Enhancing Blast Capacity of Windows." Proceedings of the Twenty-Seventh DoD Explosive Safety Seminar Held in Las Vegas, NV, August 22-26.

Belytschko, T., Wong, B. L., and Chiang, H., Y. (1989). "Improvement in low-order shell element for explicit transient analysis." Analytical and computational models of shells, Noor, A. K., Belytschko, T., and Simo, J., editors, ASME, CED-Vol. 3, pp. 383-398.

Belytschko, T., Wong, B. L., and Chiang, H., Y. (1992). "Advance in one point quadrature shell elements." Comp. Meths. Appl. Mechs Eng., 96, 93-107.

Biggs, J.M. (1964). "Introduction to structural dynamics." McGraw-Hill, New York, USA.

Block, V. (2015). "Bomb Blast Resistant Glazing: Testing and Standards." www.nibs.org/resource/resmgr/BEST/BEST1_033.pdf.

Bowles, R., and Sugarman, B. (1962). "The strength and deflection characteristics of large rectangular glass panels under uniform pressure." Glass Technology, Vol 3 pp 156-170.

Braimah, A., Contestabile, E., and Guilbeault, R. (2009). "Behaviour of Adhesive Steel Anchors under Impulse-type Loading." Canadian Journal of Civil Engineering, Vol. 36, pp. 1835-1847.

Braimah, A., Guilbeault, R., and Contestabile, E. (2014). "Strain Rate Behaviour of Adhesive Anchors in Masonry." Engineering Structures, Vol. 67, pp. 96-108.

Brown, R.,H., and Wihlock, R., A. (1983). "Strength of Anchor Bolts in Grouted Concrete Masonry." Journal of Structural Engineering, Vol. 9, No. 6, pp. 1362-1374.

Canadian Standards Association, (2012). "Design and Assessment of Buildings Subjected to Blast Loads." CSA Standard S850-12, National Standard of Canada, Ottawa, Canada.

Canadian Standards Association, (2018). "Blast-resistant window anchor systems." CSA Standard S852-18, National Standard of Canada, Ottawa, Canada.

Canadian Standards Association, (2019). "Design of concrete structures." CSA Standard A23.3-19, Canadian Standards Association, Mississauga, Ontario, Canada.

Cannon, R.W., Godfrey, D.A., and Moreadith, F.L. (1981). "Guide to the design of Anchor Bolts and Other Steel Embedments." Concrete International: Design and Construction, Vol. 3, No. 7, July, pp.28-41.

Carlsson, M., and Kristensson, R. (2012). "Structural Response with regard to explosions - Mode superposition, damping and curtailment." Masters book, Lund University, Lund, Sweden.

CERL, (2015). "Department of Foreign Affairs, Trade and Development (DFATD) Minimum Blast Design Criteria – A Guide to Using Protective Film for Security Upgrade of Glass Windows Level I." Canadian Explosives Research Laboratory.

Chen, J.B. (2004). "Static Behaviour and Strength of Adhesive Bonded Anchors in Concrete and Masonry." Master of Applied Science book, Carleton University, Ottawa, Canada.

Colak, A. (2001). "Parametric Study of Factors Affecting the Pull-Out Strength of Steel Rods Bonded into Precast Cocrete Panels." International Journal of Adhesion & Adhesives 21, pp. 487-493.

Collins, D., Klingner, R. E., and Polyzois, D. (1989). "Load-Deflection Behavior of Cast-in-Place and Retrofit Concrete Anchor Subjected to Static, Fatigue and Impact Tensile Loads." Research Report CTR 1126-1, Center for Transportation Research, University of Texas at Austin.

Cook, R.A., and Konz, R. (2001). "Factors Influencing the Bond Strength of Adhesive Anchors." ACI Structural Journal, American Concrete Institute, V.98, No.1, pp. 76-96.

Cook, R.A., Doer G. T., and Klinger, R.E. (1993). "Bond Stress Model for Design of adhesive Anchors." ACI Structural Journal, V.90, No.5, pp. 514-524.

Dawson, H., and Van, E., P. (2006). "Blast Windows and Curtainwalls: Understanding the Challenges." Design-Build Dateline, the Journal of the Design-Build Institute of America, pp 27-32.

Department of Defense Explosives Safety Board (DDESB) (2004). "DoD Ammunition and Explosives Safety Standards." DoD 6055.9-STD, Revision 5, Alexandria, VA.

Department of Defense, Naval Facilities Engineering Service Center (NFESC) (2000). "Physical Security Equipment Guide." User's Guide UG-2045-SHR, Port Hueneme: 93043-4370, California, USA.

Departments of the Air Force, Army, and Navy (1990). "Structures to Resist the Effects of Accidental Explosions." Air Force Manual 88-22, Army Technical Manual 5-1300, and Navy Publication NAVFAC P-397, Revision 1, Washington, DC.

Du Bois, P., Kolling, S., and Fassnacht, W. (2003). "Modelling of safety glass for crash simulation." Comput Mater Sci: 28:675–83.

Dussenberry, D. (2010). "Handbook for Blast-Resistant Design of Buildings." John Wiley and Sons, Inc., p. 484.

Eligehasuen, R. (2001). "Connections Between Steel and Concrete", RILEM Publucations, Vol. 1 and Vol. 2.

Eligehausen, R., and Fuchs, W. (1988). "Load-Bearing Behavior of Anchor Fastenings under Shear, Combined Tension and Shear or Flexural Loading." betonwerk + Fertigteil-Technik, No. 2, 48-56.

Fischer, K., and Häring, I. (2009). "SDOF response model parameters from dynamic blast loading experiments." Eng Struct: 31:1677–86.

Flocker, F. W., and Dharani, L. R. (1997). "Stresses in laminated glass subjected to low velocity impact." Eng Struct: 19:851–6.

Freynik, H. S. "The non-linear response of windows to random noise." NASA technical note NASA TN D-2025, 1963.

Frykberg, E., R. (2002). "Medical Management of Disasters and Mass Casualties from Terrorist Bombings: How can we cope?" Journal of Trauma, Injury, Infection, and Critical Care, 53(2), pp. 201–212.

Glass Research and Testing Laboratory. (1987). "Misty picture data: window glass experiment." TX: Texas Technical University.

Graham Architectural Products. (2012a). "Blast Mitigation Operable Aluminum Windows." http://www.grahamwindows.com/?page_id=1848.

Graham Architectural Products. (2012b). "Blast-Resistant Fixed Windows." http://www.grahamwindows.com/?page_id=1848.

GSA, (2003). "Standard Test Method for Glazing and Window Systems Subject to Dynamic Overpressure Loadings." The US General Services Administration, Washington DC, USA.

Hao, H., and Zhang, X. (2015). "Analysis and Design of Glass Windows Against Blast and Impact Loads." Proceedings of the 11th International Conference on Shock and Impact Loads on Structures, Ottawa, Canada. pp. 1-15.

Holmquist, T. J., Johnson, G. R., Lopatin, C., Grady, D., and Hertel, Jr. E. S. (1995). "High strain rate properties and constitutive modeling of glass." In: 15th International symposium on ballistics Jerusalem, Israel.

Hooper, P. A., Sukhram, R. A. M., Blackman, B. R. K., and Dear, J. P. (2012). "On the blast resistance of laminated glass." Int J Solids Struct: 49:899–918.

Hughes, T. J. R., and Liu, W. K. (1981a). "Nonlinear finite element analysis of shells: two-dimensional shells." Comp. Meths. Appl. Mechs. 27, 167-181.

Hughes, T. J. R., and Liu, W. K. (1981b). "Nonlinear finite element analysis of shells: three-dimensional shells." Comp. Meths. Appl. Mechs. 27, 331-362.

ISC, (2001). "ISC Security Design Criteria for New Federal Buildings and Major Renovation Projects." the Interagency Security Committee, May 28, 2001.

ISO 16933, (2007). "Glass in building - Explosion-resistant Security Glazing - Test and Classification for Arena Air-blast Loading." International Organization for Standardization, Geneva, Switzerland.

ISO 16934, (2007). "Glass in Building - Explosion-resistant Security Glazing - Test and Classification by Shock-tube Loading." International Organization for Standardization, Geneva, Switzerland.

Klingner, R.E., and Mendonca, J.A. (1982). "Shear Capacity-of Short Anchor Bolts and Welded Studs – A Literature Review." ACI Journal, Vol. 79, No. 5.

Kranzer, C., Gürke, G., and Mayrhofer, C. (2005). "Testing of bomb resistant glazing systems experimental investigations of the time dependent deflection of blast loaded 7.5 mm laminated glass." Glass Processing Days, The 9th International Conference on Architectural and Automotive Glas, Tampere, Finland.

Krauthammer, T. (2008). "Modern Protective Structures." CRC Press, Taylor and Francis Group, p. 509.

Kyei, C. (2014). "Effects of blast loading on seismically detailed reinforced concrete columns." Masters book, Department of Civil Engineering, Carleton University, Ottawa, Canada.

Larcher, M., Solomos, G., Casadei, F., and Gebbeken, N. (2012). "Experimental and numerical investigations of laminated glass subjected to blast loading." Int J Impact Eng: 39:42–50.

Lin, L. H., Hinman, E., Stone, H. F., and Roberts, A. M. (2004). "Survey of window retrofit solutions for blast mitigation." J Perform Constr Facil: 18:86–94.

Lin, T., and Kruger, D. (1996). "Engineering Properties of Epoxy Resins Used as Concrete Adhesive." ACI Material Journal, January-February, pp. 26-35.

Lloyd, A. (2010). "Performance of reinforced concrete columns under shock tube induced shock wave loading." Master's book, University of Ottawa, Ottawa, Canada.

Lotze, D., Klinger, R.E., and Graves, H.L. (2001). "Static Behavior of Anchors under Combinations of Tension and Shear Loading." ACI Structural Journal, Vol. 98, No. 4, pp. 525-536.

LS-DYNA® (2007). "LS-DYNA® Version 971 Keyword user's manual." Livermore Software Technology Corporation, Livermore, California, USA.

Mansfield, E., H. (1989). "The bending and stretching of plates 2nd Edition." Cambridge University Press, Cambridge, ISBN 0-521-33304-0.

Mays, G.C., and Smith, P. D. (2003). "Blast Effects on Buildings – Design of Buildings to Optimize Resistance to Blast Loading." Thomas Telford Publications Ltd, London, England. p. 121.

MCTPSM - Manual for Counter Terrorist Protective Security Measures, Supplement Four, Annex C and D. (2003). "Simplified Design Procedure for Determining the Appropriate Level of Glazing Protection." Adopted from Mays and Smith.

McVay, M., Cook, R.A., and Krishnamurthy, K. (1993). "Behavior of Chemically Bonded Anchors." Journal of Structural Engineering, American Society of Civil Engineers, V119, No.9, September Edition, pp. 2744-2762.

Meyers, G. E., (1994). "BLASTOP version 1.4." US Department of Energy.

Meyers, G.E., Baldwin, D., and Mlakar, P. (1994). "State of the Art on Blast Resistant Windows." Defense Technical Information Centre (DTIC).

Moore, D. M. (1980). "Proposed method for determining the glass thickness of rectangular glass solar collector panels subjected to uniform normal pressure loads." JPL Publication 80-34, Jet Propulsion Laboratory, Pasadena, CA.

Morison, C. (2003). "Recent developments in single degree of freedom analysis of walls and windows." Proceedings of the 11th International Symposium on the Interaction of the Effects of Munitions with Structures, Mannheim, Germany.

Morison, C. (2007). "The resistance oaf laminated glass to blast pressure loading and the coefficients for single degree of freedom analysis of laminated glass." PhD book, Defence College of Management and Technology, 549 pages.

Morison, C., and Pullan, D. (2015). "Few Degrees of Freedom Analysis of Rectangular Glazing Units Under Blast." Proceedings of the 16th International Symposium on the Interaction of the Effects of Munitions with Structures (16th ISIEMS), Destin, FL, USA.

National Counter Terrorism Security Office – NaCTSO. (2009). "Counter Terrorism Protective Security Advice for Higher and Further Education." London, U.K., p. 75.

Norville, H., S., Conrath, E., J. (2001). "Considerations for Blast Resistant Design." ASCE Journal of Architectural Engineering."

Norville, HS., Harvill, N., Conrath, EJ., Shariat, S., and Mallonee, S. (1999). "Glass-related injuries in Oklahoma City bombing." J Perform Constr Facil: 13:50.

Oda, J., and Zang, M. (1997). "Analysis of impact fracture behavior of laminated glass of bilayer type using discrete element method." Key Eng Mater: 145:349–54.

PEC, and BakerRisk. (2008). U.S. Army Corps of Engineers Protective Design Center Technical Report. Methodology Manual for the Single-Degree-of- Freedom Blast Effects Design Spreadsheets.

Peier, W. H. (1983). "Model for Pullout Strength of Anchors in Concrete." Journal of Structural Engineerings, ASCE, Vol. 109, No. 5, May, pp. 1155-1173.

Peroni, M., Solomos, G., Pizzinato, V., Larcher, M. (2011). "Experimental investigation of high strain-rate behaviour of glass." Applied Mechanics and Materials: 82: 63e8.

Protective Security Policy Committee. (2013). "Physical Security Management Guidelines – Security Zones and Risk Mitigation Control Measures." Australian Government, Business Law Branch, Attorney General's Department, Barton, ACT, Australia, p. 66.

PWGSC. (2005). "A Guide to Using Protective Film for Security Upgrade of Glass Windows." Public Works and Government Services Canada, Gatineau, Canada, p.28.

Rezaei, S. H. C. (2011). "Response of Reinforced Concrete Elements to High-Velocity Impact Load." PHD book, Purdue University, West Lafayette, Indiana, US.

RIBA. (2011). "Guidance on Designing for Counter-Terrorism." Royal Institute for British Architects, London, England, p. 21.

Rodriguez, M., D.Lotze, J. H., Gross, Y. G., Zhang, R. E., Klingner, R.E., and Graves, H.L. (2001). "Dynamic Behavior of Tensile Anchors to Concrete." ACI Structural Journal, Vol. 98, No. 4, pp. 511-524.

Saatcioglu, M., and Contastabile, E. (2015). "Review of Literature on Blast Resistant Window Anchor Systems." Submitted to Public Works and Government Services Canada.

Sankiw, G.A., and Harry B., L. (1991). "Anchors in Concrete: Design and Behaviors." American Concrete Institute, SP-130.

Smith, J. L. (2003). "Anti-Terrorism: Criteria, Tools and Technology." Applied Research Associates, Inc., Vicksburg, MS 29180, USA. p. 17.

Smith, J. L., and Renfroe, N.A. (2010). "Glazing Hazard Mitigation." National Institute of Building Science," http://www.ara.com

Standards Design Group, Inc. (2007). "Blast Resistant Glazing Design 2007." https://www.standardsdesign.com, Lubbock, Texas.

Sun, D. Z., Andrieux, F., Ockewitz, A., Klamser, H., and Hogenmuller, J. (2005). "Modelling of the failure behaviour of windscreens and component tests." Proceeding of 5th European LS-DYNA user conference, Birmingham, UK.

Technical Manual TM5-1300. (1990). "Structures to resist the effects of accidental explosions." US Department of the Army.

Timmel, M., Kolling, S., Osterrieder, P., Du Bois, P. A. (2007). "A finite element model for impact simulation with laminated glass." Int J Impact Eng: 34:1465–78.

Timoshenko, S., P., and Goodier, J., N. (1970). "Theory of elasticity, 3rd edition." McGraw-Hill, New York & London; ISBN 0-07-085805-5.

Timoshenko, S.P. (1940). "Theory of plates and shells." McGraw-Hill, New York & London.

Uddin, N. (2010). "Blast Protection of Civil Infrastructures and Vehicles using Composite." CRC, Woodhead Publishing Ltd., p. 427.

UFC 3-340-02, (2008). "Structures to Resist the Effects of Accidental Explosions." Washington, DC, USA.

UFC 4-010-01, (2003). "Structures to Resist the Effects of Accidental Explosions." Washington, DC, USA.

US Army Corps of Engineers, (1957). "Design of structures to resist the effects of atomic weapons – principles of dynamic analysis and design." EM 1110-345-415.

US Army Corps of Engineers, (1957). "Design of structures to resist the effects of atomic weapons – principles of structural elements subjected to dynamic loads." EM 1110-345-416.

Vallabhan, C., V., G., Das, Y., C., Magdi, M., Asik, M., and Bailey, J., R. (1993). "Analysis of laminated glass units." Journal of Structural Engineering, Volume 119(5), pp1572-1585, ASCE, New York.

Vallabhan, C.V.G. (1983). "Iterative analysis of nonlinear glass plates." J. Struct. Eng., 1983, 109(2): 489-502.

Ward, S. P. (2006). "Anchoring Blast Resistant Windows." www.cintec.com.

Ward, S. P., and Jordan, B. (2006). "Anchoring Blast Resistant Windows by S. P. Ward and B. Jordan." http://www.aees.org.au/wp-content/uploads

Wei, J., and Dharani, L. R. (2005). "Fracture mechanics of laminated glass subjected to blast loading." Theoret Appl Fract Mech: 44:157–67.

Wei, J., and Dharani, L. R. (2006). "Response of laminated architectural glazing subjected to blast loading." Int J Impact Eng: 32:2032–47.

Wei, J., Shetty, M. S., and Dharani, L. R. (2006). "Stress characteristics of a laminated architectural glazing subjected to blast loading." Comput Struct: 84:699–707.

Weissman, S., Dobbs, N., Stea, W., and Price, P. (1978). "Blast Capacity Evaluation of Glass Windows and Aluminum Window Frames." Defense Technical Information Centre (DTIC).

Wikipedia. (2011). "Norway attacks." <http://en.wikipedia.org/wiki/ 2011_Norway_Attacks>.

WINGARD, (2005). "Window glazing analysis response & design – WINGARD – Technical manual." Applied Research Associates Inc., ARA-TR-05-16462-2, US General Services Administration, Washington, DC, USA.

Zang, M., Chen, H., and Lei, Z. (2010). "Simulation on high velocity impact process of windshield by SPH/FEM coupling method." IEEE., p. 381–4.

Zhang, X., and Hao, H. (2011). "Laboratory test and numerical simulation of laminated glass window response to impact and blast loads." The 9th international conference on shock and impact loads on structures, Fukuoka, Japan.

Zhang, X., Hao, H., Ma, G. (2013a). "Laboratory test and numerical simulation of laminated glass window vulnerability to debris impact." Int. Journal of Impact Eng: 55:49–62.

Zhang, X., Hao, H., and Ma, G. (2013b). "Parametric study of laminated glass window response to blast loads." Engineering Structures: 56:1707–1717.

Zhang, X., and Hao, H. (2016). "The response of glass window systems to blast loadings: An overview." International Journal of Protective Structures: Vol. 7(1) 123–154.

Part V

Appendices

Appendix A:

Shock Tube Test Data for Windows on Reinforced Concrete and Steel Substrates

Appendix A contains experimental results observed during tests of 15 windows on reinforced concrete and steel substrates. Each window was subjected to two blast pressure-impulse combinations; 28 kPa – 207 kPa-ms and 69 kPa – 621 kPa-ms. A brief description of each test is given, followed by the actual recorded time histories for reflected pressures and anchor displacements. Chapter 3 provides a concise presentation of the results, analysis of test data, and discussions. Table 3.1(a) provides a summary of test parameters. This appendix presents recorded and observed performance of each window test. Each window is labelled with designations C for reinforced concrete substrates and S for steel substrates. The number that appears next to the test designation indicates the sequence of window tests conducted with odd number indicating tests under 28 kPa-207 kPa-ms and even numbers indicating tests under 69 kPa – 621 kPa-ms. This appendix presents recorded and observed performance of each window test. Displacement time-history for selected anchors, window frame edges, and substrates are potted for each test. Strain values developed in the retention anchors are presented as examples of strain time-history for selected tests (C13-C14) and (S11-S12).

A.1: Test C1

C1 was conducted on a window with aspect ratio of 1 was subjected to 4 psi (28 kPa) blast pressure. The peak pressure destroyed the unglazed outer glass, which fell into the Shock Tube in fragments of different sizes. The glazed inner pane performed well and kept all window fragments intact. The structural silicone maintained its adhesion without any sign of detachment. The window failure met the GSA performance condition 2 that indicates safe glass breakage.

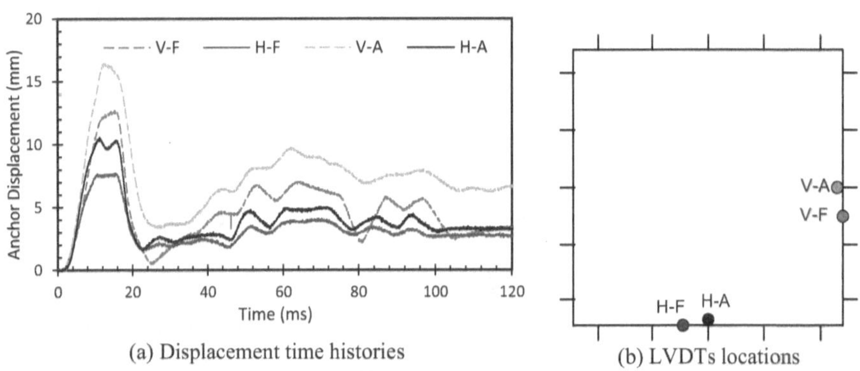

(a) Displacement time histories

(b) LVDTs locations

Figure A.1: Displacement time histories recorded in Test C1

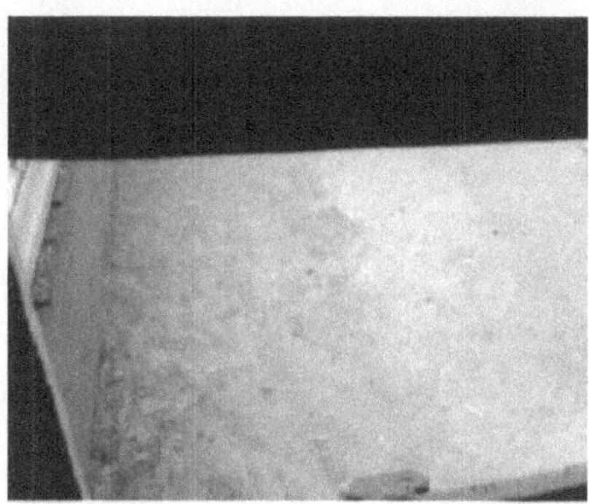

(c) Broken exterior glass inside the Shock
Tube after Test C1

(d) Glazed window after Test C1

Figure A.2: Photographs of C1 after testing

A.2: Test C2

C2 was conducted on the same window that was tested in Test C1, except for increased pressure and impulse. The pressure was increased by a factor of 2.25 to meet the GSA pressure-impulse combinations of 10 psi - 90 psi-msec. The increased level of pressure and impulse resulted in complete failure of the silicone. This caused the glazed panel to fully fly into the witness panel, damaging it slightly. Therefore, LVDTs placed on the vertical frame element and vertical mid-height anchor went out of scale at about 40 msec. Window retention anchors also remained intact without any damage. The window performance indicated high hazardous failure as the window met the GSA performance condition 5.

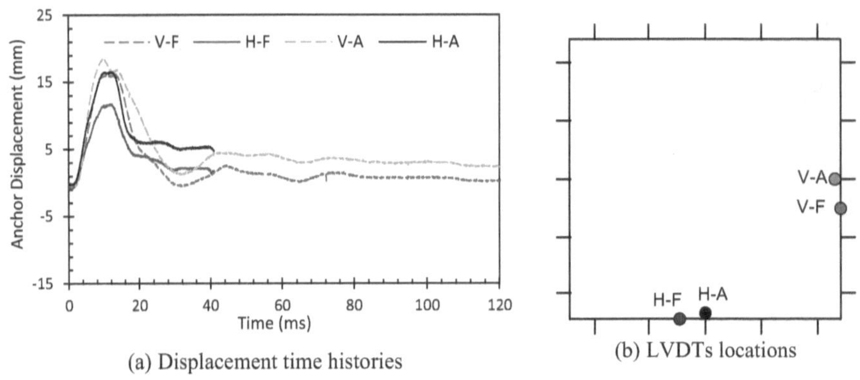

(a) Displacement time histories

(b) LVDTs locations

Figure A.3: Displacement time histories recorded in Test C2

(c) Window after Test C2

(d) Damaged witness panel and glazed pane on the floor after Test C2

Figure A.4:Photographs of C2 after testing

A.3: Test C3

C3 was conducted on a window with aspect ratio of 1 was subjected to 4 psi (28 kPa) blast pressure. The window performed in much the same manner as the previous window in Test C1. The exterior window (unglazed) pane broke into pieces and the fragments dropped into the Shock Tube. The interior pane (filmed) developed extensive fragmentation, but contained within the glazing, without any sign of glazing failure. The window failure met the GSA performance condition 2 that indicates safe glass breakage.

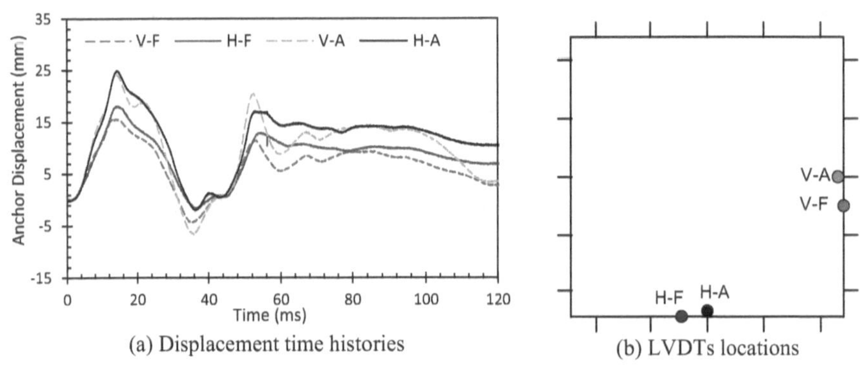

(a) Displacement time histories   (b) LVDTs locations

Figure A.5: Displacement time histories recorded in Test C3

Figure A.6: Photograph of C3 after testing

A.4: Test C4

Test C4 was conducted on the same window tested in Test C3. The increased pressure resulted in the complete failure of the wet glazing, and the window pane flew in and hit the witness panel. Therefore, the anchors did not provide increased resistance as the glazing failed prematurely. The window performance indicated high hazardous failure as the window met the GSA performance condition 5.

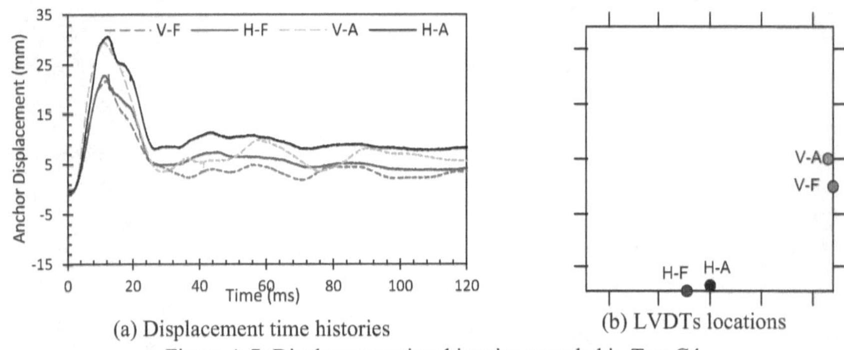

(a) Displacement time histories

(b) LVDTs locations

Figure A.7: Displacement time histories recorded in Test C4

(c) Window after Test C4

(d) Damaged witness panel after Test C4

Figure A.8: Photographs of C4 after testing

A.5: Test C5

C5 was conducted on a rectangular window mounted on a concrete substrate. There was no damage to the frame or the retention anchors. It is clear that the anchors along the long side of the frame developed about twice the displacements as those recorded along the short side. The window showed perfect performance without failure and the window met the GSA performance condition 1.

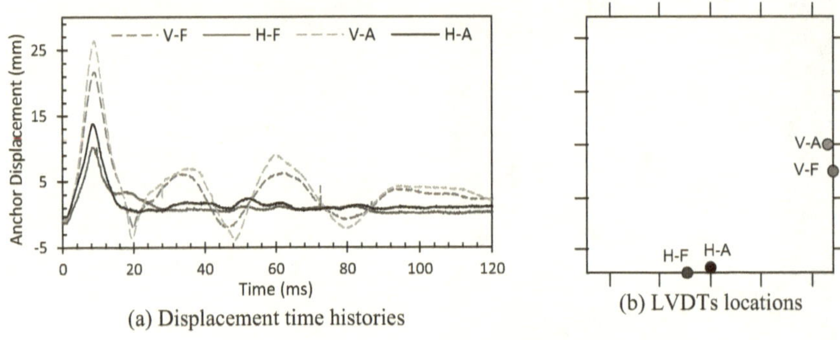

(a) Displacement time histories

(b) LVDTs locations

Figure A.9: Displacement time histories recorded in Test C5

Figure A.10: Photographs of C5 after testing

A.6: Test C6

Test C6 was conducted on the same window. The increased pressure resulted in the complete failure of the outer pane, which broke into pieces and dropped in the Shock Tube. The glazed interior pane also cracked extensively, but the films prevented the fragments from becoming loose and penetrating towards the witness panel. The window failure met the GSA performance condition 2 that indicates safe glass breakage.

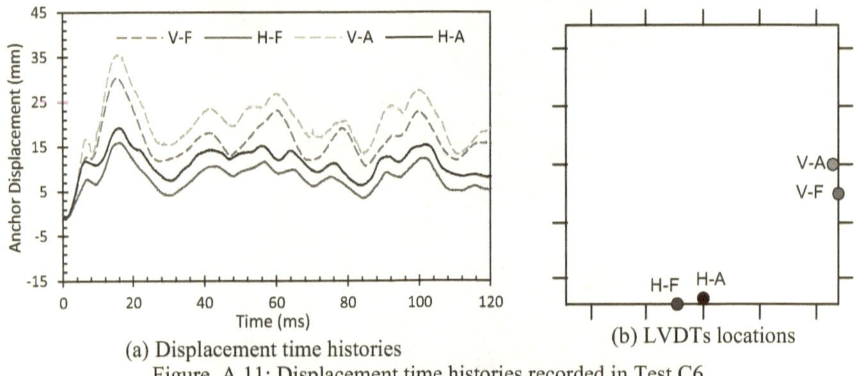

(a) Displacement time histories

(b) LVDTs locations

Figure A.11: Displacement time histories recorded in Test C6

Figure A.12: Photographs of C6 after testing

A.7: Test C7

This test was conducted on a mechanically glazed square window with a 1220 mm square dimension. The displacement measurements were taken on selected anchors and substrate locations as per Configuration 2 instrumentation setup. It was observed that the retention anchors (bolts) were bent after the test, and partially pulled out. Also, the top left side of the window frame slightly moved out of the window opening. Furthermore, the glazed inner glass pane cracked, but the glass fragments remained intact without any penetration of glass shards. However, in this test the outer glass pane (unglazed pane on the blast side) did not crack. It was also noticed that the film de-bonded in some arcas near the right edge location. The window indicated performance condition 3a of the GSA that is under the category of "very low" hazardous failure.

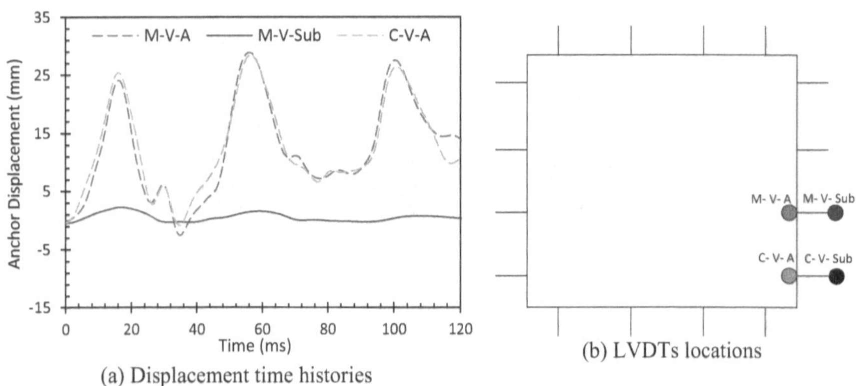

(a) Displacement time histories

(b) LVDTs locations

Figure A.13: Displacement time histories recorded in Test C7

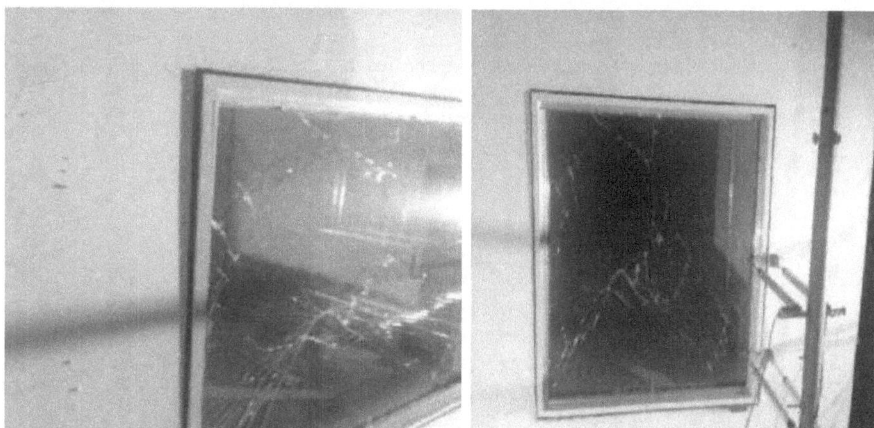

Figure A.14: Photographs of C7 after testing

A.8: Test C8

C8 indicated that this level of loading resulted in the failure of the substrate at some of the anchor locations. The window frame moved out completely causing pulling out of the bolts and the drop-in anchors from the concrete substrate. In some locations partial pull-out cone was created, chipping off the edge concrete. The failure was due to lack of sufficient embedment length as well as using only 3 anchors per side whereas the window stayed intact without any sign of failure except some premature cracks within glass panes. Even though the protective glass pane did fail and kept fragments intact, the failure of the retention anchors led to the penetration of the glass shards into the building indicating performance condition 4 of the GSA.

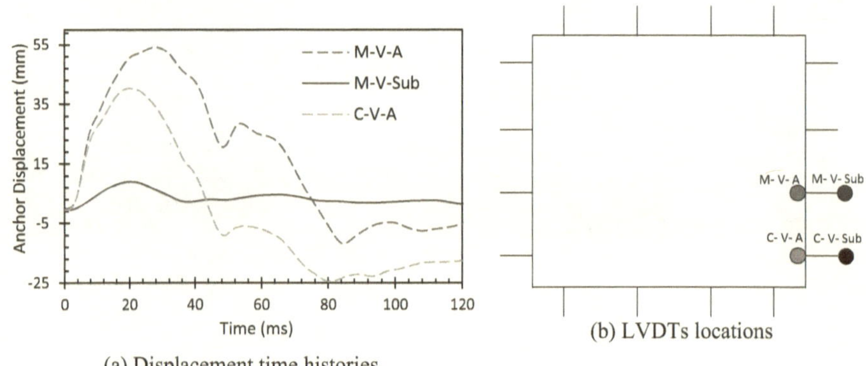

(a) Displacement time histories

(b) LVDTs locations

Figure A.15: Displacement time histories recorded in Test C8

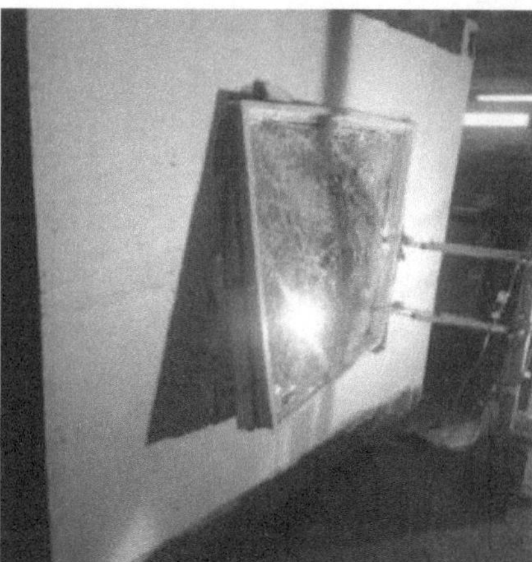

Figure A.16: Photographs of C8 after testing

A.9: Test C9

Test C9 was conducted on a square window with increased number of retention anchors and increased embedment length of the drop-in anchors. the inner glass pane cracked excessively, but the glass fragments remained intact. The outer unglazed glass pane failed completely. The data from this test was lost due to software problems. The window failure met the GSA performance condition 2 that indicates safe glass breakage.

Displacement time histories are not available

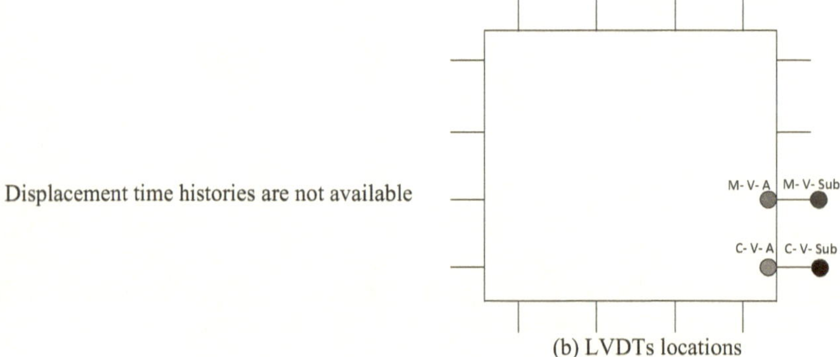

(b) LVDTs locations

Figure A.17: Displacement time histories recorded in Test C9

Figure A.18: Photographs of C9 after testing

A.10: Test C10

After test C10 it was noticed that most of the retention anchor bolts were noticeably bent and partially pulled out, also pulling out the drop-in anchors from the concrete. The 3-ply film was not sufficient for the square window area and the pressure applied to this window. The rupturing of the protective film was observed. Further, the upper horizontal window stops moved out of its original place. The rupture of the protective films led the fragments to reach the witness panel, and the performance of the window can be rated as the GSA condition 4.

Displacement time histories are not available

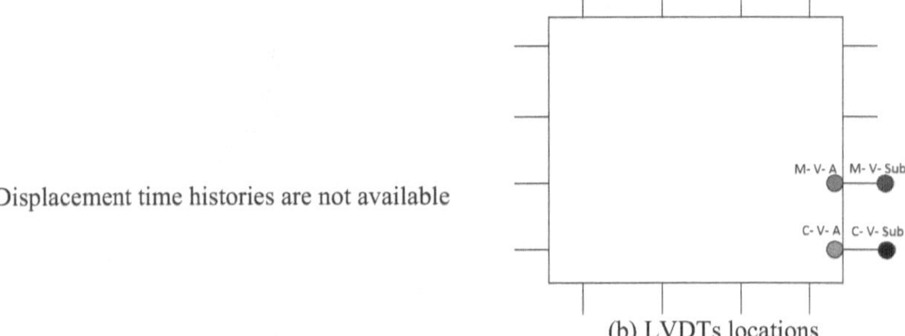

(b) LVDTs locations

Figure A.19: Displacement time histories recorded in Test C10

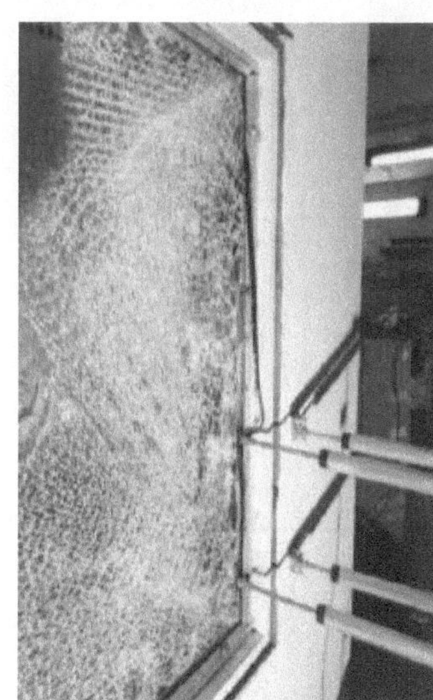

Figure A.20: Photographs of C10 after testing

A.11: Test C11

Test C11 involved a rectangular window, mechanically glazed using three plies of film. The window was subjected to 4 psi pressure, as indicated in Fig. 43(a). This level of pressure did not cause any damage neither to the glass nor the frame system. The anchor bolts remained elastic and no deformation was observed in the window frame. The window showed perfect performance without failure and the window met the GSA performance condition 1.

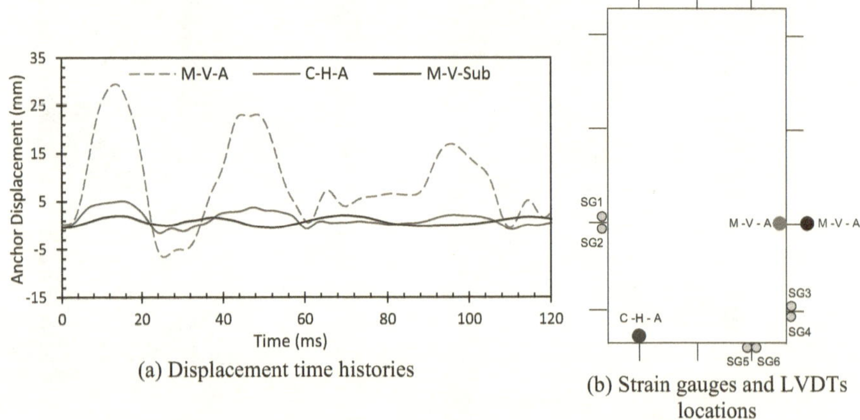

(a) Displacement time histories

(b) Strain gauges and LVDTs locations

Figure A.21: Displacement time histories recorded in Test C11

Figure A.22: Photographs of C11 after testing

A.12: Test C12

The rectangular window tested in test C11 was subjected to 10 psi-90 psi-msec pressure-impulse combination. The window did not experience any damage to the glass and the glazing system. This was the only window among all the windows tested in the experimental program that did not suffer damage to the window glass. However, many anchors became loose and partially pulled out. This window had 50 mm concrete cover over the anchors on the failure side, and 100 mm on the opposite side. The window showed perfect performance without failure and the window met the GSA performance condition 1.

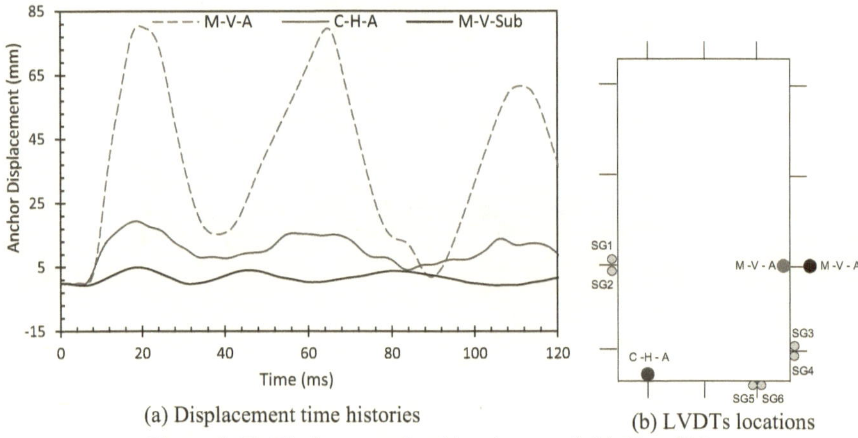

(a) Displacement time histories

(b) LVDTs locations

Figure A.23: Displacement time histories recorded in Test C12

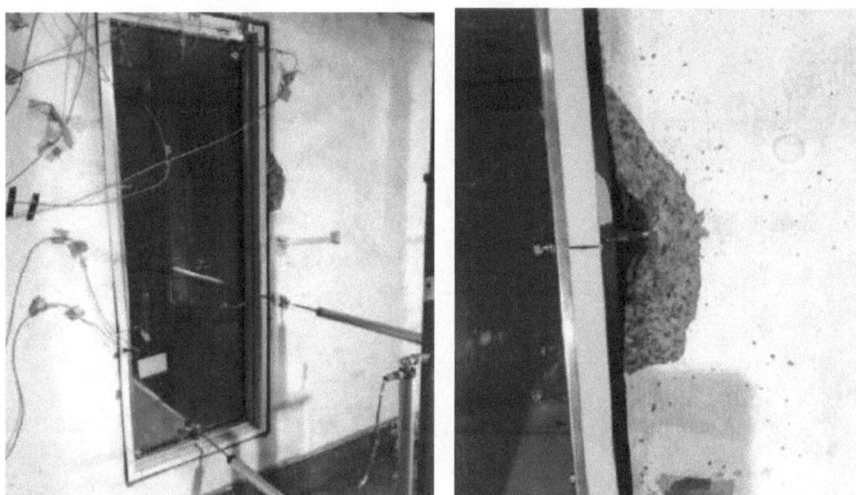

Figure A.24: Photographs of C12 after testing

A.13: Test C13

C13 was companion to the previous window used for Test C11 and C12, except for the anchor pattern. The window did not experience any damage. There was no cracking in either pane at 28 kPa level of pressure. The window showed perfect performance without failure and the window met the GSA performance condition 1.

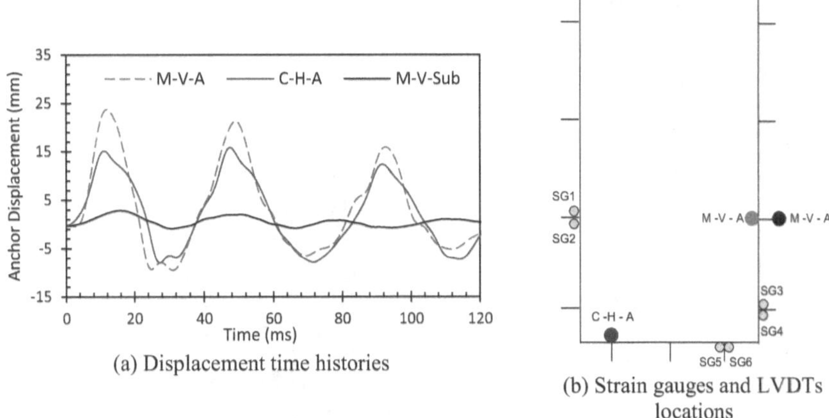

(a) Displacement time histories

(b) Strain gauges and LVDTs locations

Figure A. 25: Displacement time histories recorded in Test C13

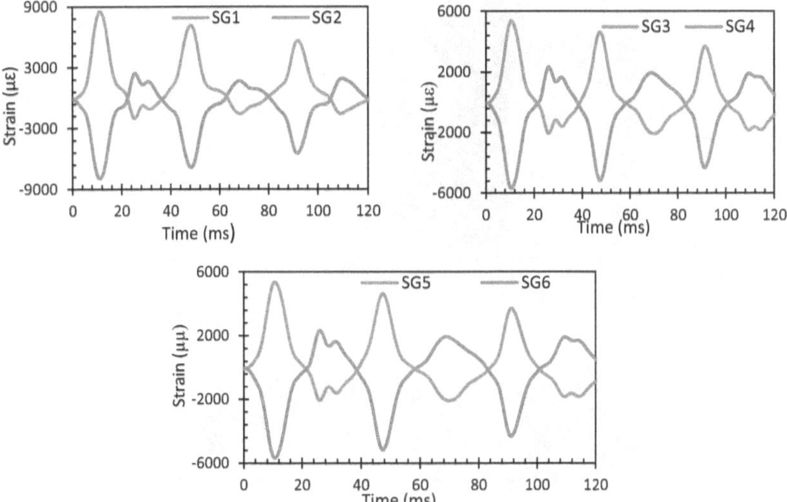

Figure A. 26: Example of strain time histories recorded in anchors (Test C13)

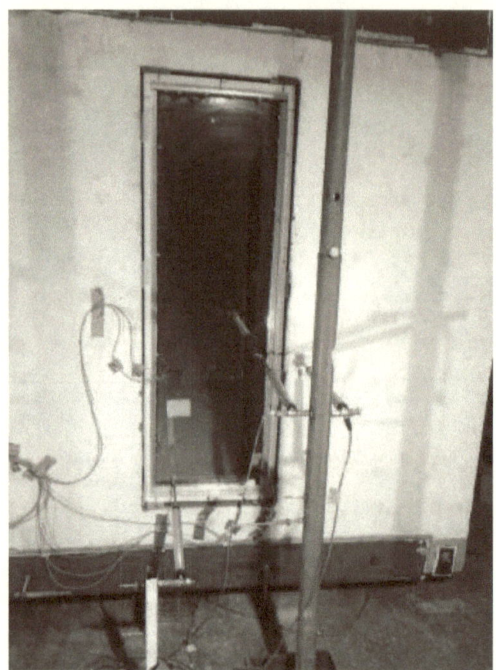

Figure A.27: Photographs of C13 after testing

A.14: Test C14

Test C14 was a retest of the rectangular window tested in test C13. The outer pane glass on the blast side was destroyed completely, but the inner pane, protected by glazing, performed well, with controlled cracking. The glazing prevented the glass fragments from penetrating inside. The window failure met the GSA performance condition 2 that indicates safe glass breakage.

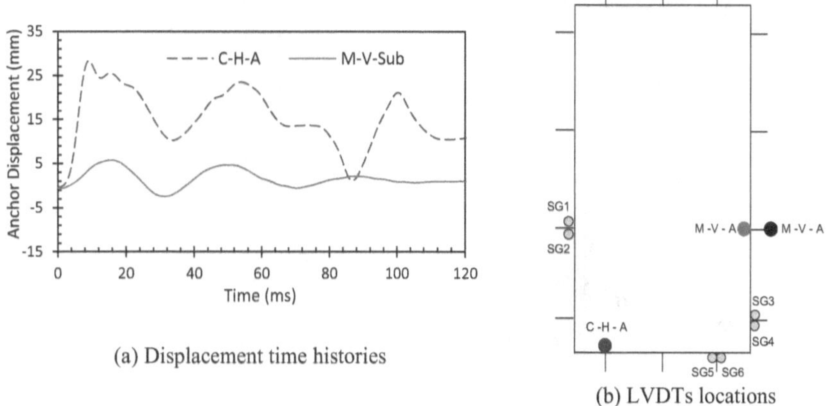

(a) Displacement time histories

(b) LVDTs locations

Figure A.28: Displacement time histories recorded in Test C14

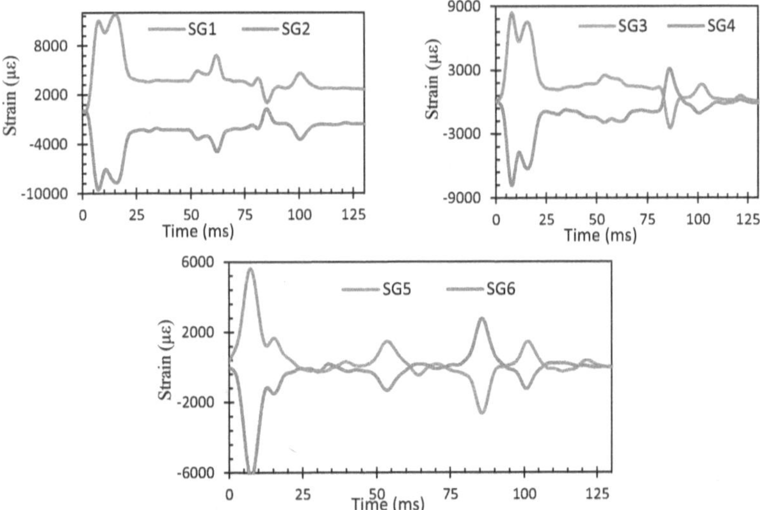

Figure A.29: Strain time histories recorded in Test C14

Figure A.30: Photograph of C14 after testing

A.15: Test S1

C1 was conducted on a rectangular window with aspect ratio of 3. During the test the window system vibrated under the influence of the primary positive pressure, but also the effects of gradually damping out positive-negative pressure cycles. The main pressure peak destroyed the unglazed outer glass, which fell into the Shock Tube in fragments of different sizes. The glazed inner pane performed well and kept all window fragments intact, without any failure of the film and the wet anchor. The window failure met the GSA performance condition 2 that indicates safe glass breakage.

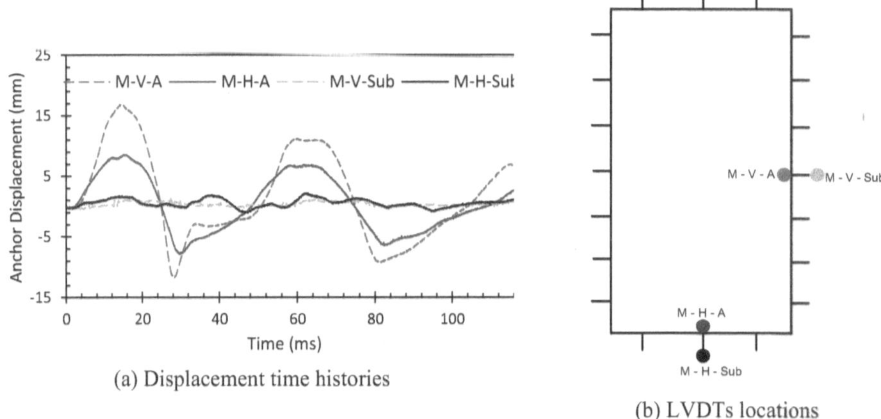

(a) Displacement time histories

(b) LVDTs locations

Figure A.31: Displacement time histories recorded in Test S1

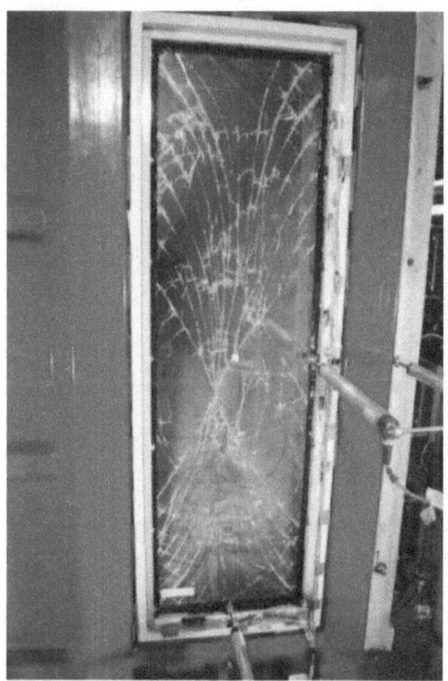

Figure A.32: Photograph of S1 after testing

A.16: Test S2

Test S2 was conducted on the same window that was tested in Test 1. The glazed glass was totally detached from the frame and a large amount of window debris was thrown on the witness panel. Subsequent examination of the frame indicated some twisting of the window stop, while remaining attached to the frame. Anchors did not experience any damage. The window performance indicated high hazardous failure as the window met the GSA performance condition 5.

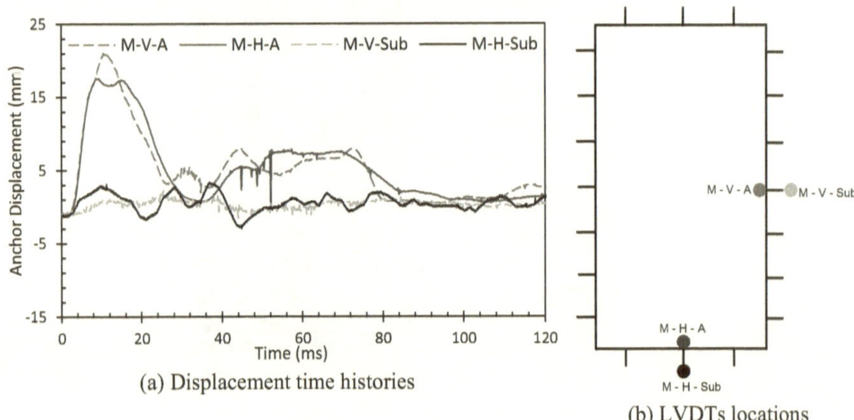

(a) Displacement time histories

(b) LVDTs locations

Figure A.33: Displacement time histories recorded in Test C2

Figure A.34: Photographs of C2 after testing

Figure A.35: Photographs of debris thrown and witness panel showing GSA demarcation line for Test S2

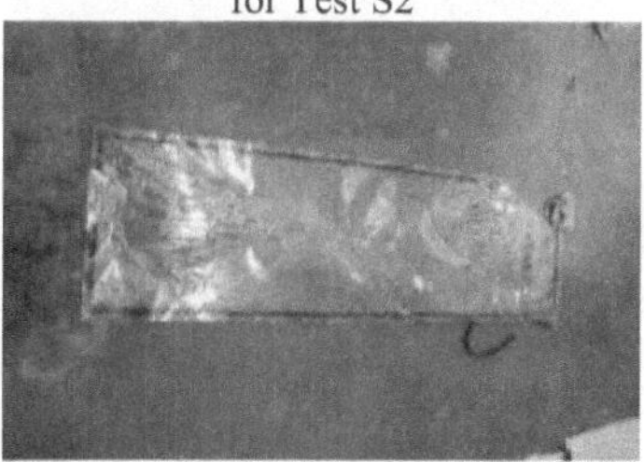

Figure A.36: Photograph of filmed window after removal, following Test S2

A.17: Test S3

Test S3 was conducted on another rectangular window. The window sustained the pressure time history without any damage. Subsequently the window was retested under Shot 1 again (under 4 psi target pressure) with a view of a possible error during the shot. However, the same pressure time history was obtained, with the same behaviour of the window, i.e., there was no damage on either of the two panes. The window showed perfect performance without failure and the window met the GSA performance condition 1.

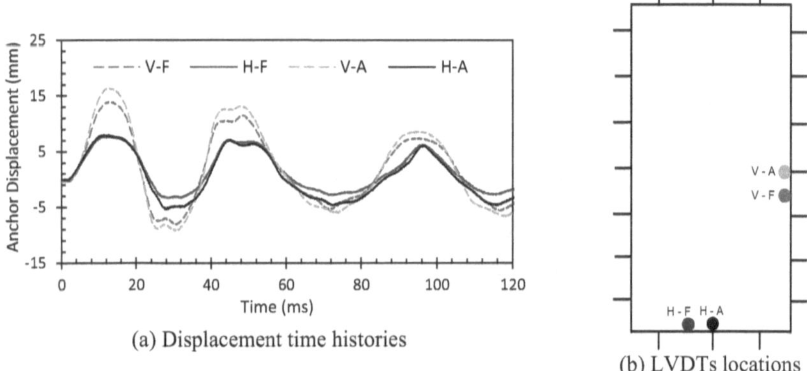

(a) Displacement time histories

(b) LVDTs locations

Figure A.37: Displacement time histories recorded in Test S3

Figure A.38: Photographs of S3 after testing

A.18: Test S4

The increased level of pressure and impulse resulted in partial failure of the silicone. This caused the glazed panel to partially detach from the left frame element at about 1/3 the height, also causing the tearing of the single-ply film. The panel remained attached to the frame, though it was significantly damaged. The window retention anchors did not experience any damage. The rupture of the protective films led the fragments to reach the witness panel, and the performance of the window can be rated as the GSA condition 4.

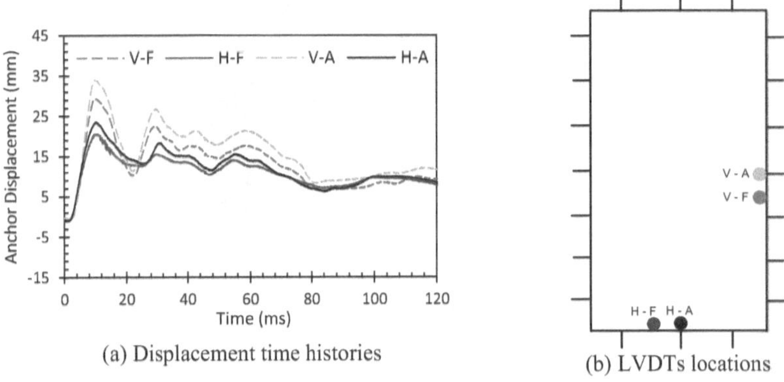

(a) Displacement time histories

(b) LVDTs locations

Figure A.39: Displacement time histories recorded in Test S4

Figure A.40: Photographs of S4 after testing

A.19: Test S5

Test S5 was conducted on a square window. The window performed well under 4 psi. The unprotected outer pane failed completely and fell into the shock tube. The wet glazing was able to keep the cracked inner pane intact without any debris flying. The window failure met the GSA performance condition 2 that indicates safe glass breakage.

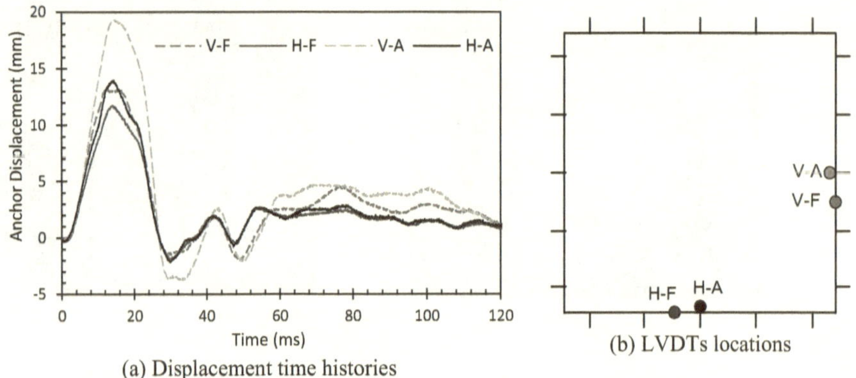

(a) Displacement time histories

(b) LVDTs locations

Figure A.41: Displacement time histories recorded in Test S5

Figure A.42: Photographs of S5 after testing

A.20: Test S6

Test S6 was a re-test of the window that had been tested earlier in Test S5. During this test the wet glazed inner pane detached from its frame and flew in towards the witness panel, hitting and damaging the panel. The is lower than the displacements of anchors observed in other square windows tested. The relatively low value of displacement can be explained by the premature failure of the window glazing, thereby limiting the force applied on the retention anchors. The window performance indicated high hazardous failure as the window met the GSA performance condition 5.

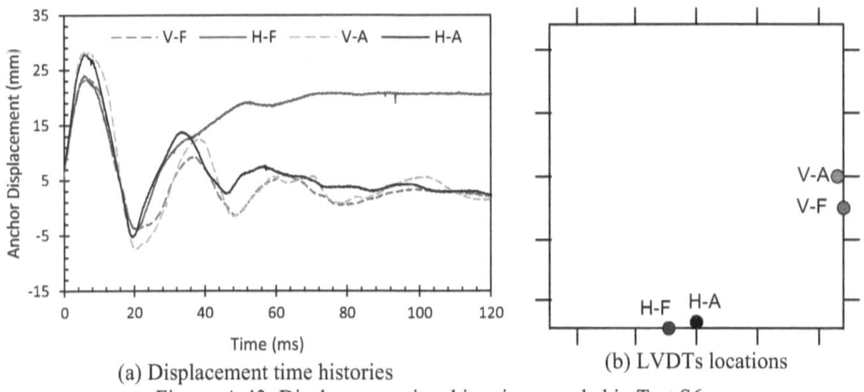

(a) Displacement time histories

(b) LVDTs locations

Figure A.43: Displacement time histories recorded in Test S6

(a) Broken outer pane

(b) Wet glazed inner pane on the floor

Figure A.44: Photographs of S6 after testing

A.21: Test S7

Test S7 was conducted on a rectangular residential window. The outer unprotected pane failed during the test. The inner wet glazed pane performed well under 28 kPa. The window failure met the GSA performance condition 2 that indicates safe glass breakage.

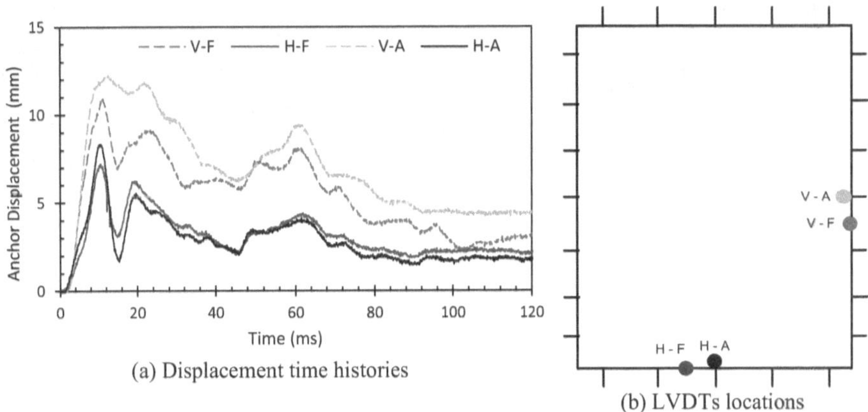

(a) Displacement time histories

(b) LVDTs locations

Figure A.45: Displacement time histories recorded in Test S7

Figure A.46: Photograph of S7 after testing

A.22: Test S8

Test S8 was a re-test of the window that had been tested earlier in Test S7. This time the pressure and impulse were increased to of 10 psi and 90 psi-msec, respectively. During the test the wet glazed inner pane got detached and flew in and hit the witness panel. The window performance indicated high hazardous failure as the window met the GSA performance condition 5.

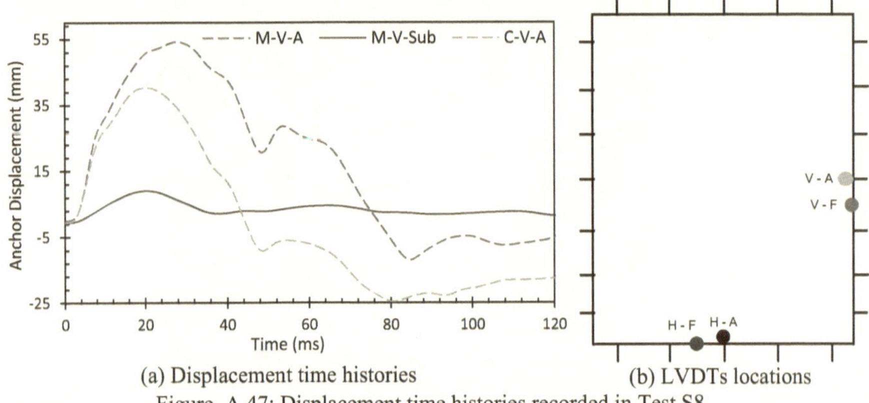

(a) Displacement time histories   (b) LVDTs locations

Figure A.47: Displacement time histories recorded in Test S8

Figure A.48: Photograph of S8 after testing

A.23: Test S9

Test S9 was conducted on a rectangular residential window. The outer unprotected pane failed during the test. The inner wet glazed pane performed well under this level of pressure. The window failure met the GSA performance condition 2 that indicates safe glass breakage.

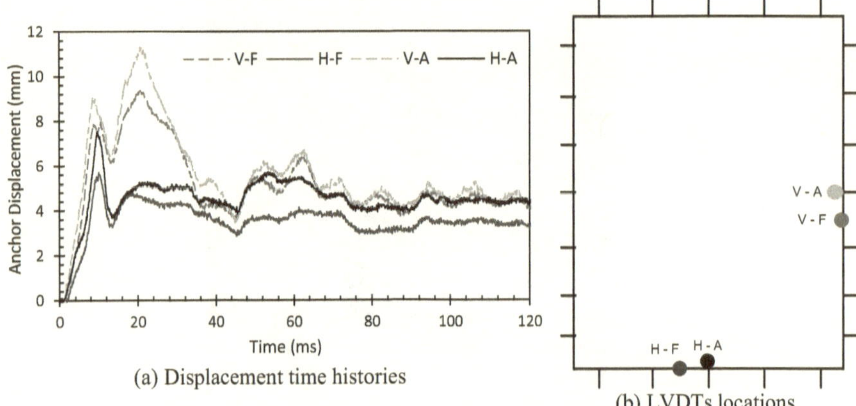

(a) Displacement time histories

(b) LVDTs locations

Figure A.49: Displacement time histories recorded in Test S9

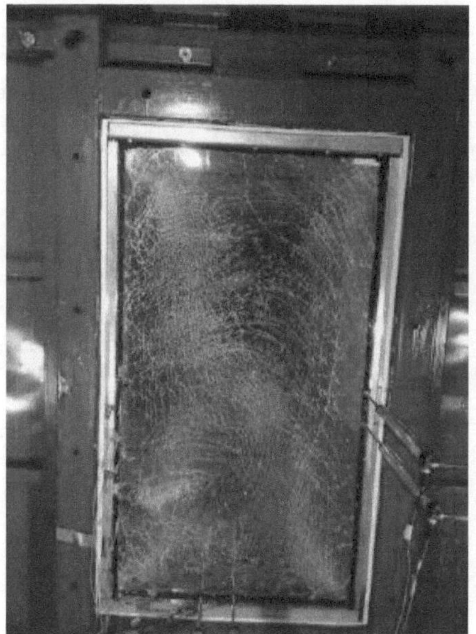

Figure A.50: Photograph of S9 after testing

A.24: Test S10

Test S10 was a re-test of the window that had been tested earlier in Test S9. During this test the unprotected outer pane broke. The wet glazed inner pane failed by rupturing of the film, as this window had only a single ply of film. The window performance indicated high hazardous failure as the window met the GSA performance condition 5.

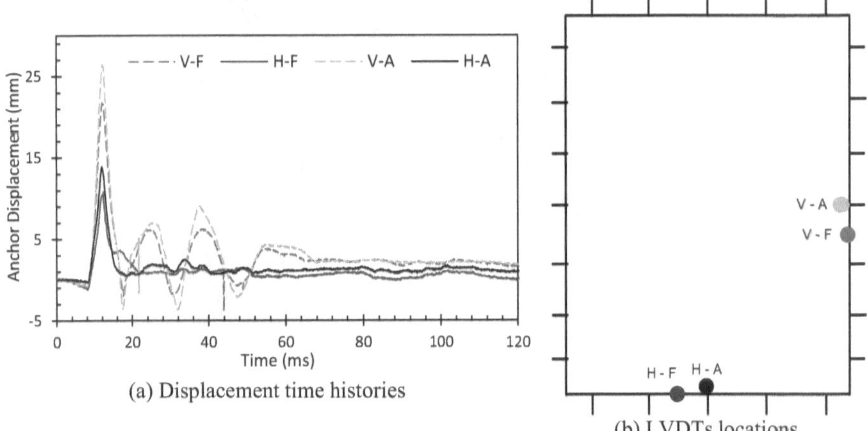

(a) Displacement time histories

(b) LVDTs locations

Figure A.51: Displacement time histories recorded in Test S10

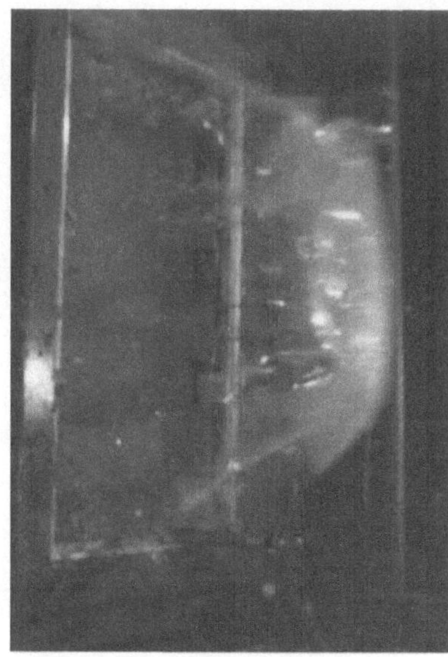

Figure A.52: Photographs of S10 after testing

A.25: Test S11

Test S11 was conducted on a square window. The window performed well under this pressure level (28 kPa). The outer unprotected pane failed, but the inner glazed pane performed well and did not allow any debris penetration. The window failure met the GSA performance condition 2 that indicates safe glass breakage.

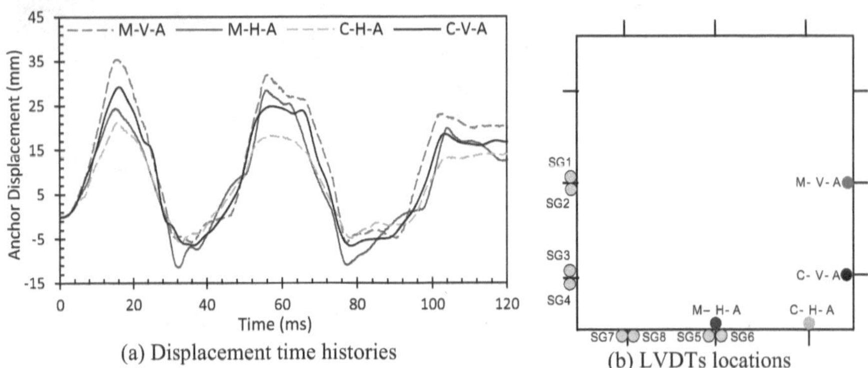

(a) Displacement time histories   (b) LVDTs locations

Figure A.53: Displacement time histories recorded in Test S11

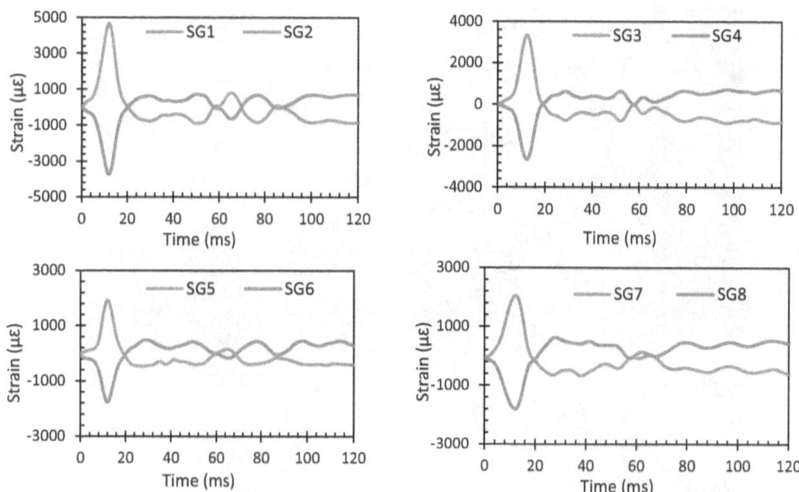

Figure A.54:An example of strain time histories recorded in anchors (Test S11)

Figure A.55: Photograph of S11 after testing

A.26: Test S12

Test S12 was a re-test of the window that had been tested earlier in test S11. Neither the four anchors used per side, nor the three plies of film used were sufficient for the window to maintain the integrity of the glazed pane. The window frame, as well as the mechanical anchors failed. The glazed pane flew into the witness panel. The window performance indicated high hazardous failure as the window met the GSA performance condition 5.

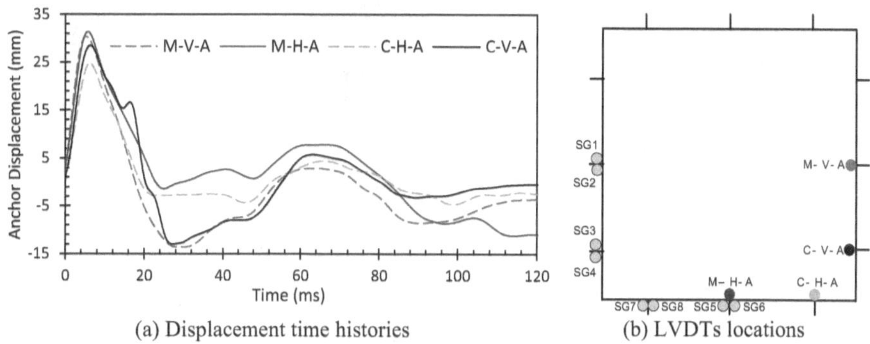

<table>
<tr><td>(a) Displacement time histories</td><td>(b) LVDTs locations</td></tr>
</table>

Figure A.56: Displacement time histories recorded in Test S12

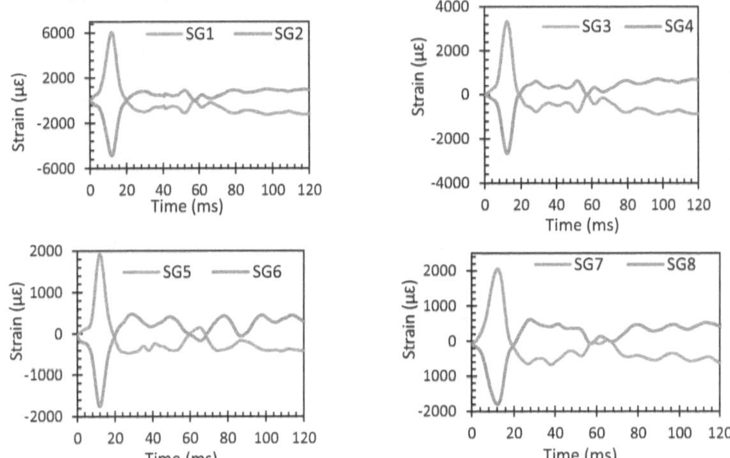

Figure A.57: Example of strain time histories recorded in anchors (Test S12)

Figure A.58: Photograph of S12 after testing

A.27: Test S13

Test S13 was conducted on a companion square window. The window performed well under this pressure level (28 kPa). The outer unprotected pane failed, but the inner glazed pane performed well and did not allow any debris penetration. The window failure met the GSA performance condition 2 that indicates safe glass breakage.

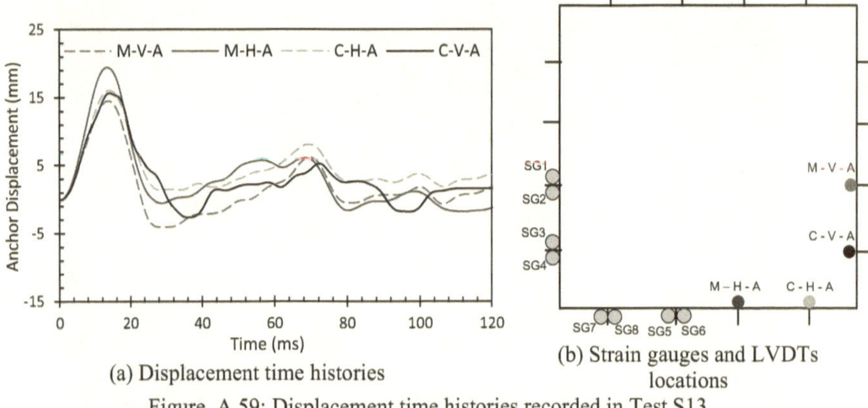

(a) Displacement time histories

(b) Strain gauges and LVDTs locations

Figure A.59: Displacement time histories recorded in Test S13

Figure A.60: Photograph of S13 after testing

A.28: Test S14

S14 was performed by applying an increased pressure of 69 kPa. The four anchors used per side were able to maintain the integrity of the overall window system, though many retention anchors failed. Three anchors on one of the vertical frame elements, and two on the other vertical element failed. One of the anchors at the top horizontal frame element also ruptured. The window system attained its full capacity, while sacrificing some of the retention anchors. The window failure met the GSA performance condition 2 that indicates safe glass breakage.

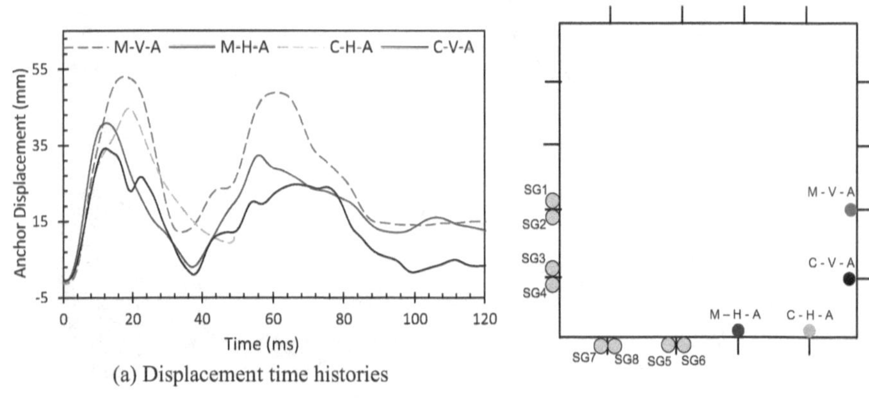

(a) Displacement time histories

(b) LVDTs locations

Figure A.61: Displacement time histories recorded in Test C14

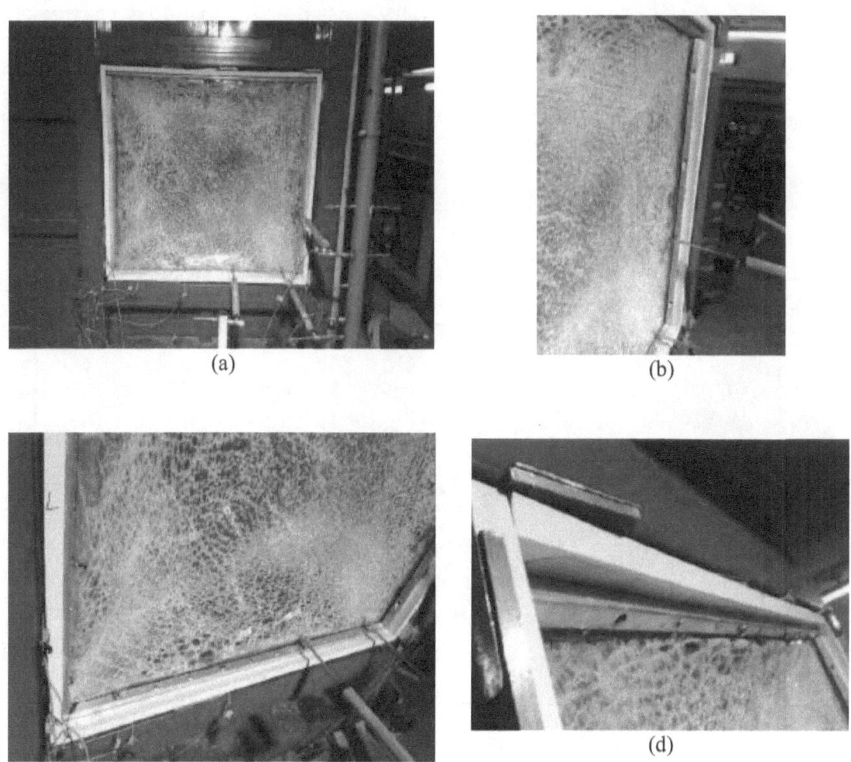

(a)

(b)

(c)

(d)

Figure A.62: Photographs of performance of window retention anchors after Test S14 and the failure locations for window retention anchors

A.29: Test S15

Test S15 was conducted on a rectangular window with three plies of protective films of a total thickness of 14 mils. The window performed well under this pressure level (28 kPa). The outer unprotected pane failed, but the inner glazed pane performed well and did not allow any debris penetration. The window failure met the GSA performance condition 2 that indicates safe glass breakage.

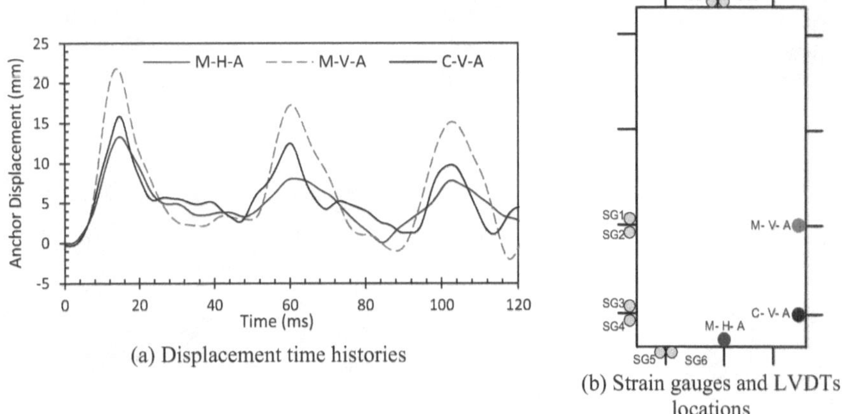

(a) Displacement time histories

(b) Strain gauges and LVDTs locations

Figure A.63: Displacement time histories recorded in Test S15

Figure A.64: Photograph of S15 after testing

A.30: Test S16

The same rectangular window was re-tested tested with target pressure value of 69 kPa. The retention anchors were sufficient to maintain the integrity of the window system, but they were damaged significantly. Four anchors along the vertical sides sheared off and all the remaining anchors bent significantly, indicating substantial yielding. Both the frame and the remaining anchors developed significant deformations. The glazing suffered from localized damage. The films delaminated from the glass at several locations, while locally pulling out of the frame along the edges. The window failure met the GSA performance condition 2 that indicates safe glass breakage.

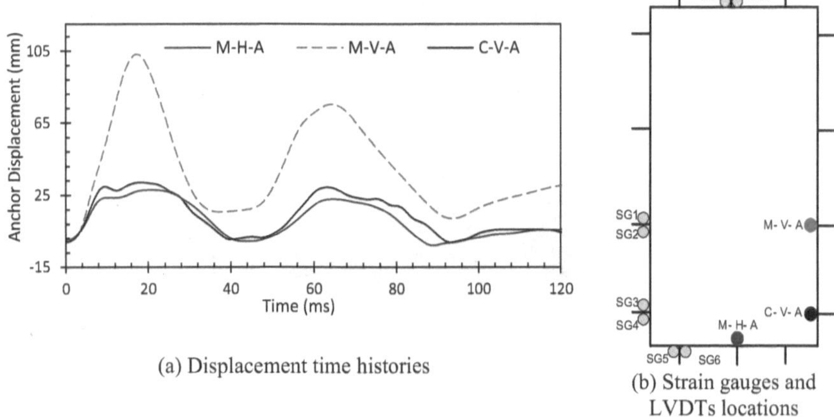

(a) Displacement time histories

(b) Strain gauges and LVDTs locations

Figure A.65: Displacement time histories recorded in Test S16

(a)

(b)

(c)

Figure A.66: Photographs of window after Test S16

Appendix B:

Shock Tube Test Data for Windows on Concrete Block and Stone Masonry Substrates

Appendix B contains the results of 16 shock tube tests conducted on windows secured on concrete block and stone masonry walls as substrates. Each window was subjected to two blast pressure-impulse combinations; 28 kPa – 207 kPa-ms and 69 kPa – 621 kPa-ms. A brief description of each test is given, followed by the actual recorded time histories for reflected pressures and anchor displacements. Chapter 3 provides a concise presentation of the results, analysis of test data, and discussions. Table 3.1(b) provides a summary of test parameters. This appendix presents recorded and observed performance of each window test. Each window is labelled with designations B for concrete block substrates and ST for stone masonry substrates. The number that appears next to the test designation indicates the sequence of window tests conducted with odd number indicating tests under 28 kPa-207 kPa-ms and even numbers indicating tests under 69 kPa – 621 kPa-ms. Displacement time-history for selected anchors, window frame edges, and substrates are potted for each test. Strain values developed in the retention anchors are presented as examples of strain time-history for selected tests.

B.1: Test B1

Test B1 was conducted on a double pane square window with 1220 x 1220 mm (48" by 48") frame dimensions. The unprotected outer pane failed and fell into the Shock Tube. After the test, the inner glazed pane cracked, but the glazing sustained the broken glass without any penetration of the debris. There were hairline cracks observed in the substrate along some of the mortar joints. Fig. 86 also shows the glazed pane after the test. The window failure met the GSA performance condition 2 that indicates safe glass breakage.

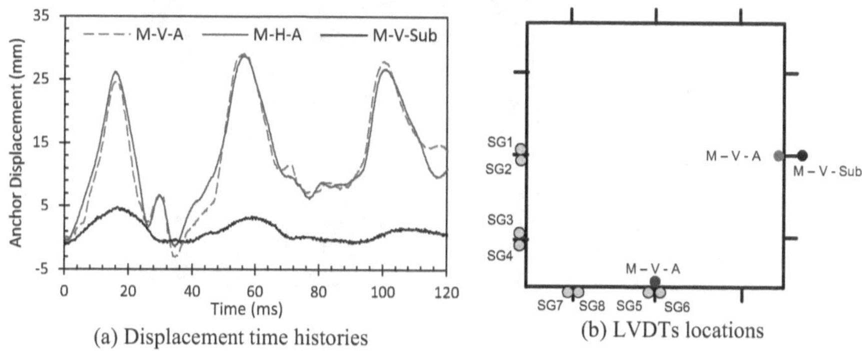

(a) Displacement time histories   (b) LVDTs locations

Figure B.1: Displacement time histories recorded in Test B1

Figure B.2: Photograph of B1 after testing

B.2: Test B2

Test B2 was conducted on the same square window with 1220 x 1220 mm frame dimensions, tested earlier as Test B1. The window did not perform well under this level of pressure. The film ruptured during the test, resulting in the penetration of significant glass debris towards the witness panel. The substrate showed increased hairline cracks along the mortar joints, but otherwise did not suffer any damage. The rupture of the protective films led the fragments to reach the witness panel, and the performance of the window can be rated as the GSA condition 4.

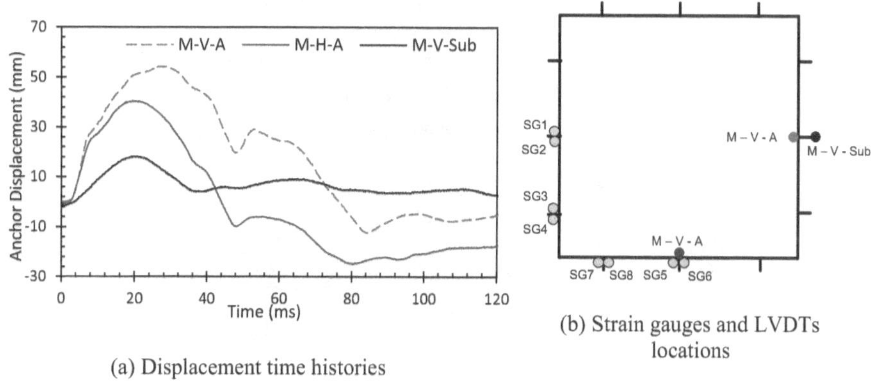

(a) Displacement time histories

(b) Strain gauges and LVDTs locations

Figure B.3: Displacement time histories recorded in Test B2

Figure B.4: Photograph of B2 after testing

B.3: Test B3

Test B3 was companion to the previously tested square window (Test B1) except for the increased number of plies of protective film. The unprotected outer pane failed and fell into the Shock Tube. The inner glazed pane cracked, but the glazing sustained the broken glass without any penetration of the debris. Unfortunately, there were instrumentation problems during the test, and no data was recorded. The window failure met the GSA performance condition 2 that indicates safe glass breakage.

Displacement time histories are not available

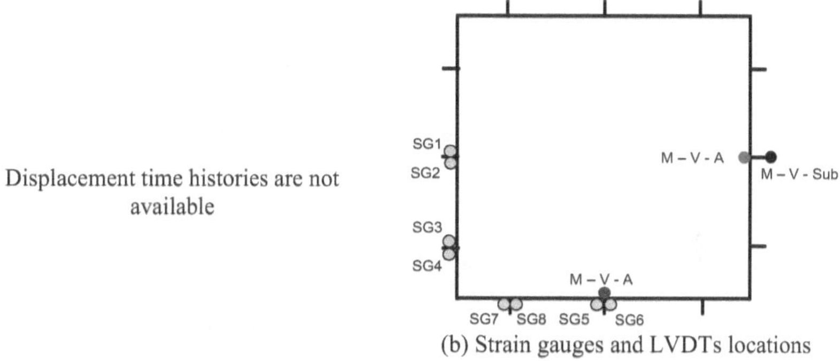

(b) Strain gauges and LVDTs locations

Figure B.5: Displacement time histories recorded in Test B3

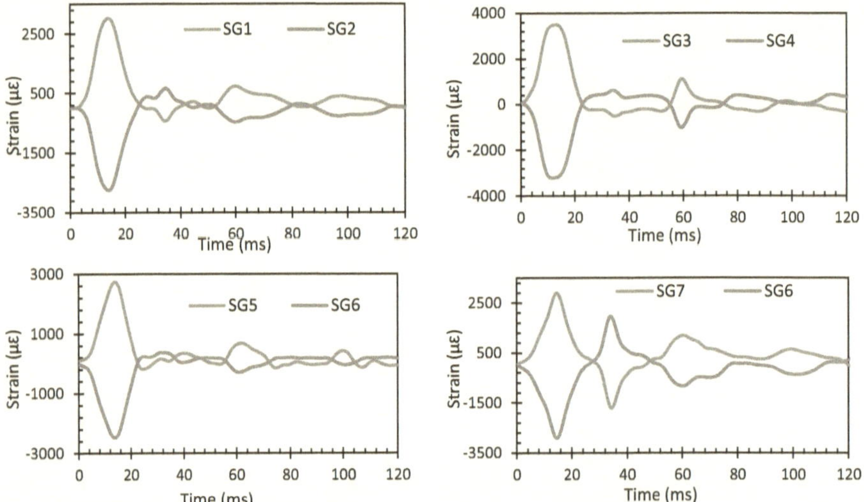

Figure B.6: Strain time histories recorded in Test B3

Figure B.7: Photograph of B3 after testing

B.4:   Test B4

Test B4 was conducted on the previous square window tested earlier (Test B3). The increased number of plies improved the behaviour in this test, and unlike the companion Test B2 with 3 plies of protective film, the glazing did not fail. The mechanical glazing with 5 plies of protective film was able to contain broken glass shards. Unfortunately, there were instrumentation problems during the test, and no data was recorded. The window failure met the GSA performance condition 2 that indicates safe glass breakage.

Displacement time histories are not available

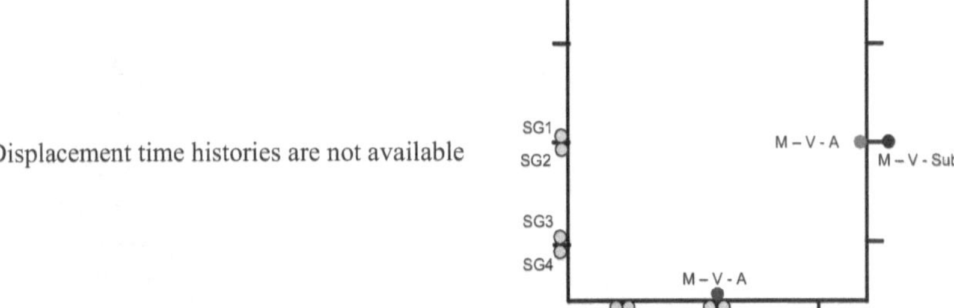

(b) Strain gauges and LVDTs locations

Figure B.8: Displacement time histories recorded in Test B4

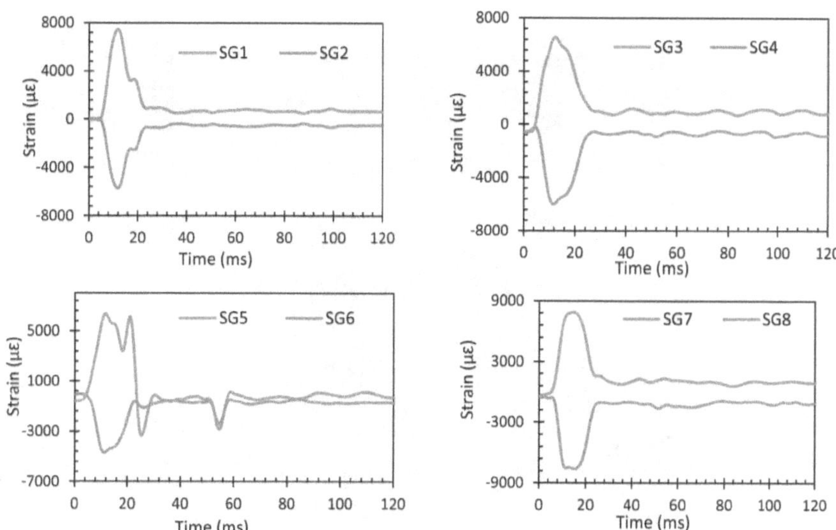

Figure B.9: Strain time histories recorded in Test B4

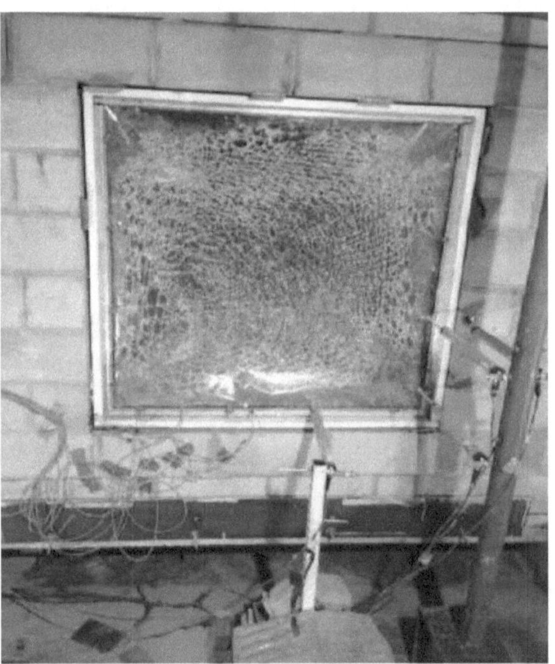

Figure B.10: Photograph of window after Test B4

B.5:   Test B5

Test B5 was conducted on a rectangular window with 560 mm by 1676 mm frame dimensions. The window performed well during the test under this level of pressure. The unprotected outer pane failed and fell into the Shock Tube. The inner glazed pane cracked, but the glazing sustained the broken glass without any penetration of the debris. The window failure met the GSA performance condition 2 that indicates safe glass breakage.

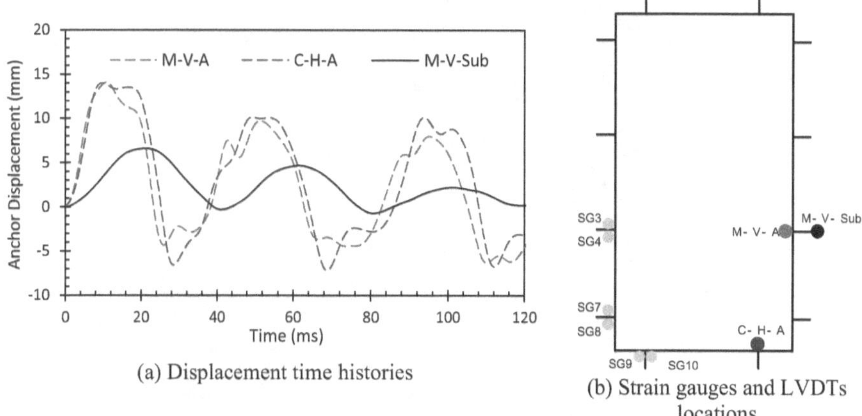

(a) Displacement time histories

(b) Strain gauges and LVDTs locations

Figure B.11: Displacement time histories recorded in Test B5

Figure B.12: Photograph of B5 after testing

B.6:   Test B6

Test B5 was conducted on the same rectangular window that was tested in test B5. It performed well and the glazing did not allow the broken glass shards to penetrate inside. The window failure met the GSA performance condition 2 that indicates safe glass breakage.

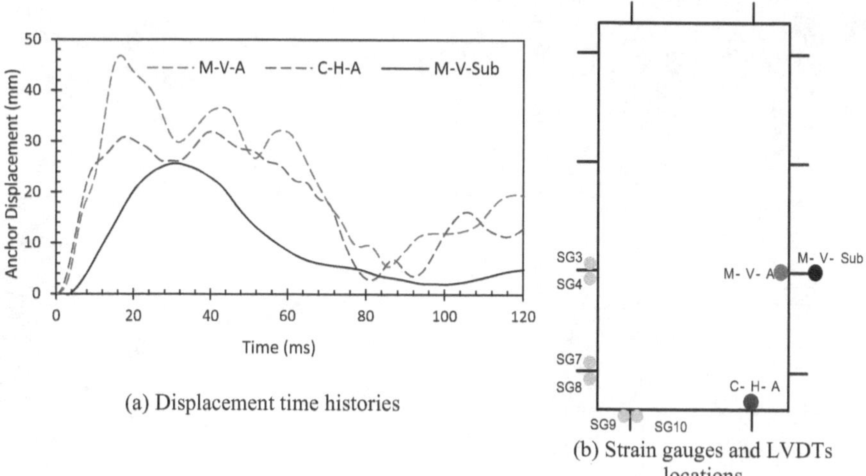

(a) Displacement time histories

(b) Strain gauges and LVDTs locations

Figure B.13: Displacement time histories recorded in Test B6

Figure B.14: Photographs of window and anchors after Test B6

B.7: Test B7

Test B7 was conducted on a rectangular window with 560 mm by 1676 mm frame dimensions. As before, the window performed well during this level of pressure. The unprotected outer pane failed and fell into the Shock Tube. The inner glazed pane cracked, but the glazing maintained the broken glass in place without any penetration of debris. The window failure met the GSA performance condition 2 that indicates safe glass breakage.

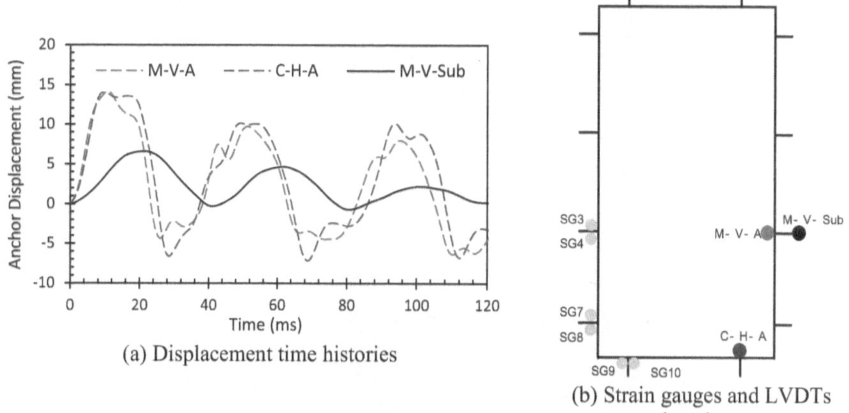

(a) Displacement time histories

(b) Strain gauges and LVDTs locations

Figure B.15: Displacement time histories recorded in Test B7

Figure B.16: Photograph of B7 after testing

B.8:   Test B8

Test B8 was conducted on the same rectangular window that was tested in test B7. This time rupturing of the films was observed in the short (horizontal) direction of the window pane. The anchors experience significant bending, implying post-yield behaviour. Some of the anchors partially pulled out, indicating the rupturing of the film occurred close to the capacity of the anchors. The premature rupturing of the films was attributed to relatively poor installation of the films, as few pockets of delamination of the films were observed prior to testing. The rupture of the protective films led the fragments to reach the witness panel, and the performance of the window can be rated as the GSA condition 4.

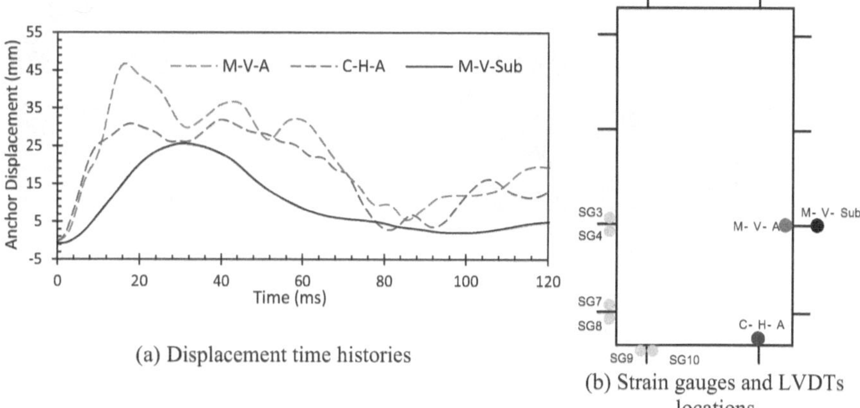

(a) Displacement time histories

(b) Strain gauges and LVDTs locations

Figure B.17: Displacement time histories recorded in Test B8

 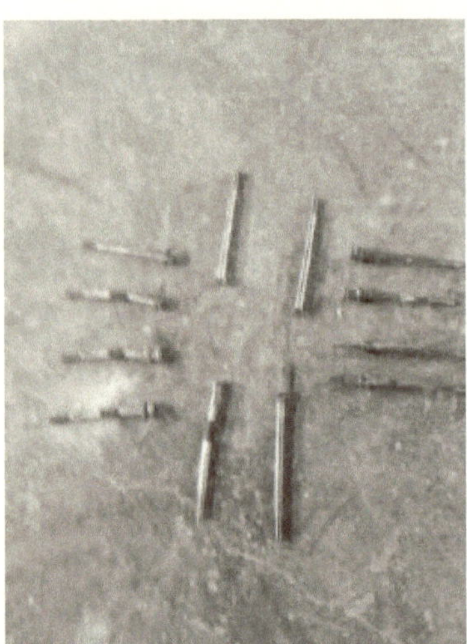

Figure B.18: Photograph of window after Test B8

B.9: Test B9

The window tested in Test B9 was companion to the previous two rectangular windows. The window did not experience any damage. Neither pane was cracked. This may be explained by the fact that the substrate used had been tested under 6 previous shots with observed cracks forming in the mortar joints, becoming softer. As if was consistently observed, and as it will be discussed under Sec. 4, softer substrates were less critical as they would experience more displacement at window anchor locations, and would tend to move along with the window, without stressing the windows excessively. The window showed perfect performance without failure and the window met the GSA performance condition 1.

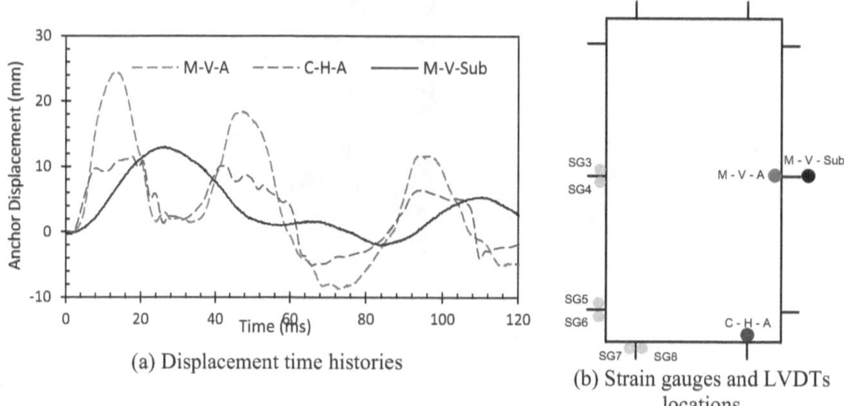

(a) Displacement time histories

(b) Strain gauges and LVDTs locations

Figure B.19: Displacement time histories recorded in Test B9

Figure B.20: Photograph of B9 after testing

B.10: Test B10

Test B10 was conducted on the same rectangular window that was tested in Test B9. The window performed well with failure of the outer unprotected pane and cracking of the glazed inner pane, while maintaining the integrity of the overall system. There was no penetration of glass shards. The retention anchors experienced significant bending, especially along the long sides. There was some penetration of small glass shards, reaching up to the witness panel. The window failure met the GSA performance condition 2 that indicates safe glass breakage.

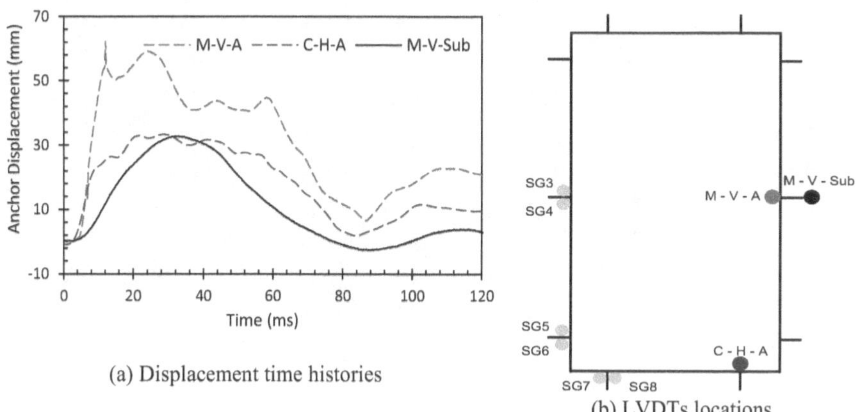

(a) Displacement time histories

(b) LVDTs locations

Figure B.21: Displacement time histories recorded in Test B10

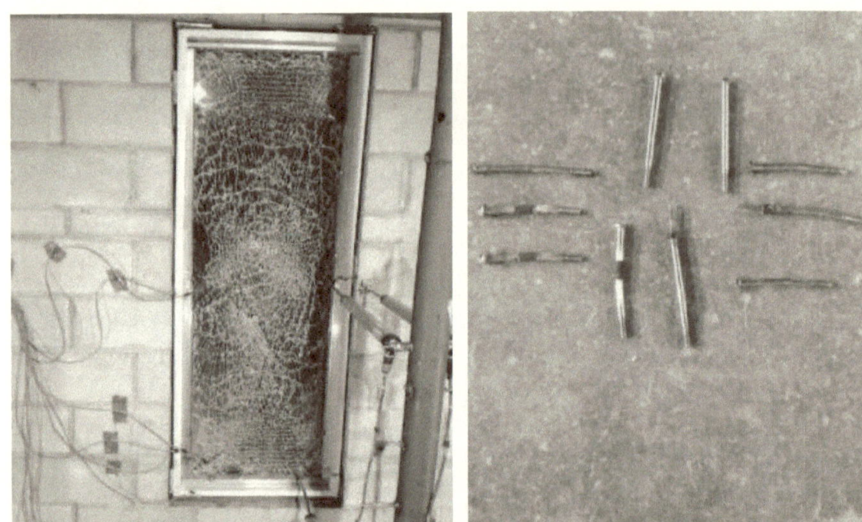

Figure B.22: Photographs of window and anchors after Test B10

B.11: Test ST1

Test ST1 was conducted on a square double pane window with 1220 x 1220 mm (48" by 48") frame dimensions. Upon applying 28 kPa blast pressure, the window performed well under this pressure-impulse combination. The unprotected outer pane failed and fell into the Shock Tube. The inner glazed pane cracked, but the glazing maintained the broken glass in place without any penetration of debris. The window failure met the GSA performance condition 2 that indicates safe glass breakage.

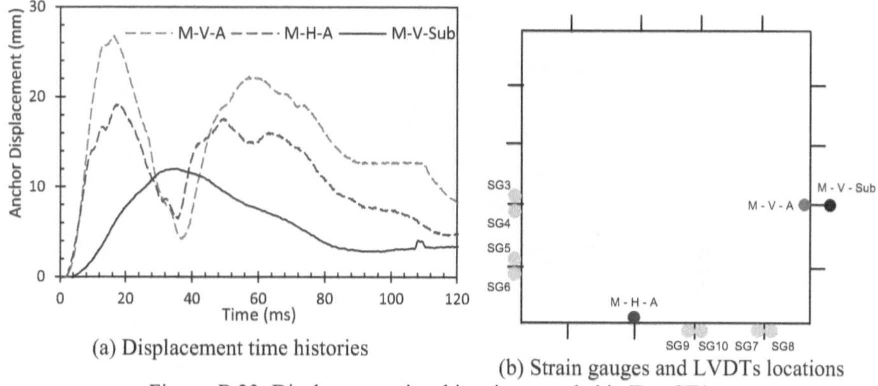

(a) Displacement time histories

(b) Strain gauges and LVDTs locations

Figure B.23: Displacement time histories recorded in Test ST1

Figure B.24: Photograph of ST1 after testing

B.12: Test ST2

Test ST2 was conducted on the same square window that was tested earlier as test ST1. Under increased pressure and impulse, the window suffered from anchorage failure. The anchors embedded in stones triggered the failure of individual stone units. This resulted in the separation and warping of the window frame. The glazing also suffered damage, as the films delaminated from the window in a number of places. This caused the high magnitude of displacements recorded during testing. Even though the protective glass pane did fail and kept fragments intact, the failure of the retention anchors led to the penetration of the glass shards into the building indicating performance condition 4 of the GSA.

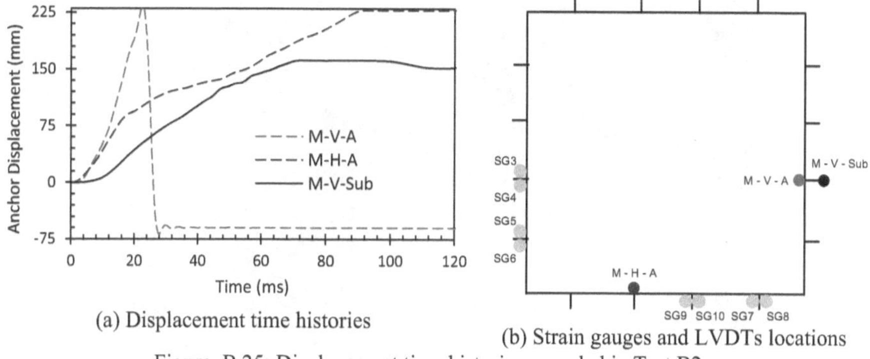

(a) Displacement time histories

(b) Strain gauges and LVDTs locations

Figure B.25: Displacement time histories recorded in Test B2

Figure B.26: Photograph of ST2 after testing

B.13: Test ST3

Test ST3 was conducted on a rectangular double pane window with 560 x 1676 mm frame dimensions. When the 28 kPa pressure was triggered, the window performed well under this pressure-impulse combination. The unprotected outer pane failed and fell into the Shock Tube. The inner glazed pane cracked, but the glazing maintained the broken glass in place without any penetration of debris. The window failure met the GSA performance condition 2 that indicates safe glass breakage.

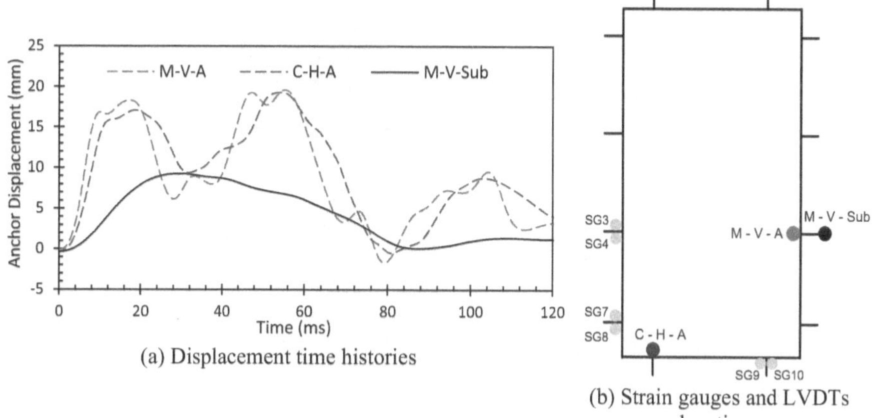

(a) Displacement time histories

(b) Strain gauges and LVDTs locations

Figure B.27: Displacement time histories recorded in Test ST3

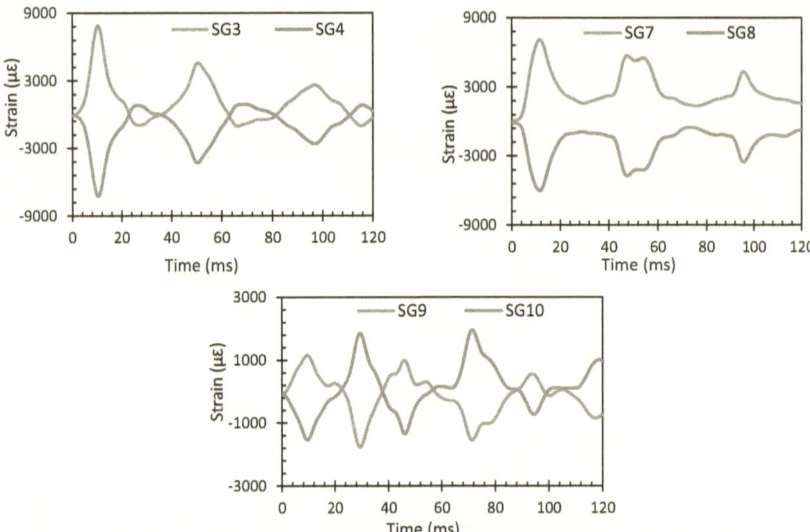

Figure B.28: Example of strain time histories recorded in retention anchors (Test ST3)

Figure B.29: Photographs of ST3 after testing

B.14: Test ST4

Test ST4 was conducted on the same rectangular window that was tested earlier as test ST3. While the glazing fulfilled its function, the substrate showed signs of significant deterioration. Two of the stones next to the window displaced. A large piece of stone flew towards the witness panel and landed close to the panel. The window failure met the GSA performance condition 2 that indicates safe glass breakage.

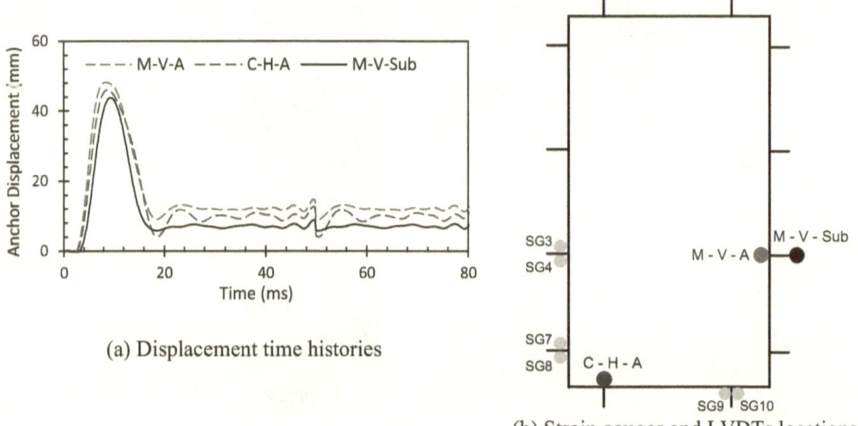

(a) Displacement time histories

(b) Strain gauges and LVDTs locations

Figure B.30: Pressure and displacement time histories recorded in Test ST4

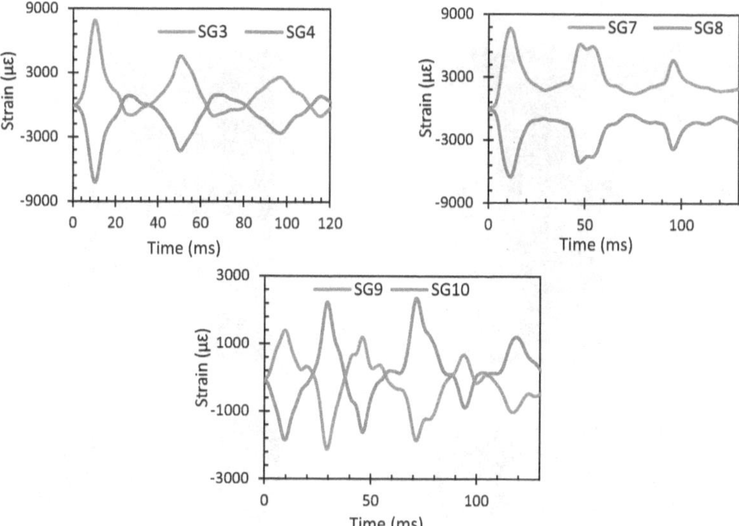

Figure B.31: Example of strain time histories recorded in anchors (Test ST4)

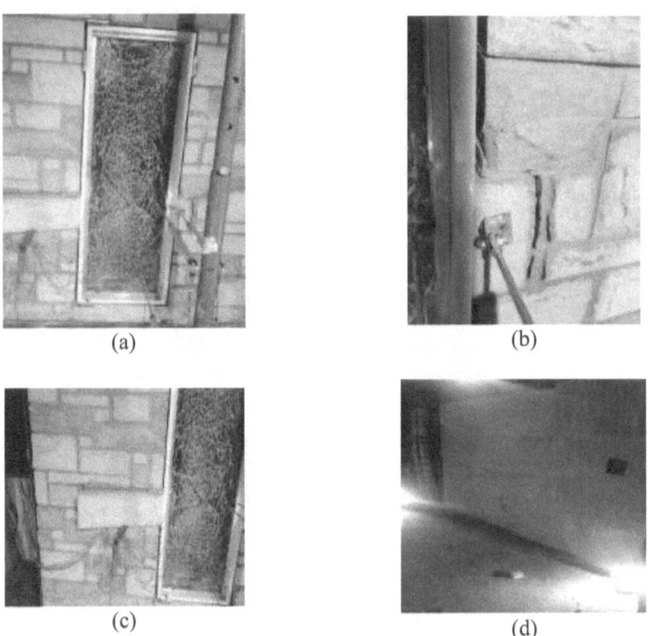

(a)

(b)

(c)

(d)

Figure B.32: Photographs of window after Test ST4

B.15: Test ST5

Test ST5 was conducted on a rectangular double pane window with 560 x 1676 mm frame dimensions. It did not experience any damage in the window. There was no cracking in the outer and inner panes once 28 kPa of reflected pressure was applied on the window. The window survived the blast pressure without and damage. A similar behaviour was also observed in test B9 when concrete block masonry was used as the substrate. In this case the block masonry substrate had been tested 4 times before and had undergone significant softening. The stone masonry substrate used in the current test had also been tested earlier (twice), with significant cracking of the mortar joints, dislodging of stones, necessitating repair of the wall. Softer substrates tend to move along with the window, transferring lower stresses to the window. The window showed perfect performance without failure and the window met the GSA performance condition 1.

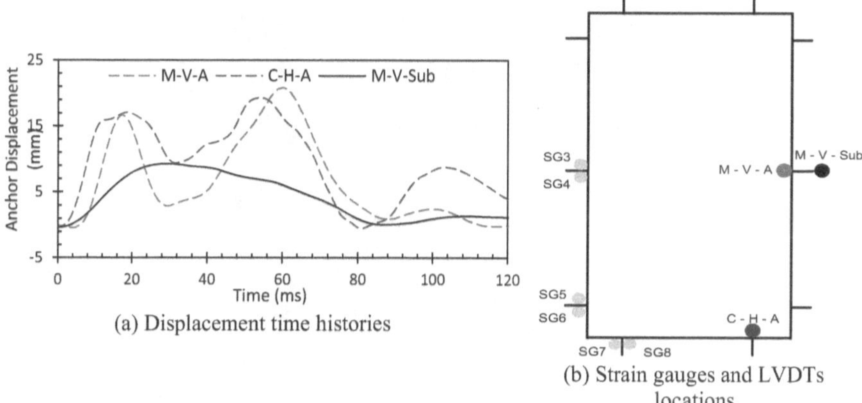

(a) Displacement time histories

(b) Strain gauges and LVDTs locations

Figure B.33: Displacement time histories recorded in Test ST5

Figure B.34: Photograph of ST5 after testing

B.16: Test ST6

Test ST6 was conducted on the same rectangular window that was tested earlier in test ST5. While the glazing fulfilled its function, the substrate showed signs of significant deterioration. Some of the stones moved significantly and at least one stone split into two, exposing the retention anchor inside. There was extensive cracking along the mortar joins, as well as movements of some of the other stones, even at locations away from the window. The substrate was demolished after the test, as it was found to be unsafe to handle, repair and retest. The window anchors were observed to have bent significantly, indicating inelastic behaviour. There was no rupturing of the anchors. The window failure met the GSA performance condition 2 that indicates safe glass breakage.

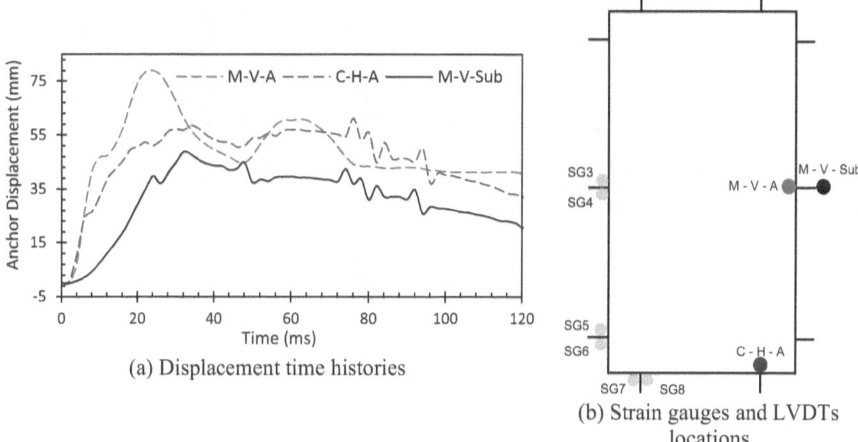

(a) Displacement time histories

(b) Strain gauges and LVDTs locations

Figure B.35: Displacement time histories recorded in Test ST6

Figure B.36: Photographs of window after Test ST6

Appendix C:

Details of Finite Element Method (FEM) and Modelling Techniques Employed

This Appendix contains the details of the numerical investigation conducted using software LS-DYNA. The windows were modelled and analyzed for model validation and for undertaking an analytical parametric study. The models consisted of insulated glass units (IGU) tested in the experimental phase, which were comprised of two glass panes with an air gap between the two. The inner glass pane was glazed by a film that was mechanically anchored to the aluminum frame of the IGU. In addition, the aluminum frame was secured to different substrates using Grade 8 steel anchors. The Appendix contains the details of the (FEM) modeling, including the geometry of window models, the construction of the models, the selection of appropriate element models, the generation of FEM mesh, load applications, boundary conditions, and sample response of glass panes and retention anchors to blast loads at different stages of loading.

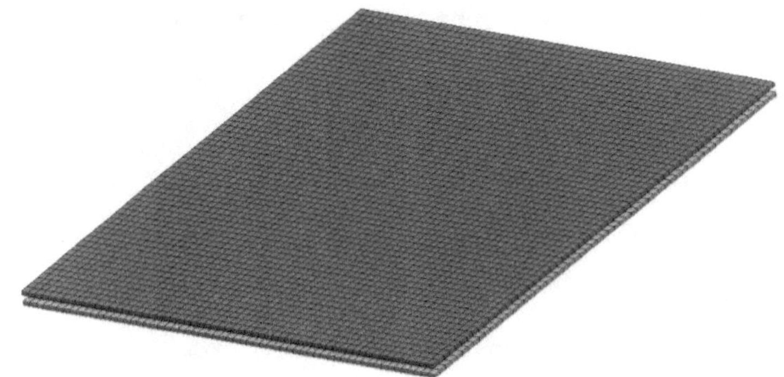

Figure C.1: Solid mesh elements for square glass

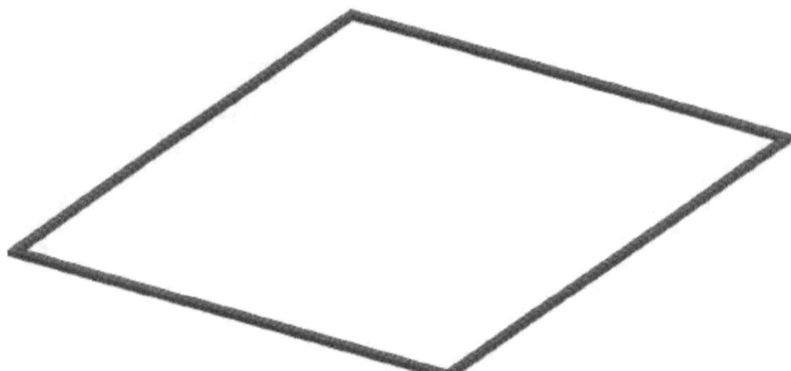

Figure C.2: Edge glass between the glass layers for square model

Figure C.3: Beam element mesh for anchor bolts

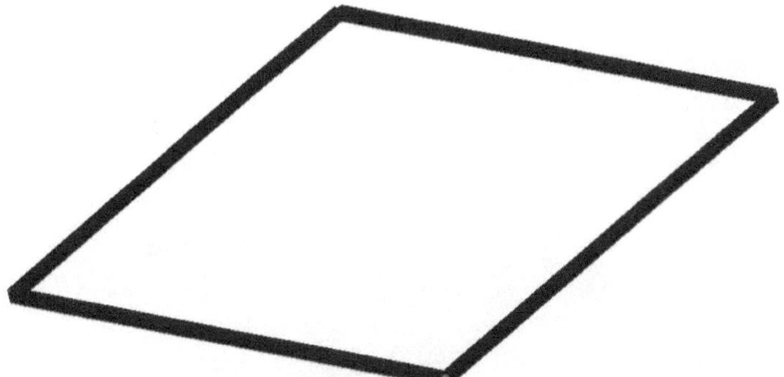

Figure C.4: Beam element mesh for the frame

Figure C.5: Shell mesh for the film element

Figure C.6: Discrete spring element

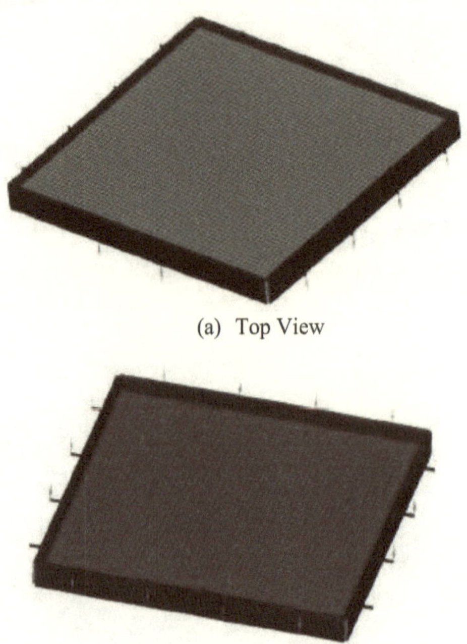

(a) Top View

(b) Bottom View
Figure C.7: Full geometry of square FEM model

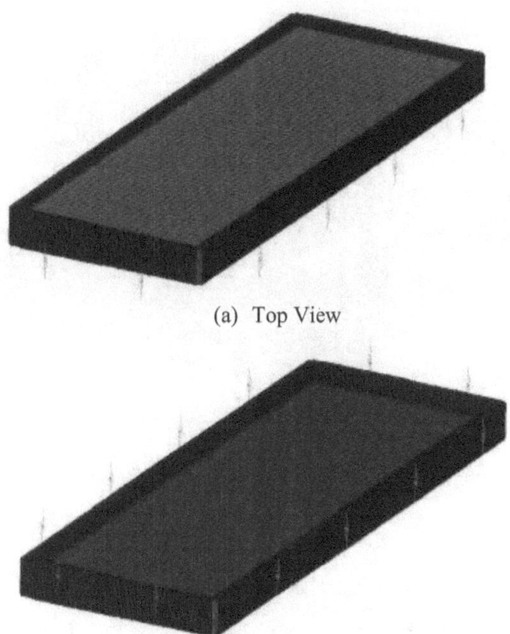

(a) Top View

(b) Bottom View

Figure C.8: Full geometry of rectangular FEM model

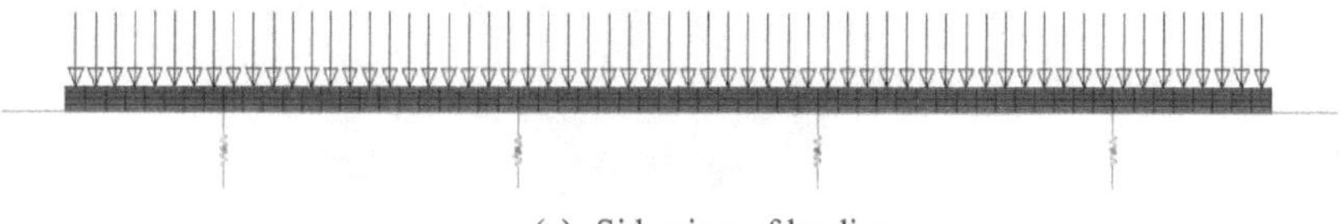

(a) Side view of loading

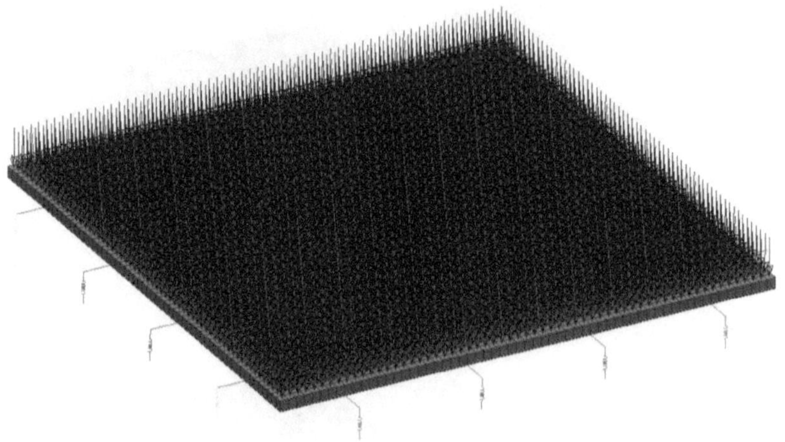

(b) 3-D view of loading

Figure C.9 Blast pressure application on square FEM model

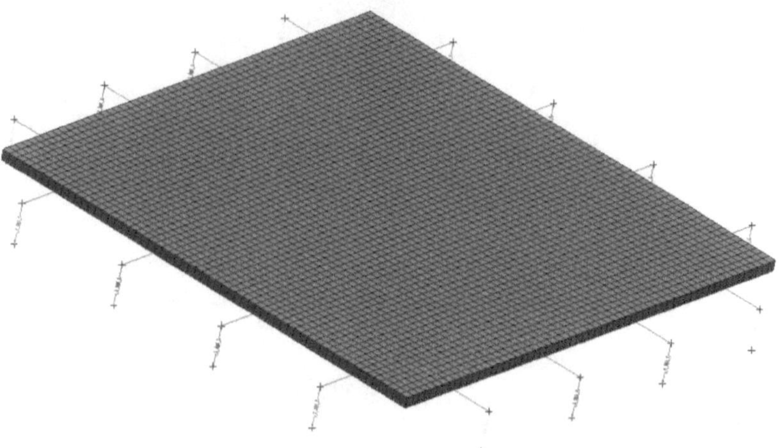

Figure C.10: Boundary condition location for square FEM Model

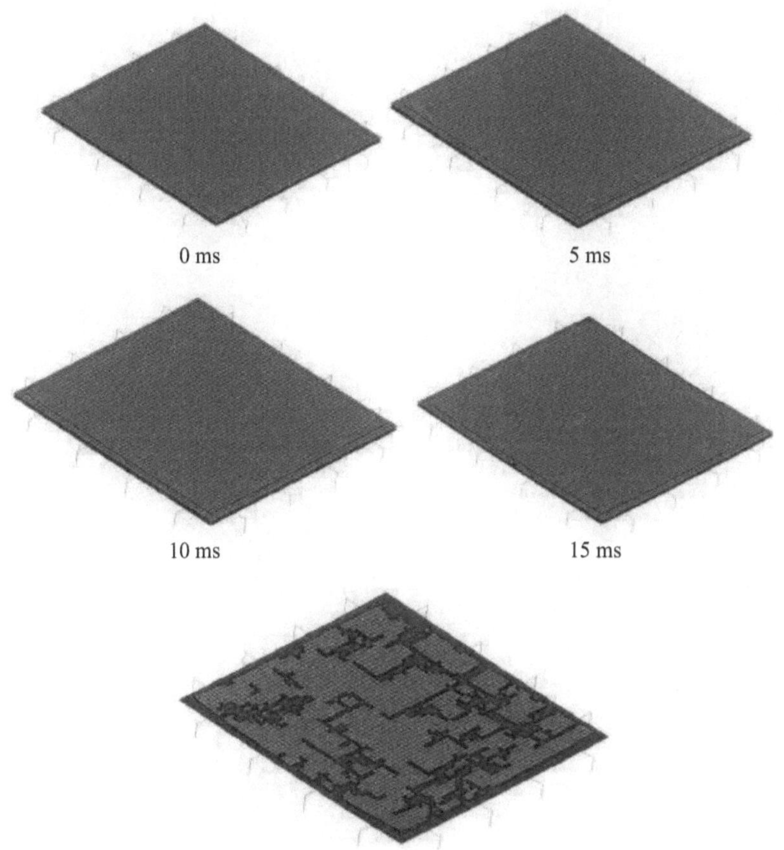

Figure C.11: Typical response of top glass pane

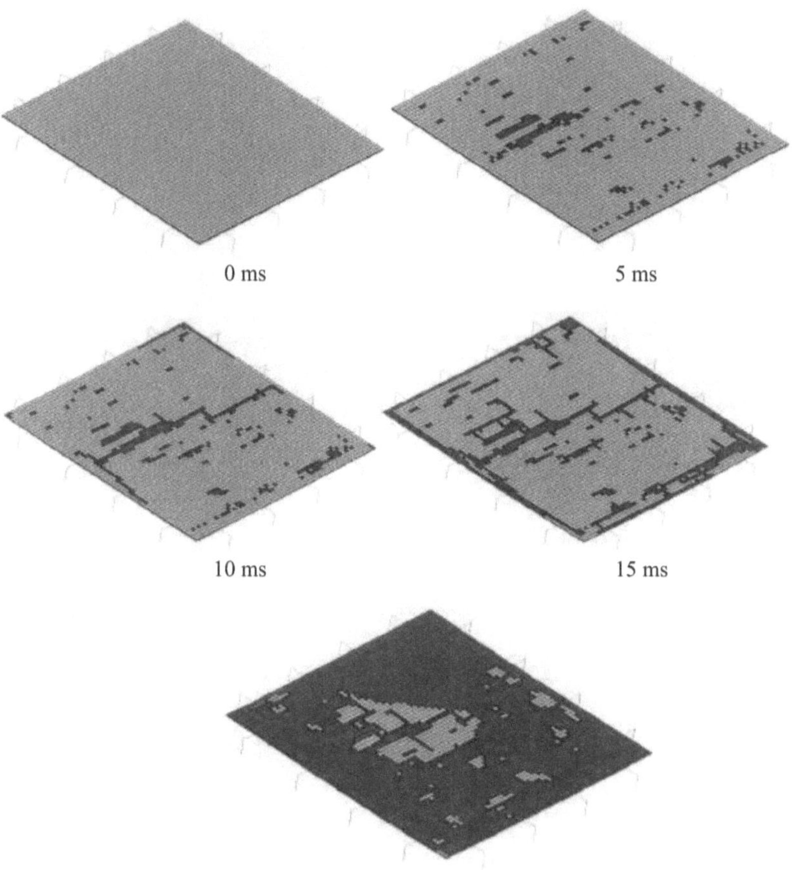

Figure C.12: Typical response of bottom glass pane (yellow glass; red film)

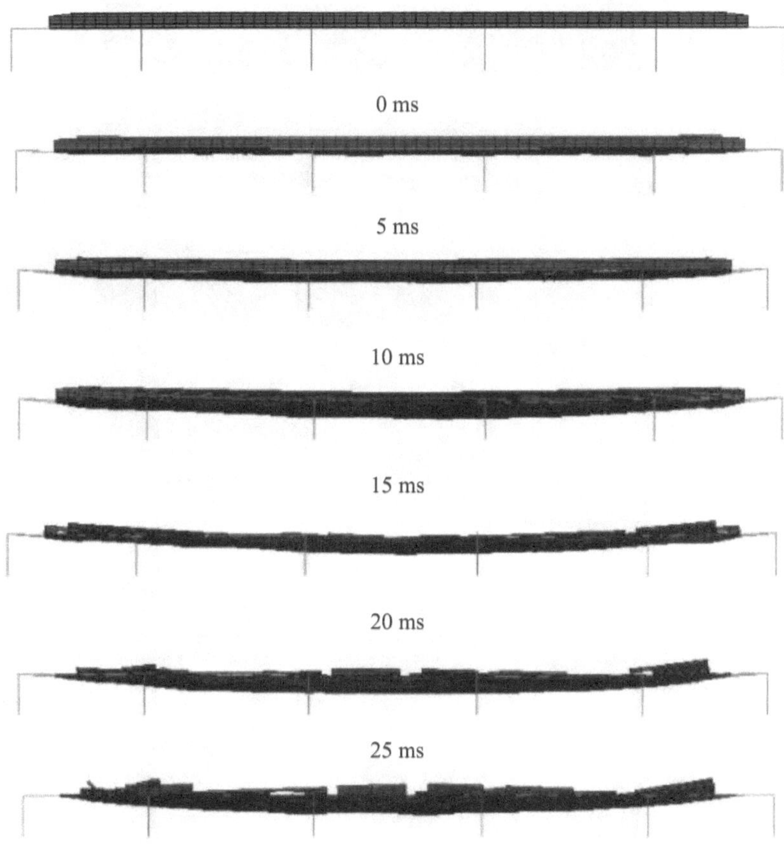

Figure C.13: Side view of typical window response to blast shock waves

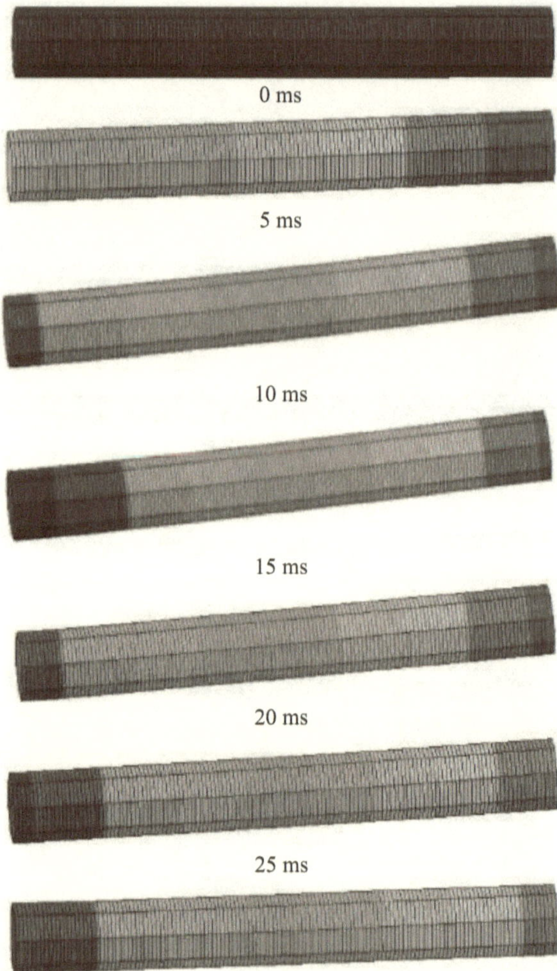

Figure C.14: Typical deflected shape of window retention anchor at different time steps